Andrew T. Scull

MUSEUMS OF MADNESS

**The Social Organization of Insanity
in Nineteenth-Century England**

St. Martin's Press
New York

For Nancy and Anna

Contents

List of Plates

The author and publishers make grateful acknowledgement to the sources mentioned above for permission to reproduce the illustrations.

Acknowledgements

I have received very generous help from many people in the course of writing this book, and I wish to thank all of them for their kindness. Robert Scott first introduced me to the sociological study of deviance and encouraged me to embark on this study. He and Donald Light Jr read an earlier version of this work and provided much valuable criticism and advice. Subsequently, a number of other friends and colleagues have discussed my research with me and have improved the manuscript considerably: I am particularly grateful to William Bynum and Steven Spitzer; and to Magali Larson, Jan Smith, and John Moffett. Jill Norman and Sandy Thatcher have given me invaluable editorial advice and encouragement.

For permission to consult materials in their possession, I should like to thank: the Library of the Royal College of Psychiatrists and Dr Alexander Walk; the archivists at the London (Middlesex and London Divisions), Bedfordshire, and Sussex County Record Offices; and the medical directors of the following mental hospitals: Stone, Bucks; St Luke's Woodside, London; St Dunstan's and St Andrew's, Northampton; the Littlemore and the Warneford, Oxford; and Devizes, Wiltshire. I should particularly like to thank the medical director and the library staff at the Institute of Living, Hartford, Connecticut, for allowing me access to their invaluable Norman collection.

My last, and by far my greatest, debt is to my wife Nancy, who has assisted me at every stage in so many ways. Her contribution to this work has quite simply been incalculable.

Chapter One

The Rise of the Asylum

Men make their own history, but they do not make it just as they please; they do not make it under circumstances chosen by themselves, but under circumstances directly encountered, given and transmitted from the past. The tradition of all the dead generations weighs like a nightmare on the brain of the living.

(Karl Marx, *The Eighteenth Brumaire of Louis Bonaparte*)

No medical advance, no humanitarian approach was responsible for the fact that the mad were gradually isolated, that the monotony of insanity was divided into rudimentary types. It was the depths of confinement itself that generated the phenomenon; it is from confinement that we must seek an account of this new awareness of madness.

(Michel Foucault, *Madness and Civilization*)

1. The Social Control of the Mad

The typical response to the deranged underwent dramatic changes in English society between the mid-eighteenth and mid-nineteenth centuries. At the outset of this period, mad people for the most part were not treated even as a separate category or type of deviants. Rather, they were assimilated into the much larger, more amorphous class of the morally disreputable, the poor, and the impotent, a group which also included vagrants, minor criminals, and the physically handicapped. Furthermore, just as in the case of the indigent generally, the societal response to the problems posed by the presence of mentally disturbed individuals did not involve segregating them into separate receptacles designed to keep them apart from the rest of society. The overwhelming majority of the insane were still to be found at large in the community. By the mid-nineteenth century, however, virtually no aspect of this traditional response remained intact. The insane were clearly and sharply distinguished from other 'problem populations'. They found themselves incarcerated in a specialized, bureaucratically organized, state-supported asylum system which isolated them both physically and symbolically from the larger society. And within this segregated environment, now recognized as one of the major varieties of deviance in English society, their condition had been diagnosed as a uniquely and essentially medical problem. Accordingly, they had been delivered into the hands of a new group of professionals, the so-called 'mad-doctors'. This book seeks to provide a critical account and understanding of this major historical shift in the styles and practices of social control, and an assessment of its major consequences.

Conventionally, of course, this transformation process is known to historians as the 'reform' of the treatment of the 'mentally ill'. The very language that is used thus reflects the implicit assumptions which have hitherto marked most historians' treatment of the subject – a naïve Whiggish view of history as progress, and a failure to see key elements of the reform process as sociologically highly problematic. For those writing from this perspective, lunacy reform reflects two converging forces. On the one hand, the rise of an urbanized, industrial society is seen as producing a social order whose very complexity forced the adoption of some form of institutional response. On the other, the acceptance of state 'responsibility' for the insane, the advent of the asylum, and the developing link between medicine and insanity are pictured as the 'natural' outcome of the growing civilization of social existence, the rise of humanitarian concern for one's fellow citizens, and the advances of science and human understanding. The direction taken by lunacy reform is thus presented as at once inevitable and basically benign – both in intent and in consequences.

In this and subsequent chapters, I shall endeavour to show that almost all aspects of this purported 'explanation' are false, or provide a grossly distorted and misleading picture of what lunacy reform was all about. Reform did indeed have deep structural roots in the changing nature of English society, but these roots were embedded to a far greater extent and in far more complex ways in the nature of capitalism as a social phenomenon than conventional simplistic references to urbanization and industrialization have managed to grasp. The reformers did indeed profess to be actuated by 'humane' concern with the well-being of the lunatic. (I have yet to meet a reformer who conceded that his designs on the objects of his attentions were malevolent.) But whatever the Victorian haute bourgeoisie's degree of sympathy with the sufferings of the lower orders, and however convinced one may or may not be of the depth of their interest in the latter's welfare, it remains the case that to present the outcome of reform as a triumphant and unproblematic expression of humanitarian concern is to adopt a perspective which is hopelessly biased and inaccurate: one which relies, of necessity, on a systematic neglect and distortion of the available evidence. It is time to transfer our attention away from the rhetoric of intentions and to consider instead the actual facts about the establishment and operation of the new apparatus for the social control of the mad. Similarly with the notion that the medical capture of insanity reflected and was somehow caused by some mysterious advance in scientific understanding: as an ideological prop for the professional claims of psychiatry, this claim has obvious merits; as an historical analysis of the process itself, it has none. Quite regardless of one's opinions on the extent of scientifically-based psychiatric knowledge of mental illness today, there would, I think, be a widespread consensus on the dearth of almost any real knowledge base in early nineteenth-century medicine which would have given the medical profession a rationally defensible claim to special expertise vis-à-vis the insane.

Among those committed to (or trapped within) the conventional account of psychiatric history, central elements of the reform process become 'obvious', taken for granted, insulated from critical scrutiny. And where reality is too insistent and diverges too sharply from their mythical representation of it, the discrepancies between the ideal and the real are dismissed as the predictable out-come of human imperfection or the unintended, 'accidental' consequences of well-intended actions. Mere facts are thus re-ordered so as to leave the myth intact. Nor should this surprise us. As Gilbert Ryle once pointed out, 'A myth is, of course, not a fairy story. It is the presentation of facts belonging in one category in the idioms belonging to another. To explode a myth is accordingly not to deny the facts but to reallocate them.'[1] My task, indeed, far from being one of denying the facts, must be to re-emphasize them, and to show how they lead to an interpretation of lunacy reform widely at variance with that traditionally offered.

My primary concerns in the chapters which follow will be to establish how and why insanity came to be exclusively defined as an illness, a condition within the sole jurisdiction of the medical profession; to answer the related question of why the mad-doctors and their reformist mentors opted for the asylum as the domain within which the insane were to receive their 'treatment'; and to delineate the effects of these choices. Such questions deserve to be raised and answered in the first instance because the adoption of the state-run asylum system, the transformation of madness into mental illness, and the subsequent reverberations of these developments represent the most striking and lasting legacy of the reform movement. Furthermore, it is not at all obvious on the face of things why these changes took the form that they did. Since the initial and continuing costs of making this separate provision for the mentally ill were obviously high, and apparently cheaper means of sustaining them were already in existence (for example, in the general mixed workhouses which the Webbs found to be such a characteristic feature of the nineteenth-century English response to poverty and dependency, or through a system of outdoor relief providing for maintenance in the community), the successful 'capture' of such a group by the medical profession and the large-scale and costly construction of mental hospitals in which to incarcerate them must be seen as inherently problematic phenomena.

Even apart from their historical importance, such questions have an obvious contemporary relevance, not least because, as Paul Rock has put it, 'modes of social control exerted in the past become part of the moral and definitional context [of the present] . . . This propensity to preserve earlier moral reactions means not only that much contemporary deviance is a fossilized or frozen residue from the past, but that contemporary control is constrained and oriented

[1] Gilbert Ryle, *The Concept of Mind*, New York, Harper & Row, 1949. (London, Penguin, 1970.)

by the past. Each new generation does not rewrite the social contract.'[1] As it happens, since the mid-1950s we have been moving away from one aspect of the nineteenth-century legacy in the field of mental health – the primary reliance on the asylum. But even here a historical context is vital if we are to grasp what is being abandoned and why.[2] The significance of the nineteenth-century experience is still more incontestable in those areas – state intervention to control problem populations and the 'medicalization' of deviance – where the application of nineteenth-century approaches continues to grow in scope and importance.

Sociologically speaking, the answers to these questions possess in addition a potentially much wider significance. For the developments I shall analyse here have obvious parallels with changes occurring almost contemporaneously in other sectors of the social control apparatus. Thus the key elements which distinguish deviance and its control in modern societies from the shapes which such phenomena assume elsewhere likewise grew to maturity in the period stretching from the late eighteenth through the nineteenth century. Of major importance in this respect were: (1) the substantial involvement of the state, and the emergence of a highly rationalized, centrally administered and directed social control apparatus; (2) the treatment of many types of deviance in institutions providing a large measure of segregation from the surrounding community; and (3) the careful differentiation of different sorts of deviance, and the subsequent consignment of each variety to the ministrations of experts – which last development entails, as an important corollary, the emergence of professional and semi-professional 'helping occupations'. From this perspective, the differentiation of the insane, the rise of a state-supported asylum system, and the emergence of the psychiatric profession can be seen to represent no more than a particular, though very important, example of this much more general series of changes in the social organization of deviance. Accordingly, a more adequate understanding of lunacy reform can be expected to provide us with important clues as to the structural sources of this wider transformation of the mechanisms for the

[1] Paul Rock, *Deviant Behaviour*, London, Hutchinson, 1973, pp. 156, 159.
[2] See Andrew T. Scull, *Decarceration: Community Treatment and the Deviant – A Radical View*, Englewood Cliffs, N.J., Prentice-Hall, 1977.

social control of problem populations, and as to the kinds of effects bureaucratic processing, state intervention, and 'expert' involvement have produced.

Before proceeding directly to a discussion of the reform movement and its ramifications, however, I think one must address a logically prior set of issues: namely, what were the social preconditions of élite receptivity to the idea of an asylum system as the primary, almost the sole, response to the problems posed by insanity? How did the changing relationship between the state and civil society contribute to both the possibility and the pressures for state intervention in the control of the mad? And what social and cultural climate had to exist before claims on anyone's part to possess an expertise allowing of the reconstruction and rehabilitation of the deviant would be taken seriously? In the remainder of this chapter, I shall attempt to answer these questions, and in the process to show that the resolution of each of these issues is closely interconnected with the resolution of the others. Ultimately, I shall argue, they can all be seen to rest in one way or another on the same underlying set of changes in the social structure and intellectual climate of English society.

2. Changing Responses to Insanity: Their Nature and Sources

In medieval England, the dependent classes relied principally on a haphazard and often ineffectual tradition of Christian charity and almsgiving. Poverty, particularly if it were voluntarily assumed, was a status invested with considerable religious significance and meaning. But neither the Church nor private individuals made any serious effort to match aid to need or to provide an organized response to specific problems of dependency. On the contrary, such a measured, calculated approach was clearly foreign to a society where the impulse to give was governed largely by the desire to ensure one's own salvation.

The insane were affected by this general, unsystematic approach to the deviant. Some were left to their own devices: the deranged beggar was a familiar part of the medieval landscape, wandering from place to place, community to community in search of alms.

Other lunatics relied on their families as a primary means of support. '[Since] the public did not make itself responsible for the custody of the lunatic, his own people were required to guard him and others from harm . . .',[1] sometimes with some temporary or permanent financial assistance from the community. In only a small minority of cases was any effort made to relieve the family of this burden by gathering lunatics together in institutions. At least until the seventeenth century, Bethlem remained the only specialized receptacle of this kind, and provision there was on an exceedingly modest scale. (In 1403-4, the inmates consisted of six insane and three sane patients, and this number grew only slowly in the following centuries. In 1632, for example, it was reported to contain twenty-seven patients, and in 1642, forty-four.)[2] In other parts of the country, some of the insane who posed a particularly acute threat to the social order, or who lacked friends or family on whom they could call for support, were likely to find themselves, along with the 'sick, aged, bedridden, diseased, wayfaring men, diseased soldiers, and honest folk fallen into poverty', cared and provided for within the walls of one of the many small medieval 'hospitals'.[3] Custody for others who proved too violent or unmanageable to maintain in the community was provided by the local gaol.

The first (largely abortive) attempts to break with medieval precedent in dealing with the poor came in the sixteenth century. Throughout Western Europe in this period, the efforts of centralizing monarchs to augment state power produced a series of clashes between Church and state. In England this conflict led to a decisive subordination of the former to secular political authority, and greatly accelerated the diminution of the Church's role in civil society. The dissolution of the monasteries and the redistribution of monastic lands were both symptoms and cause of this decline, a decline which rendered a Church-based response to the indigent increasingly anachronistic and unworkable. At the same time,

[1] R. M. Clay, *The Mediaeval Hospitals of England*, London, Methuen, 1909, p. 32.

[2] W. K. Jordan, *The Charities of London 1480-1660*, New York, Russell Sage, 1960, pp. 189-90.

[3] The medieval hospital was 'an ecclesiastical, not a medical institution' and, like Bethlem, 'it was for care rather than for cure'. R. M. Clay, *Mediaeval Hospitals*, 1909, pp. xvii-xviii, 13.

demands for the maintenance of internal order were if anything still more acutely felt than in the past. Rising population, coupled with the growing commercialization of agriculture and the spread of enclosures, was spawning a volatile 'army' of vagrants, beggars, and idlers, no longer needed on the land. And the threat these groups posed to the power of the central royal authorities was heightened by the still precarious nature of the latter's control, both vis-à-vis potential challengers from within, and in the context of the ever-intensifying international rivalries of the emerging European state system. Forced to attend to the demands of internal order, the Tudor monarchs found themselves increasingly compelled to supplement religious with secular control of the poor.

As part of their efforts to cope with this problem, the Tudors and their Stuart successors made tentative attempts to make local administrators responsible and subject to central authority, and to encourage the establishment of institutions in which a portion of the threatening army of idle vagrants and beggars could be confined and kept under surveillance. (The most famous of these places was the Bridewell, or house of correction, established in London in 1555 in an old royal palace.) But the new institutions were often short-lived, and the drive for increased central control ultimately collapsed at the outbreak of the English Civil War.[1]

The contrast with the rest of Western Europe is an instructive one. Here, the same imperatives produced an initially similar response: the primitive beginnings of an institutional approach to the deviant. In Europe, though, these first institutions continued to receive royal encouragement and to grow in size and numbers during the seventeenth century, a process which culminated in the establishment of the French Hôpitaux Généraux from 1656 onwards, and the inauguration of what some historians have called the Great Confinement.[2] The difference clearly reflects the divergent path taken by the English state apparatus in this period.

---

[1] Sidney and Beatrice Webb, *English Poor Law History: Part I The Old Poor Law*, London, 1927, pp. 65–100.

[2] Michel Foucault, *Madness and Civilization*, New York, Mentor Books, 1965 (London, Tavistock Publications, 1971); Georg Rusche and Otto Kirchheimer, *Punishment and Social Structure*, New York, Russell & Russell, 1968.

In the rest of Western Europe, the ever-present spur of military conflict (actual or threatened) prompted the establishment of large standing armies, which had as their corollary a massive build-up of royal power. Continental Absolutisms, with their ever larger bureaucratic apparatus and their ever greater fiscal exactions, thus possessed the capacity to continue to promote the confinement of the troublesome. They also possessed the incentive to do so, since a volatile mass of half-starved paupers, vagabonds, and minor criminals posed an obvious threat to state stability which, given the persistence and intensity of other internal and external threats, could scarcely be ignored.

While incentive and capacity were far from entirely absent in England, neither was present to anything like the same degree. Largely protected by its island status from the dangers of external assault, the royal administration could afford to adopt a somewhat less repressive policy towards its poor. Moreover, spared the need to extract massive taxes to support a modernized apparatus of war, the English state did not need to exploit its poor as harshly, so that English sovereigns had far less need to fear the periodic explosions of the lower orders, goaded beyond the limits of endurance by the exactions of the tax collectors – rebellions which were so recurrent a feature of the continental monarchies' experience in this period.[1] If the English monarchy was thus spared the political necessity of encouraging confinement as a means of disciplining the poor, this was fortunate, since by and large it lacked the institutional *capacity* to do so. '[In the absence of] the forcing house of warfare on land which had speeded the development of Absolutism on the Continent . . .', the royal administration, already deprived of a standing army, could develop neither the centrally controlled bureaucracy nor the fiscal resources vital to the successful long-run pursuit and enforcement of such a policy. As a consequence, what limited English experiments there were with state-directed confinement of the poor fell by the wayside with the collapse of the first two Stuarts' attempts to build an indigenous English Absolutism. For

[1] See Gabriel Ardant, 'Financial Policy and Economic Infrastructure of Modern States and Nations', in Charles Tilly (ed.), *The Formation of National States in Western Europe*, Princeton, N.J., Princeton University Press, 1975, pp. 164–242.

this larger failure necessarily also meant the collapse of efforts by men like Cecil and Laud to extend a greater measure of central control over the treatment of the 'disreputable poor'.[1]

Thus, after a brief flurry of activity in the late sixteenth and early seventeenth centuries, the poor, including the insane, continued to be dealt with on a local, parish level – though under the Poor Law Act of 1601 (43 Eliz. c. 2) they were now acknowledged to be a secular rather than a religious responsibility. This meant that as many as 15,000 separate administrative units were involved in the management of the poor; and this pervasive emphasis on localism was further reinforced by the custom of restricting aid to those belonging to one's own parish, a custom which received statutory recognition in the 1662 Act of Settlement (14 Charles II c. 12). Yet despite this wide scope for the exercise of local discretion, most parishes continued to provide for the derelict in essentially similar ways. Of all the funds expended for such purposes during this period, 'by far the largest amounts were dedicated to uses which we may fairly describe as household relief . . . for the support at the subsistence level of needy and worthy poor, legally resident in the parish'.[2] Lunatics were simply one group among many who received such support. Those who remained permanently insane did not pose a unique problem, but formed part of the larger class of the really poor and impotent: the senile, the incurably ill, the blind, the crippled, and the maimed. Efforts were made to keep these people in the community, if necessary by providing their relatives or others who were prepared to care for them with permanent pensions for their support.[3]

From the end of the sixteenth century and throughout the

[1] Perry Anderson, *Lineages of the Absolutist State*, London, New Left Books, 1974, p. 129 and *passim*, for a superb comparative treatment of European Absolutism. For a provocative collection of essays on European state-building in this period, see C. Tilly (ed.), *The Formation of National States in Western Europe*, Princeton, N.J., Princeton University Press, 1975.

[2] W. K. Jordan, *Philanthropy in England 1480–1660. A Study of the Changing Pattern of English Social Aspirations*, New York, Russell Sage, 1959, p. 256.

[3] Samuel Mencher, *Poor Law to Poverty Program: Economic Security Policy in Britain and the United States*, Pittsburgh, University of Pittsburgh Press, 1967, p. 39; A. Fessler, 'The Management of Lunacy in Seventeenth Century England', *Proceedings of the Royal Society of Medicine, Historical Section* 49, 1956, pp. 901–7.

seventeenth (perhaps stimulated by the lack of alternative outlets for the investment of capital), this system of household relief was gradually supplemented by 'a steadily mounting attempt to provide for the care of the hopelessly indigent, the permanent casualties of society, in carefully constituted almshouse foundations' created by private charity.[1] At first, these were no more than substitute households, supplementary provision along familiar lines for the care of those in need. No efforts were made to classify inmates according to the (supposed) underlying causes of their pathology, or to impose a new and radically different routine on them. The almshouse was simply one more household among many; its inmates continued to mix indiscriminately with one another and with the community at large. More frankly punitive functions were assumed by the houses of correction or 'Bridewells', modelled on the original London foundation. As well as 'vagrants and beggars who could not be convicted of any crime save that of wandering abroad or refusing to work',[2] such places served as houses of confinement for the more dangerous or troublesome lunatics.

More extensive and wide-ranging changes in what was still a policy of placing primary reliance upon non-institutional means for controlling deviance did not begin to be discussed and implemented until the eighteenth century. There then emerged an increased emphasis on providing for the indigent and disreputable in institutions, a trend which was most marked in London. Defoe, listing twenty-seven 'public gaols' and 125 'tolerated prisons' (a general term for all types of institutions for deviants), commented that 'there are in London, notwithstanding we are a nation of liberty, more public and private prisons, and houses of confinement, than in any city in Europe, perhaps as many as in all the capital cities of Europe put together'.[3] Many were long-established

[1] W. K. Jordan, *Philanthropy in England*, p. 257; Christopher Hill, *Reformation to Industrial Revolution: A Social and Economic History of Britain 1530–1780*, London, Weidenfeld & Nicolson, 1967, p. 47; W. J. Ashley, *An Introduction to English Economic History and Theory Part II: The End of the Middle Ages*, New York, Putnam, 1893, p. 364.

[2] Kathleen Jones, *Lunacy, Law, and Conscience 1744–1845*, London, Routledge & Kegan Paul, 1955, p. 22.

[3] Daniel Defoe, *A Tour through the Whole Island of Great Britain*, London, 1724–6; London, Penguin, 1971, p. 321.

institutions, such as Bethlem and Bridewell, but almost all of these were now considerably enlarged. (Bethlem, for instance, had moved to a new site in 1676. It now contained between 130 and 150 inmates and was being extended to provide for a large number of incurables.) These were supplemented by a large number of new institutions, many of them charitable foundations. Hospitals provide one example of the growing tendency to isolate the indigent from the rest of society. In this period they were used almost exclusively by the poor. Between 1719 and 1751, seven hospitals were added to the ancient foundations of St Bartholomew's, St Thomas's, and Bethlem in London alone. Others were founded in major provincial cities such as Liverpool, Manchester, and Leicester. Similarly, workhouses, first established on an experimental basis in a few towns in the 1630s, spread rapidly following the more successful example of the Bristol workhouse, founded in 1696. 'By the middle of the eighteenth century the urban community of market town size or above, which had no workhouse, was a rarity . . .', and from 'about 1760 onwards' these institutions were increasingly purpose-built.[1]

By modern standards, most of these eighteenth-century institutions possessed a peculiarly mixed character. Workhouses, for example, despite their name and the intentions of their founders, became dumping grounds for the decrepit and dependent of all descriptions. Prisons mixed young and old, men and women, debtors and felons, in a single heterogeneous mass. Hospitals, while more and more concentrating on caring for the sick, also made provision for lunatics, orphans, and the aged. The distinctions between the various categories making up the disreputable classes continued to be very imprecise, but there had begun to emerge a number of institutions specifically concerned with the insane.

In the vicinity of London the private madhouse trade, as it was then called, was largely concentrated in two areas, Hoxton and Chelsea. In the provinces, such places as Gateshead and Henley-in-Arden became centres of this new industry. Records of these early madhouses are almost non-existent, but there are passing references to them in contemporary books and pamphlets, and local evidence

[1] G. W. Oxley, *Poor Relief in England and Wales 1601–1834*, Newton Abbot, David & Charles, 1974, p. 84.

of a fragmentary kind sometimes survives. On this basis, one may surmise that madhouses originated in at least two distinctive ways. One of the origins of the madhouse system, at least so far as pauper lunatics were concerned, was the practice which developed in some parishes from the mid-seventeenth century onwards of boarding them out, 'at the expense of the parish, in private dwelling houses, which gradually acquired the description of "mad" houses'. Among the more affluent classes, insane relatives were most often cared for on an individual basis, for which purpose they were frequently placed 'in the custody of medical men or clergymen'.[1] As there was both a strong demand on the part of the upper classes for some system of private care which would relieve them of the burden of their unmanageable relatives, and the ability to provide substantial rewards for those who obliged them in this way, this sector of the private madhouse system grew rapidly in the early part of the eighteenth century.

Besides these private institutions run for profit, by the end of the century there were also a number of charitable institutions, most of which were set up to provide for the poor but respectable classes. The earliest of these were the small receptacle at Norwich, founded in 1713, and the ward for incurable lunatics established at Guy's Hospital in 1728. More important than these, inasmuch as it provided a model for other institutions established later in the century and also (as we shall see) represented a major attempt to assert medical control over the problem of insanity, was the establishment of St Luke's Hospital in London in 1751. Subsequently, a second St Luke's opened in 1764 at Newcastle upon Tyne, and in 1766 a 'lunatic hospital' with twenty-two cells opened in Manchester, attached to the existing Infirmary. These were followed by similar institutions at York, Liverpool, Leicester, and Exeter. By the standards of the nineteenth century, none of these was a very large institution, and they never contained more than a minor portion of the insane population. Their primary importance lay in the fact that they helped to legitimate the notion of institutionalization as a response to the problems posed by the presence of mentally disturbed individuals in the community.

[1] William Parry-Jones, *The Trade in Lunacy*, London, Routledge & Kegan Paul, 1972, pp. 7–8.

One must be careful not to exaggerate the extent to which provision for the insane had assumed an institutional form, for what evidence we have suggests that most lunatics, until well into the nineteenth century, continued to be supported by some system of outdoor relief. Nonetheless, these developments illustrate that the traditional family-based response to insanity (and indeed to all forms of deviance) was beginning to be abandoned. Those who see this process, and the asylum's ultimate triumph in the nineteenth century, as a relatively direct and uncomplicated consequence of the rise of an urban-industrial society argue that the rise of segregative forms of social control represented a 'natural' response to the inability of a community- and household-based relief system to cope with the vastly greater problems created by this new form of social organization. In Mechanic's words, 'Industrial and technological change . . ., coupled with increasing urbanization brought decreasing tolerance for bizarre and disruptive behavior and less ability to contain deviant behavior within the existing social structure.'[1] The increased geographical mobility of the population and the anonymity of existence in the urban slums were combined with the destruction of the old paternal relationships which went with a stable, hierarchically organized rural society. Furthermore, huddled together in the grossly overcrowded conditions which accompanied the explosive, unplanned growth of urban and industrial centres, the situation of the poor and dependent classes became simultaneously more visible and more desperate. In a period in which society as a whole grew richer, the rise of industry is blamed for creating for the first time an extensive proletariat, 'cut off from the ever-sustaining resources of an uncomplicated rural parish, and living at the mercy of an employment subjected to periodic intervals of slump or complete stagnation'.[2]

The suggestion is that families in these conditions were much less capable of sustaining a non-productive member, and that both the scale of the problems and the anonymity of urban existence threatened the easy and uncomplicated system of relief which had sufficed in earlier times. Though for a long time the implications of

[1] David Mechanic, *Mental Health and Social Policy*, Englewood Cliffs, N.J., Prentice-Hall, 1969, p. 54.
[2] W. K. Jordan, *Philanthropy in England*, pp. 66–7.

these developments were evaded, and 'the whole frame of historical and economic reference remained agrarian in an economy undergoing an industrial revolution',[1] eventually the new problems posed by poverty and dependence in an urban environment had to be faced. For the structural foundations of an effective system of parochial relief were undermined and brought close to collapse by the rise of an urban-industrial order. Despite the fact that they were no longer concerned with individuals, but with an amorphous mass, and despite their growing conviction that many of the poor were 'undeserving', the new class of entrepreneurs could not wholly avoid making some provision for them, if only because of the revolutionary threat they posed to the social order. The asylum – and analogous institutions such as the workhouse – allegedly constituted their response to this situation.

But there are serious problems with this line of argument. While the proportion of town-dwellers in England rose sharply from the late eighteenth century onwards, the process of urbanization was simply not as far advanced as this account necessarily implies when pressures developed to differentiate and institutionalize the deviant population. In the early stages of the Industrial Revolution, 'cotton was the pacemaker of industrial change, and the basis of the first regions which could not have existed but for industrialization, and which expressed a new form of society, industrial capitalism'.[2] Though technical innovations introduced into the manufacturing process in the latter half of the eighteenth century, together with the application of steam power, soon resulted in factory production, the technology of cotton production remained comparatively simple; and much of the industry remained decentralized and scattered in a variety of small local factories, as likely located in 'industrial villages' as concentrated in large urban centres. Even in other industries, initially 'most of the new industrial units were small and highly localized'.[3] Consequently, although large towns absorbed an increasing proportion of the English population, city dwellers remained a distinct minority during the first decades of the

[1] ibid., p. 67.

[2] Eric Hobsbawm, *Industry and Empire*, London, Penguin, 1969, p. 56.

[3] Asa Briggs, *The Making of Modern England 1783–1867*, New York, Harper & Row, 1965, p. 18.

Table 1   The Growth of Large Urban Centres in England 1801–21

	1801	1811	1821
Manchester	109,218	137,201	155,707
Liverpool	77,635	94,376	118,972
Birmingham	73,760	85,755	106,722
Bristol	63,645	76,433	97,779
Halifax	62,425	73,315	91,930
Leeds	54,162	62,534	83,758
Plymouth		56,000	61,112
Sheffield		53,231	62,275
Blackburn			53,330
Bradford			52,954
Oldham			52,510
Norwich			51,188

Source: Adapted from Eli Halevy, *England in 1815*, London, Benn, 1949, p. 257.

Table 2   Percentage of the Population of England and Wales Living in Cities of 20,000 and up

1801	1811	1821	1831	1841	1851	1861	1871	1881	1891
16·94	18·11	20·82	25·05	28·90	35·00	38·21	42·00	48·00	53·58

Source: A. F. Weber, *The Growth of Cities in the Nineteenth Century*, New York, Columbia University Press, 1899, p. 47.

nineteenth century, by which time powerful pressures were already being exerted to secure the establishment of lunatic asylums (and other forms of segregative control) on a compulsory basis. London, it is true, already had a population of 840,000 in 1801, and grew to contain more than a million people by 1811 – but it remained unique. In 1801, there were only six other cities with a population of more than 50,000; by 1811, there were eight; by 1821, there were twelve, including three which had passed the 100,000 mark. More significantly, at the turn of the century, 'only one third [of the English population] lived in a town of any size, only one in six in a town over 20,000'.[1]

By themselves, these figures suggest that the notion that it was *urban* poverty which forced the adoption of an institutional response to deviance is by no means as self-evident as is commonly assumed.[2] And when one looks for direct, concrete evidence of such a connection, one's faith in the traditional wisdom is still further diminished. As we shall see, in 1808 local magistrates were given discretionary power to provide asylum accommodation at county expense for pauper lunatics. Whether any given county adopted this solution to the problem of the dependent insane bore little or no relationship to the degree of urbanization of its population. While Lancashire and the West Riding of Yorkshire, two of the most heavily populated counties in England, were among the first to plan and open county asylums, Middlesex, the most densely populated county in the country, made no effort to do so until 1827, and then acted only under the spur of direct Parliamentary pressure. None of the counties in the West Midlands, along with the North the most industrialized and urbanized region of England, built an asylum until 1845, when they were compelled to do so. At the other end of the scale, the second county to open an asylum under the 1807 Act (in 1812) was small, rural Bedfordshire. Other rural counties exhibited a similar enthusiasm for the institutional solution at a comparatively early date. Indeed the majority of the asylums built on the basis of the permissive act were situated in rural counties: Norfolk (1814), Lincolnshire (1820), Cornwall (1820), Gloucestershire (1823), Suffolk (1829), Dorset (1832), Kent (1833).

[1] Harold Perkin, *The Origins of Modern English Society 1780-1880*, London, Routledge & Kegan Paul, 1969, p. 117. In fact, at the first census of 1801, there were only fourteen towns in the country with a population of more than 20,000.

[2] A comparative perspective enables one to make this point still more emphatically. As David Rothman has shown in his *The Discovery of the Asylum* (Boston, Little Brown, 1971), during the first half of the nineteenth century, the United States too moved rapidly to embrace a policy of segregative control – at a period when, as even the most avid proponent of the urbanization thesis must concede, the American population remained overwhelmingly rural.

No clear-cut connection exists, therefore, between the rise of large asylums and the growth of large cities. Instead, I suggest that the main driving force behind the rise of a segregative response to madness (and to other forms of deviance) can much more plausibly be asserted to lie in the effects of the advent of a mature capitalist market economy and the associated ever more thorough-going commercialization of existence. While the urban conditions produced by industrialization had a direct impact which was originally limited in geographical scope, the market system observed few such restrictions, and had increasingly subversive effects on the whole traditional rural and urban social structure. These changes in turn prompted the abandonment of long-established techniques for coping with the poor and troublesome.

Some may object that these contentions rest upon a chronological confusion: that the rise of capitalism in England occurred too early to be plausibly invoked as the explanation of events occurring in the late eighteenth and the first half of the nineteenth century.[1] But such criticism is itself confused and misplaced, for I am concerned here not simply with the initial moves towards commercialized production and the rise of a market of national reach and scope, but with the massive reorganization of an entire society along market principles – what Karl Polanyi has termed 'the running of society as an adjunct to the market'. And this takes place only in the late eighteenth and early nineteenth century.

The rise of market-oriented production in England can, of course, be traced back at least as far as the fifteenth century. Slowly, though at an increasing pace from the early seventeenth century onwards, the market system spread to incorporate all but the Celtic fringe, so that by 1750, England was already in essence a single national market economy.[2] But it was a market riddled with imperfections, which in consequence 'exercised a weak pull on the economy'[3] and had only a limited impact on the English social structure. The reasons for this were many. Difficulties of transport

[1] David Roberts suggested this objection to me.

[2] E. Hobsbawm, op. cit., pp. 27–8; Pierre Mantoux, *The Industrial Revolution in the Eighteenth Century*, London, Cape, 1928, p. 74.

[3] L. A. Clarkson, *The Pre-Industrial Economy in England 1500–1750*, London, Batsford, 1971, p. 22.

and communications hampered the market's effectiveness. Like-wise, the underdevelopment of credit mechanisms, together with the customary and institutional barriers to the reorganization of the land and labour markets along capitalistic lines,[1] meant that the rationalizing impact of capitalism, though present, only operated within strict limits. And precisely 'because the mass of consumers was poor and their effective demand restricted by low incomes', the incentives to prompt producers to overcome those limits were still insufficient.[2]

The consequences of this situation are plain. The weak pull of the market allowed the persistence of a relatively unchanging agriculture and the survival of a social order which, reformulated in terms of eighteenth-century philosophy, exhibited substantial continuities with the past. Market determination of wages and prices coexisted alongside and at times was substantially inhibited by traditional conceptions of the just wage and the just price, as well as customary ideas about what constituted a fair day's work. Moreover, 'wage-earners of a modern type were to be found only in isolated groups . . . [though] a large proportion, perhaps a majority, of workers had reached what may be considered a half-way stage between peasant and proletarian'.[3] From prince to pauper, society was held together by what Cobbett referred to as 'the chain of connection'. Social subordination rested upon reciprocal bonds of patronage, deference, and dependence, and 'permanent vertical links . . ., rather than the horizontal solidarities of class, bound society together . . . a social nexus . . . less formal and inescapable than feudal homage, more personal and comprehensive than the contractual, employment relationships of capitalist "Cash Payment".'[4]

The changing structure of the English economy from the late

[1] 'Mercantilism, with all its tendency towards commercialization, never attacked the safeguards which protected these two basic elements of pro-duction – labor and land – from becoming the objects of commerce.' Karl Polanyi, *The Great Transformation*, Boston, Beacon, 1957, p. 70.

[2] L. A. Clarkson, op. cit., p. 22.

[3] H. Perkin, op. cit., p. 90.

[4] ibid., p. 49. As E. P. Thompson (*Whigs and Hunters*) and Douglas Hay (*Albion's Fatal Tree*) have recently reminded us, one must not romanticize this social system. Beneath the emphasis on patronage and dependence lay a ruling class skilled and ruthless in manipulating force and terror.

eighteenth century onwards undermined and then destroyed the old order. Profound shifts occurred in the relationships between the superordinate and the subordinate classes, and in upper-class perceptions of their responsibilities towards the less fortunate – changes which can be summarized as the transition from a master-servant to an employer-employee relationship; from a social order dominated by rank, order, and degree to one based on class.[1] There emerged a 'general sense of betrayal of paternal responsibilities by the naked exercise of the power of property'.[2] As part of the general change from regulated to self-regulating markets, centuries-old legislation protecting workers' standard of living and conditions of work was abolished. Increasingly, 'the process of acquisition set the terms on which other social processes were allowed to operate'.[3] Capitalism broke the social bonds which had formerly held it in check.

The impetus for these changes had a number of sources. Substantially improved transport had reduced costs and widened internal markets. But more importantly, domestic population had begun to rise very rapidly indeed from the 1770s onwards (in the fifty years from 1780, it roughly doubled). This, coupled with the impact of the growing industrial sector of the economy, produced a large and continuing expansion of demand. Nowhere was this development more marked than in the demand for food. Given an extra stimulus between 1793 and 1815 by the Napoleonic Wars, the market for foodstuffs entered upon a phase of permanent boom. (During the Wars, wheat prices, for example, reached double their pre-war levels, and they remained substantially above their pre-war peak even when the artificial spur of military conflict was removed.) These conditions provided rural producers with sustained pressures and incentives to rationalize agricultural production. In Asa Briggs's words, 'businesslike farming became a reasonable economic proposition'.[4] Along with the cultivation of new land, the

---

[1] Cf. Asa Briggs, 'The Language of "Class" in Early Nineteenth Century England', in A. Briggs and J. Saville (eds.), *Essays in Labour History*, London, Macmillan, 1960, pp. 43–73.

[2] H. Perkin, op. cit., p. 126.

[3] A. Briggs, *The Making of Modern England*, pp. 64–5.

[4] ibid., p. 40.

application of systematic business calculation to farming was perhaps as important as anything in bringing about the remarkable early nineteenth-century rise in agricultural output.

Rationalization, of course, had its costs. Marginal smallholders and cottagers with some alternative sources of support than wage labour were squeezed out and proletarianized, in part by the Parliamentary enclosures of the late eighteenth century but also by the harsh competitive realities of an economic system dominated by industrial manufactures and an ever more thoroughly rationalized agriculture. In-servants, who had formerly lived as part of the farmer's family, were increasingly transformed into labourers, since at a time of rising prices and over-abundant labour this was cheaper. And labourers were hired for shorter and shorter terms, because that was more economically rational: the farmer did not have to pay them when, for whatever reason, they were idle.[1] The economy as a whole came under the sway of the notion that '[the employer] owed his employees wages, and once these were paid, the men had no further claim on him'.[2]

Thus, just as surely as urbanization, the market when given its head destroyed the traditional links between rich and poor which had characterized the old order. The 'great transformation' wrought by the advent of a thoroughly market-oriented society sharply reduced the *capacity* of the lower orders to cope with economic reverses. Wage-earners, whether they were agricultural labourers or the early representatives of an urban proletariat, shared a similar incapacity to make adequate provision for periods of economic depression. Quite apart from the centres of urbanization and industrialization, and to a much greater degree than the geographically limited scope of those processes would indicate, the burgeoning market economy was rendering anachronistic the idealized conception of a population living amidst 'the ever-sustaining resources of an uncomplicated rural parish'. To make matters worse, along with the closing off of alternatives other than wage work as a means of providing for subsistence went the

[1] The last two paragraphs are heavily indebted to the analysis in Eric Hobsbawm and George Rudé, *Captain Swing*, London, Penguin, 1969, Chapters 1 and 2.

[2] P. Mantoux, op. cit., p. 428.

tendency of the primitive capitalist economy to oscillate wildly and unpredictably between conditions of boom and slump.

All in all, among the lower classes in this period, family members unable to contribute effectively towards their own maintenance must have constituted a serious drain on family resources. In the situation which they faced, 'any interruption of the ability to work or the availability of a job spelt dire want . . . The aged and children became a greater burden . . .',[1] as of course did the insane. Consequently, while the family-based system of caring for the insane and other types of deviants may never have worked especially well, one suspects that by the turn of the century it was likely to have been functioning particularly badly.

These changes in structures, perceptions, and outlook which marked the transition from the old paternalist social order to a fully capitalist social system provided a direct source of bourgeois dissatisfaction with the traditional, non-institutional response to the indigent; but they were by no means the only ones. Another derived from the dislocations of the social structure associated with the rapid rise in population and the transition to an industrial economy. Not the least of these dislocations was the sizeable late-eighteenth-century expansion in the proportion of the population in temporary or permanent receipt of poor relief – an expansion which took place at precisely that point in time when the growing power of the bourgeoisie and their increasing dominance of intellectual life was reducing the inclination to tolerate such a state of affairs. By 1803, 'over a million people, one in nine of the population, were said to be in receipt of poor relief, casual or permanent'.[2] Doubtless alarmed by this situation, the upper classes readily convinced themselves that laxly administered systems of household relief promoted poverty rather than relieved it, a position for which they found ample ideological justification in the writings of Malthus and others.[3] Instead, they were increasingly attracted towards an

---

[1] Gaston Rimlinger, *Welfare Policy and Industrialization in Europe, America, and Russia*, New York, Wiley, 1971, p. 8.

[2] H. Perkin, op. cit., p. 22.

[3] T. R. Malthus, *An Essay on the Principle of Population*, London, Johnson, 1798, esp. Chapter V; John MacFarlan, *Inquiries Concerning the Poor*, Edinburgh, Longman and Dickson, 1782, pp. 34–6; William Temple, *An Essay on Trade and Commerce*, London, 1770, p. 258.

institutionally-based system. Workhouses, asylums, and the like were not only expected to provide an efficient and economical solution to the problem; they enabled a close and continuing watch to be kept on who was admitted. By making living conditions in the workhouses sufficiently unattractive, all save the truly needy and 'deserving' poor could be deterred from applying for relief; and the treatment of those so confined could always serve as an example *pour encourager les autres*. In this way, the whole system might be made efficient and economical.[1]

Institutions seemed to promise still other advantages. A labour force composed primarily of displaced peasants was ill-disposed to submit to the rigours of discipline demanded by a wage labour system – and, more especially, by the requirements of wage labour in a factory. In Andrew Ure's words, the problem was 'to subdue the refractory tempers of work people accustomed to irregular paroxysms of diligence . . .',[2] and to teach them to conform to the impersonal dictates of power-driven machinery. In devising techniques to secure these ends, there can be little question but that 'the most available [human] material was that large element of the people whose dependence upon charity had surrendered them bodily into the hands of the civil power'.[3] Here the appeal of the institution was obvious: for it appeared to provide the opportunity for the most intensive and thorough-going control over the lives of its inmates. The quasi-military authority structure which it could institute seemed ideally suited to be the means of establishing 'proper' work habits among those marginal elements of the work force who were apparently most resistant to the monotony, routine, and regularity of industrialized labour, providing 'rigorous life conditions to discipline the laborer and purge his character of the evil habits of "luxury" and "sloth" . . .'[4] Workhouses and the like would thus 'perform the double service of administering punishment for idleness and providing training in the habits of thrift and

[1] Edgar S. Furniss, *The Position of the Laborer in a System of Nationalism*, New York, Kelly, 1965, p. 107; W. Temple, op. cit., pp. 151–269.

[2] Andrew Ure, *The Philosophy of Manufactures*, London, 1835, p. 16.

[3] E. Furniss, op. cit., p. 117.

[4] ibid., p. 107; William Bailey, *A Treatise on the Better Employment and More Comfortable Support of the Poor in Workhouses*, London, 1758.

industry'.[1] They would function, in Bentham's caustic phrase, as 'a mill to grind rogues honest and idle men industrious . . .',[2] and as a stark warning to those tempted to stray from the path of labour and virtue.

Thus, on the most general level, the receptivity of the English ruling class to the notion of an institutional response to problem populations can be traced to the underlying structural transformations of their society. But what were the sources of the increasing tendency, not only to institutionalize the deviant, but also to depart from the traditional practice of treating the indigent, troublesome, and morally disreputable as part of a single amorphous mass? More specifically, given my present concerns, how and why did insanity come to be differentiated from the previously inchoate mass of deviant behaviours, so that it was seen as a distinct problem requiring specialized treatment in an institution of its own, the asylum? For it should be obvious that before the asylum could emerge as a specialized institution devoted to the problems of coping with insanity, the latter had to be distinguished as a separate variety of deviant behaviour. Insanity could not be a term narrowly applied to cases of furious mania or reserved for demented members of the upper classes. It had to be seen as a condition existing more pervasively among the lower classes of the community – a distinct species of pathology which could not be considered as just one more case of poverty and dependency.[3]

The establishment of a market economy and, more particularly,

---

[1] W. Temple, op. cit.

[2] Bentham to Brissot in Jeremy Bentham, *Works*, Vol. X (ed. J. Bowring), Edinburgh, 1843, p. 226.

[3] Of course, I am not suggesting here that prior to this process of differentiation the population at large were naïvely unaware of any and all differences between the various elements making up the disreputable classes – between, say, the raving madman and the petty criminal, or the blind and the crippled. Obviously, on a very straightforward level such distinctions were apparent and could linguistically be made – and in extreme cases made some practical differences to the way individuals were dealt with. The critical question, however, is when and for what reasons such perceived differences rigidified and came to be seen as *socially significant* – i.e., began routinely to provoke differential responses and to have consequential impact on the lives of the deviant. The question of the definition of insanity is discussed in Chapter 7 below.

the emergence of a market in labour, provided the initial incentive to distinguish far more carefully than hitherto between different categories of deviance. If nothing else, under these conditions, stress had to be laid for the first time on the importance of distinguishing the able-bodied from the non-able-bodied poor. One of the most basic prerequisites of a capitalist system, as both Marx and Weber have emphasized, was the existence of a large mass of wage labourers who were not merely 'free' to dispose of their labour power on the open market, but who were actually forced to do so. In Marx's words, 'Capital presupposes wage labour, and wage labour presupposes capital. One is the necessary condition of the other'.[1] Indeed,

all the peculiarities of Western capitalism have derived their significance in the last analysis only from their association with the capitalist organization of labour. Even what is generally called commercialization – the development of negotiable securities and the rationalization of speculation, the exchanges, etc. – is connected with it. For without the rational capitalist organization of labour, all this, so far as it was possible at all, would have nothing like the same significance, above all for the social structure and all the specific problems of the modern Occident connected with it. Exact calculation – the basis of everything else – is only possible on the basis of free labour.[2]

But to provide aid to the able-bodied threatened to undermine in a radical fashion and on many different levels the whole notion of a labour market.

Parochial provision of relief to the able-bodied interfered with labour mobility.[3] In particular, it encouraged the retention of a 'vast inert mass of redundant labour', a stagnant pool of underemployed labouring men in rural areas, where the demand for labour was subject to wide seasonal fluctuations. It distorted the operations of the labour market and, thereby, of all other markets, most especially on account of its tendency, via the vagaries of local

[1] Karl Marx, *Capital*, Vol. I, New York, International Publishers, 1967, pp. 578, 717–33. (London, Penguin, 1976.)

[2] Max Weber, *The Protestant Ethic and the Spirit of Capitalism*, London, Allen & Unwin, 1930, p. 22.

[3] J. MacFarlan, op. cit., pp. 176ff.; Adam Smith, *The Wealth of Nations*, New York, Modern Library, 1937, pp. 135–40 (London, Penguin, 1970).

administration, to create cost differentials between one town or region and another. Late eighteenth-century economic writers complained that relief to the able-bodied 'renders the price of labour in England very unequal, in some places so low as to afford little encouragement to industry; in others so exorbitantly high as to become ruinous to manufactures . . .' – a complaint later echoed by the Poor Law Commission.[1] Finally, by its removal of the threat of individual starvation, such relief had a pernicious effect on labour discipline and productivity, an outcome accentuated by the fact that the 'early labourer abhorred the factory, where he felt degraded and tortured . . .'[2]

Instead, it was felt that want ought to be the stimulus to the capable, who must therefore be distinguished from the helpless. Such a distinction is deceptively simple; but in a wider perspective, this development can be seen as a crucial phase in the growing rationalization of the Western social order and the transformation of prior *extensive* structures of domination into the ever more intensive forms characteristic of the modern world. Traditional pre-capitalist conceptions viewed the domestic population as a largely unchangeable given from which an effort was made to squeeze as large a surplus as possible; the emergent modern conception of the labour pool viewed it as modifiable and manipulable human material whose yield could be steadily enlarged through improvements in use and organization, rationally designed to transform qualitatively its value as an economic resource. As Moffett has shown, during this process, 'the domestic population came increasingly to be regarded as an industrial labor force – not simply a tax reservoir as formerly – and state policies came increasingly to be oriented to forcing the entire working population into remunerative employment'.[3] The significance of the distinction between the able-bodied and non-able-bodied poor thus increases *pari passu* with the rise of the wage labour system.

[1] J. MacFarlan, op. cit., p. 178; *Report of the Poor Law Commission 1834*, London, Penguin, 1971, p. 43.

[2] Karl Polanyi, op. cit., pp. 164–5; E. P. Thompson, *The Making of the English Working Class*, London, Penguin, 1963.

[3] John T. Moffett, 'Bureaucracy and Social Control: A Study of the Progressive Regimentation of the Western Social Order', unpublished Ph.D. dissertation, Columbia University, 1971.

The beginnings of such a separation are evident even in the early phases of English capitalism. The great Elizabethan Poor Law, for example, classified the poor into the able but unemployed, the aged and impotent, and children; and a number of historians have been tempted to see in this and in the Statute of Artificers (1563) a primitive labour code of the period, dealing respectively with what we would call the unemployed and unemployable, and the employed. But, as Polanyi suggests, in large measure 'the neat distinction between the employed, unemployed, and unemployable is, of course, anachronistic since it implies the existence of a modern wage system which was absent [at this time]'.[1] Until much later, the boundaries between these categories remained in practice much more fluid and ill-defined than the modern reader is apt to realize. Moreover, though it is plain that the Tudors and Stuarts did not scruple to invoke harsh legal penalties in an effort to compel the poor to work, these measures were undertaken at least as much 'for the sake of political security' as for more directly economic motives.[2]

Gradually economic considerations became more and more dominant. As they did so, it became increasingly evident that 'no treatment of this matter was adequate which failed to distinguish between the able-bodied unemployed on the one hand, the aged, infirm, and children on the other'.[3] The former were to be compelled to work, initially through the direct legal compulsion inherited from an earlier period. But the upper classes came to despair of the notion that they 'may be compelled [by statute] to work according to their abilities . . .',[4] and were increasingly attracted towards an alternative method according to which, in the picturesque language of John Bellers, 'The Sluggard shall be cloathed in Raggs. He that will not work shall not eat.'[5] The superiority of this approach was put most bluntly by Joseph Townsend:

[1] K. Polanyi, op. cit., p. 86.

[2] Dorothy Marshall, *The English Poor in the Eighteenth Century*, London, Routledge, 1926, p. 17; Maurice Dobb, *Studies in the Development of Capitalism*, New York, International Publishers, 1963, pp. 233ff.

[3] K. Polanyi, op. cit., p. 94.

[4] J. MacFarlan, op. cit., p. 105.

[5] John Bellers, *Proposals for Raising a College of Industry*, London, 1696, p. 1.

Hunger will tame the fiercest animals, it will teach decency and civility, obedience and subjection to the most perverse. In general, it is only hunger which can spur and goad [the poor] on to labour; yet our laws have said they shall never hunger. The laws, it must be confessed, have likewise said, they shall be compelled to work. But then legal constraint is attended with much trouble, violence and noise; creates ill-will, and can never be productive of good and acceptable service; whereas hunger is not only peaceable, silent, unremitting pressure, but, as the most natural motive to industry and labour, it calls forth the most violent exertions.[1]

The whiplash of hunger, that is, appeared as 'a purely economic and "objective" form of compulsion'; a suprahuman law of nature. And, as Malthus was quick to point out, 'When nature will govern and punish for us, it is a very miserable ambition to wish to snatch the rod from her hands and draw upon ourselves the odium of the executioner.'[2]

Thus the functional requirements of a market system promoted a relatively simple, if crucial, distinction between two broad classes of the indigent. Workhouses and the like were to be an important *practical* means of making this vital theoretical separation, and thereby of making the whole system efficient and economical. However, although workhouses were initially intended to be just that – institutions to remove the able-bodied poor from the community in order to teach them the wholesome discipline of labour – they swiftly found themselves depositories for the decaying, the decrepit, and the unemployable. And an unintended consequence of this concentration of deviants in an institutional environment was that it produced an exacerbation of the problems of handling some of them.[3] More specifically, it rendered problematic the whole question of what was to be done with those who could not or would not abide by the rules of the house – among the most important of whom were the acutely disturbed and refractory insane.

A single mad or distracted person in the community produced problems of a wholly different sort from those the same person

---

[1] [Joseph Townsend], *A Dissertation on the Poor Laws*, London, 1786.

[2] T. R. Malthus, *Essay on Population*, 6th edn, London, Murray, 1826, Book II, p. 339.

[3] J. MacFarlan, op. cit., pp. 97ff.

would have produced if placed with other deviants within the walls
of an institution. The order and discipline of the whole workhouse
were threatened by the presence of a madman who, even by
threats and punishment, could neither be persuaded nor induced to
conform to the regulations. And besides, by its very nature, the
workhouse was ill-suited to provide a secure safe-keeping for those
who might pose a threat to life or property. In the words of a
contemporary appeal for funds to set up a second charity asylum in
London, 'The law has made no particular provision for lunaticks
and it must be allowed that the common parish workhouse (the
inhabitants of which are mostly aged and infirm people) are very
unfit places for the Reception of such ungovernable and mischievous persons, who necessarily require separate apartments.'[1]
Advocates of similar institutions in the provinces also sought to
capitalize upon this situation, pointing out that 'when the Poor-
house shall be relieved of the insane . . . the respectable magistrates
. . . will then find it easier to extirpate vice, disorder, and guilty
idleness, from this great family of the lowest and most ignorant
class of society'.[2] The local gaol, which was frequently resorted to
as a substitute place of confinement for violent maniacs, proved
scarcely more satisfactory, the dislocations which the madmen's
presence produced provoking widespread complaints from both
prisoners and their gaolers. And faced by similar problems, general
hospitals began to respond by refusing to accept lunatic inmates
'on Account of the safety of other Patients'.[3]

Clearly, the adoption of an institutional response to all sorts of
problem populations greatly increased the pressures to elaborate
the distinctions amongst and between the deviant and dependent.
By making separate institutional provision for a troublesome group
like the insane, a source of potential danger and inconvenience to
the community could be removed to a place where such people
could no longer pose a threat to the social order. So that by the late

[1] St Luke's Hospital, *Considerations upon the usefulness and necessity of
establishing an Hospital as a further provision for poor Lunaticks*, in manuscript
at St Luke's Woodside, London, 1750, p. 1.

[2] Letter to the *Liverpool Advertiser*, cited in Michael Fears, 'Moral Treatment and British Psychiatry', paper presented at the Conference of the British
Sociological Association, 1975, p. 5.

[3] St Luke's, op. cit., p. 2.

2*

eighteenth century, many were becoming convinced of the need for specialized institutions. After all, one must surely concede that

the case of the unhappy objects afflicted with this disorder is in a peculiar manner distressful, since besides their own sufferings, they are rendered a nuisance and a terror to others; and are not only themselves lost to society, but take up the time and attention of others. By placing a number of them in a common receptacle, they may be taken care of by a much smaller number of attendants; and at the same time they are removed from the public eye to which they are multiplied objects of alarm, and the mischiefs they are liable to do to themselves and others, are with much greater certainty prevented.[1]

Initially, with respect to the insane, this situation provided no more than an opportunity for financial speculation and pecuniary profit for those who set up private madhouses and asylums. Such, indeed, was the general character of the eighteenth-century 'trade in lunacy', which, even in the sector concerned with pauper lunatics, was a frequently lucrative business dealing with the most acutely disturbed and refractory cases – those who in the general mixed workhouse caused trouble out of all proportion to their numbers. While claims to provide cures as well as care were periodically used as a means of drumming up custom, the fundamental orientation of the system (besides profit) was towards restraint in an economical fashion of those posing a direct threat to the social order.[2] Indeed, the revelations of the nineteenth-century parliamentary inquiries into the system were to reveal that almost every other consideration, including the welfare of the inmates, was willingly sacrificed to the requirements of order and restraint with the least trouble to the keeper. As we shall see, however, in the long run such a differentiation of deviance provided the essential social preconditions for the establishment of a new organized profession, claiming to possess a specific expertise in the management of insanity, and oriented towards a rehabilitative ideal.

On the most general level, the English élite's receptivity to the notion that a particular occupational group possessed a scientifically based expertise in dealing with lunacy reflected the growing secular rationalization of Western society at this time, a development

[1] John Aikin, *Thoughts on Hospitals*, London, Johnson, 1771, pp. 65–6.
[2] W. Parry-Jones, op. cit.

which, following Weber, I would argue took place under the dominant, though not the sole, impetus of the development of a capitalist market system. More specifically, it reflected the penetration of this realm of social existence by the values of science, the idea that 'there are no mysterious incalculable forces that come into play, but rather that one can, in principle, master all things by calculation'.[1] Linked to this change in perspective was a fundamental shift in the underlying paradigm of insanity, away from an emphasis on its demonological, non-human, animalistic qualities towards a naturalistic perspective which viewed the madman as exhibiting a defective *human* mechanism, and which therefore saw this condition as at least potentially remediable.[2]

What was emerging at the end of the eighteenth century was a growing market or trade in lunacy; and those operating in this developing market were at work in a social context in which claims to possess expertise and special competence were on general grounds likely to find a receptive audience. It is thus not surprising that the development and consolidation of institutional means of coping with madness parallels that of a professionalized group of managers of the mad. For it was the existence of the institutions which permitted, or perhaps it might be more accurate to say, formed the breeding ground for, this emerging 'professionalism'. On the one hand (and particularly once the state was led to invest directly in the asylum solution), the institutions provided the incentive, in the form of a guaranteed market for the experts' services; and on the other, they provided a context within which, isolated from the community at large, the proto-profession could develop empirically based craft skills in the management of the distracted.[3] As I have

[1] Max Weber, *From Max Weber: Essays in General Sociology*, London, Oxford University Press, 1946, p. 139.

[2] In the next chapter we shall examine in more detail the social sources and appeal of the ideology of rehabilitation; and the impact of this shift in the cultural meaning of madness (and hence in what was considered appropriate treatment for the lunatic) on the reform movement as a whole.

[3] The distinction I want to emphasize here is between skills largely learned by a process of trial and error and transmitted from one generation to the next through a system of apprenticeship; and those resting on an elaborate rational-scientific basis, allowing of a standardized, routine transmission of expertise. Ideological protestations and smokescreens notwithstanding, the former remains the basis for most controllers' claims to expertise.

already noted, one of my major concerns in what follows will be with *how* one particular group captured and organized this market, defining the problem as one they were uniquely qualified to deal with and in the process decisively shifting insanity into the medical arena. Equally important for my analysis is a further implication of the fact that they were able to do so. The emergence in the nineteenth century of what was to become the psychiatric profession lent scientific legitimacy to the process through which the various sub-categories of deviance were established and institutionalized. Or, to put it another way, this development played a critical role in transforming the vague cultural construct of madness into what now purported to be a formally coherent, scientifically distinguishable entity, which reflected and was caused by a single underlying pathology.

This was a self-reinforcing system, for the key dimensions of the emergent profession's claims to expertise came to revolve around questions of institutional management. The very essence of their approach lay in its emphasis on order, rationality, and self-control; goals which could only be reached in an institutional setting. A dialectical process was at work, whereby the separation of the insane into madhouses and asylums helped to create the conditions for the emergence of an occupational group laying claim to expertise in their care and cure, and the nature and content of the restorative ideal which the latter fostered reinforced the commitment to the institutional approach. Thereafter, the existence of both asylums and psychiatry was to testify to the 'necessity' and 'naturalness' of distinguishing the insane from other deviants.

Analysing these developments from a slightly different perspective, we can see that in a number of ways the emergence of medically run asylums for the mad was predicated upon important changes in the relationship between the state and civil society, for a vital feature of this radically novel social control apparatus as it emerged and consolidated itself in the nineteenth century was the degree to which its operations became subject to central control and direction, and dependent upon state power and patronage. Until very late in its history, English society remained overwhelmingly localized in its social organization, characterized by a fragmentation of power and loyalties, and as we have already seen, the mechanisms for coping with deviance in pre-nineteenth-century England placed a corresponding reliance upon an essentially communal and family-based system of control. The assumption of direct state responsibility for these functions, which took place over the first four or five decades of the nineteenth century, thus marked a sharp departure from these traditional emphases.

While the administrative centralization and rationalization which are crucial elements of this transformation are not wholly the consequence of economic rationalization, it seems inescapable that in England, and elsewhere in Western Europe in the later and most critical phases of these processes, the advance of the capitalist economic order and the growth of the central authority of the state are twin processes intimately connected with each other.

On the one hand, were it not for the expansion of commerce and the rise of capitalist agriculture, there would scarcely have been the economic base to finance the expanded bureaucratic state structures. But on the other hand, the state structures were themselves a major economic underpinning of the new capitalist system (not to speak of being its political guarantee).[1]

In a very literal sense, institutional control mechanisms were impracticable earlier, because of the absence both of the necessary administrative techniques and also of the surplus required to establish and maintain them.

The creation of more efficient administrative structures, which was both the precondition and the consequence of the growth of the state and of large-scale capitalist enterprise, possessed a dual importance. It allowed for the first time the development of a tolerably adequate administrative apparatus to mediate between the central and local authorities, and thus to extend central control down to the local level. It also provided the basis for the development of techniques for the efficient handling of large numbers of people confined for months or years on end, without which the institutional mechanisms of social control could scarcely have achieved the importance that they did.

[1] Immanuel Wallerstein, *The Modern World System*, New York, Academic Press, 1974, p. 133.

Financially speaking, state construction and operation of institutions for the deviant and dependent was very costly. Hence the importance as a transitional arrangement of the state contracting with private entrepreneurs to provide gaols, madhouses, and the like. By this method, the state allows the 'deviant farmer' to extort his fees and control his costs in whatever ways he can, and turns a blind eye to his methods; in return the latter relieves the state of the capital expenditure (and often even of many of the running costs) required by a system of segregative control. This is the structural underpinning of the free market in lunacy which formed such a noteworthy feature of eighteenth- and early nineteenth-century responses to the mad. The change to a system directly run by the state was obviously conditioned by, though by no means the automatic product of, the development of large stable tax revenues and the state's ability to borrow on a substantial scale.

In Jean Boudin's famous words, 'Financial means are the nerves of the state.' The 'nervous system' of the English state, lacking the spur of military competition, without a standing army to enforce and require efforts to extract taxes, and dominated by a gentry class fearful of the expansion of the power of the central authority, was for a long time only poorly developed when compared with the Continental Absolutisms of the period.[1] Everywhere, however, in Europe as well as in England, 'until we approach the nineteenth century . . . fiscal possibilities were strictly limited by the structure and trend of the economy'.[2] In the absence of a developed market economy, the structure of economic life militated against the effective levying of taxes. Subsistence economies offer systematic obstacles to both the estimation and the collection of taxes. Where there is only limited exchange, value and net earnings cannot be estimated with any degree of accuracy, and intervening in the tight cycle of production and consumption becomes very difficult. Furthermore, the fact that so much economic activity does not take a monetarized form hinders the collection of taxes – which by now are levied in money, not in kind. In these and other ways, '*tax collection and assessment are indissolubly linked to an exchange*

[1] P. Anderson, op. cit., Chapter 5.
[2] G. Ardant, op. cit., p. 174.

economy.[1] State borrowing and the rise of the so-called national debt are likewise intimately tied to the expansion of the monetarized sector of the economy – to the development of capital markets and the growth of the sophisticated credit and accounting mechanisms characteristic of capitalist economic organization. In the circumstances, one can readily understand why for more than a century and a half, the taxes in support of the poor authorized by the Elizabethan Poor Law (1601) 'were enforced in any community only as a last resort, for these rates were extremely unpopular and they were most difficult to raise'.[2] And while the growing commercialization of the English economy in the eighteenth century gradually began to break down the technical obstacles to larger state appropriation of the social product, political barriers did not dissolve as fast.

In the long run, the development of national and international markets produced a diminution, if not a destruction, of the traditional influence of local groups (especially kinship groups), which formerly played a large role in the regulation of social life. But local opposition to centralized intervention in an increasing range of social activities did not, of course, simply disappear in the face of these developments. Indeed, as we shall see, it proved remarkably tenacious, particularly in the politically sensitive area of the size and reach of 'the central coercive machinery at the disposal of the State'.[3] Central control of the social control apparatus – whether of the facilities for the surveillance and restraint of the poor,[4] the apparatus for the policing of the criminal,[5] or the machinery for certifying and managing the mad – was not won easily, and we shall

[1] ibid., p. 166, emphasis in the original.
[2] W. K. Jordan, *Philanthropy in England*, p. 141; W. J. Ashley, op. cit., p. 360.
[3] P. Anderson, op. cit., p. 139.
[4] N. C. Edsall, *The Anti-Poor Law Movement 1834–44*, Manchester, University of Manchester Press, 1971.
[5] D. Hay, 'Property, authority and the criminal law', in D. Hay, P. Linebaugh, J. G. Rule, E. P. Thompson, and C. Winslow (eds.), *Albion's Fatal Tree: Crime and Society in Eighteenth Century England*, New York, Pantheon, 1975 (London, Allen Lane, 1975 and Penguin, 1977); Steven Spitzer and Andrew T. Scull, 'Social Control in Historical Perspective: From Private to Public Responses to Crime', in D. Greenberg (ed.), *Corrections and Punishment: Structure, Function, and Process*, Beverly Hills, Sage Publications, 1977, pp. 281–302.

have occasion to notice the retarding impact of this factor on the lunacy reformers' project.

Nevertheless, the underlying thrust of the changes in the English social structure in this period is clear: the growth of a single national market and the rise of allegiance to the central political authority to a position of over-riding importance ultimately undermined the rationale of a locally-based response to deviance, based as that was on the idea of settlement and the exclusion of strangers. As local communities came to be defined and to define themselves as part of a single over-arching political and economic system, it made less and less sense for one town to dispose of its problems by passing them on to the next. There was a need for some substitute mode of exclusion. All of which contributed to 'the monopolization of all "legitimate" coercive power by one universalist coercive institution . . .',[1] and to the development of a state-sponsored system of segregative control.

[1] Max Weber, *Economy and Society*, Vol. I, Totowa, N.J., Bedminster Press, 1968, p. 337.

Chapter Two

The Social Context of Reform

> ... Poor Ophelia
> Divided from herself and her fair judgment,
> Without which we are pictures, or mere beasts;
>
> (William Shakespeare, *Hamlet*)

> [In] either the public, or the minor and more clandestine Bethlems ...
> such a mode of management is used with men, as ought not to be,
> although it too generally is, applied even to brutes.

> Derangement is not to be confused with destruction ... [The lunatic's]
> unfortunate state ... for the most part ought to be regarded not as an
> abolition, but as a suspension merely of the rational faculties.
>
> (John Reid, *Essays on Hypochondriasis and Other Nervous Affections*)

The differentiation of the insane from the wider category of the
merely indigent and troublesome was made irrevocable by the
events of the first half of the nineteenth century. This final phase of
the process was marked by the efforts of a relatively small group of
laymen to alleviate the conditions of those they saw as an oppressed
segment of society. Simultaneously, however, it marked a highly
significant redefinition of the moral boundaries of the community.
Insanity was transformed from a vague, culturally defined
phenomenon afflicting an unknown, but probably small, proportion
of the population into a condition which could only be authorita-
tively diagnosed, certified, and dealt with by a group of legally
recognized experts; and which was now seen as one of the major
forms of deviance in English society. Whereas in the eighteenth
century only the most violent and destructive amongst those now

labelled insane would have been segregated and confined apart from the rest of the community, with the achievement of lunacy reform the asylum was endorsed as the sole officially approved response to the problems posed by mental illness. And, in the process, the boundaries of who was to be classified as mad, and thus was to be liable to incarceration, were themselves transformed.

1. Free Trade in Lunacy

Not until the end of the 1840s did a network of publicly financed and state-run asylums assume a dominant position in the institutional management of the mad. The first four decades of the new century did witness a sharp expansion in the number of lunatics confined in specialized institutions, but such expansion for the most part followed eighteenth-century precedents and occurred in the private, profit-making sector of the mad business. Between 1807 (when a House of Commons Select Committee collected and published the first nationwide figures on the number of private madhouses) and 1844 (when the Metropolitan Commissioners in Lunacy published the report which finally persuaded the legislature to compel local justices to set up publicly run asylums), the number of private licensed houses in England more than tripled. From a total of forty-five establishments in 1807, the private system had grown to encompass 139 madhouses by 1844. For the remainder of that decade the size of this sector stayed relatively constant; thereafter, as the expansion of the public sector siphoned off almost all the pauper patients – the majority of the insane population – it declined slowly, though as many as ninety-one private houses still received patients in 1890.

In some respects, it may be misleading to speak of early nineteenth-century madhouses as a system; for there was an extraordinarily wide variability in the character of the houses and those who ran them. During the first half of the century, the greater number of provincial madhouses contained up to approximately twenty-five patients. Most of those in the London area, the so-called Metropolitan houses, were also small. Of the thirty-six operating in 1816, nine were licensed to take fewer than ten patients each; and most of the remainder contained well under a hundred.

On the other hand, institutions such as Hoxton House, Haydock Lodge, or Warburton's Bethnal Green Houses provided for four or five hundred in a single establishment. While places like Ticehurst and Brislington House catered almost exclusively to an upper-class and aristocratic clientele, the large London houses swarmed with a mixture of paupers and a smattering of the marginal middle class.

Similarly, there were wide disparities in the ratio of staff to patients, and in the kind of treatment the patients received. The magistrates charged with visiting Ticehurst reported that many patients 'spoke with pleasure of their residence at Ticehurst, and expressed unwillingness to quit it; all expressed themselves well satisfied with the arrangements made for their comfort and convenience'. Here, for fifty patients, there were as many as thirty-six attendants. At Brislington House, Edward Fox was among the first to demonstrate that the insane could be managed in a more humane and less violent fashion than had hitherto been believed possible. He provided for the segregation and classification of patients according to the degree of their disorder and his management of them involved little or no restraint. At the other extreme, by the standards the nineteenth-century lunacy reformers were to apply (and which we largely still share), conditions in many, perhaps a majority, of the houses were appalling. Particularly early in the century, inmates suffered extremes of barbarity and neglect.

Reflecting the continuing administrative weakness of the English state bureaucratic apparatus (especially on the local level), there was an almost total absence of legal restrictions on entry into or the subsequent conduct of the mad business.[1] At the same time the market for the madhouse keepers' services was expanding, as the tendency to incarcerate all sorts of problem populations grew ever more marked and as the corresponding recognition that 'the Practice of confining such lunatics and other insane persons as are chargeable to their respective Parishes in Gaols, Houses of Correction, Poor Houses, and Houses of Industry, is highly

---

[1] Until 1828, the only legislation purporting to regulate the care of lunatics in these institutions was an Act of 1774, providing for the licensing and inspection of Metropolitan madhouses by members of the Royal College of Physicians and of provincial madhouses by local magistrates.

dangerous and inconvenient'[1] spread ever more widely. Undoubtedly, this permissive legal climate and the demand for places of confinement to which lunatics could be removed, encouraged speculators with no other qualifications than a little capital and an interest in quick returns to enter the mad business. A contemporary observer commented: 'Few speculations can be more unpleasant than that of a private madhouse, and it is seldom if ever undertaken, unless with the hope of receiving large returns on the capital invested.'[2] Concerned solely with maximizing the return on their investment, such men were sometimes prepared to go to extreme lengths to increase their profits. Displaying few scruples, these proprietors became 'wholesale dealers and traffickers in this species of human misery'.[3] A doubtless unintentional by-product of their activity was to provide the lunacy reformers with some of their most powerful ammunition.

Primarily because of the desire to reduce the comparatively large investment needed to enter the trade, at this period 'lunatic houses are mostly common dwelling houses, fitted to the purpose not originally built for it'.[4] Not only were few madhouses of the time purpose-built; but as an economy measure in those that had to be adapted to accommodate lunatics, the necessary alterations were kept to a minimum. A particularly common practice was to buy an old, abandoned country mansion, to turn the impressive-looking central structure into accommodation for the more profitable patients, and to relegate the paupers to the stables and outbuildings.

The scenes of the greatest abuses were the asylums which accommodated paupers. The profit that could be made out of a single pauper was comparatively negligible, given the pittance which the parish overseers allowed for the support of pauper lunatics. In the absence of legal restraint, however, there were no restrictions on the number of patients that could be entrusted to a

---

[1] *Report of the Select Committee on Criminal and Pauper Lunatics*, 1807, p. 6.

[2] Andrew Duncan, *Observations on the Structure of Hospitals for the Treatment of Lunatics as a Branch of Medical Police*, Edinburgh, 1809, p. 18.

[3] Andrew Halliday, *A General View of the Present State of Lunatics and Lunatic Asylums*, London, 1828, p. 10.

[4] *Report of the Select Committee on Madhouses*, 1815, p. 77.

single keeper. To ensure a sufficient return on their capital, therefore, and to take advantage of these potential economies of scale,
madhouses which took pauper patients were generally very large.
This explains the growth in the number of large establishments up
to the middle of the nineteenth century, and their subsequent decline
as the opening of county asylums drained off the pauper patients.
(More licensed houses disappeared between 1850 and 1860, the
decade during which most county asylums built under the 1845
Asylums Act first opened their doors, than during the next thirty
years; and those that disappeared included all the largest houses.)
While such large establishments were not confined to the London
area – Haydock Lodge in Lancashire was licensed for 400 pauper
and fifty private patients – the metropolis contained a number of
the more famous (or infamous) houses. In 1815, Miles' House at
Hoxton contained 486 patients, three-quarters of whom were
paupers; at Warburton's two houses in Bethnal Green, the White
House contained 360 patients (230 paupers) and the Red House
275 patients (215 paupers). In 1844, of the Metropolitan Houses
taking paupers, Hoxton House contained 396 patients, Peckham
House 251, and Warburton's two establishments 562.

Even to our eyes, institutions containing three, four, and five
hundred seem like sizeable concentrations of people. Placed in their
proper historical context, however, they were simply enormous. In
the early nineteenth century, few institutions, including factories,
approached this size. For with any concentration of numbers, the
employer had to 'submit to the constant trouble and solicitude of
watching over a numerous body of workmen . . .', and were he to
try to employ a workforce of two or three hundred men, not only
did this mean that he could no longer directly supervise his own
employees, but it even became 'exceedingly difficult to supervise
his supervisors'.[1] Given the scarcity of trained managers and the
poverty of the management techniques of the period, most commercial enterprises perforce remained comparatively small. The
size of the madhouses is the more remarkable, then, since, unlike
the factory owner, the proprietor of a madhouse faced the further

[1] Cited in Sidney Pollard, *The Genesis of Modern Management*, Harmonds-
worth, Penguin, 1965, pp. 21–2.

problem of managing *all* aspects of the lives of an inmate population confined in his buildings for months, if not years, at a time. Moreover, this was a population composed of people who by definition had failed to respond to conventional efforts to manage and control their behaviour.

To make matters worse, these houses had to compete against one another for patients. And given the parsimony of parish Poor Law officials and their lack of concern with anything save efficient custody, madhouse keepers catering to the pauper trade were forced to reduce their charges for such patients to a bare minimum. Most of these institutions were, as a result, no more than convenient receptacles for the most troublesome and socially inept. They were characteristically overcrowded, and attendants were few and far between. At Warburton's White House, for example, there were at times as few as two paid attendants for 170 male pauper lunatics; inmates were kept alive only with the help of convalescent patients.

The dearth of attendants and the unsuitability of those who were employed – together with the structural deficiencies of the buildings and the absence of effective techniques of managing or supervising either inmates or staff – produced an overwhelming reliance upon chains and other forms of mechanical restraint. In Warburton's houses, to save trouble and expense, and to allow the attendants some free time at the week-end, patients were placed in cribs at three o'clock on a Saturday afternoon, secured with chains, and left there until Monday morning. In the worst pauper establishments, 'fetters and chains, moppings at the morning toilet, irregular meals, want of exercise, the infliction of abusive words, contemptuous names, blows with the fist, or with straps, or with keys, formed an almost daily part of the lives of many unprotected beings'.[1]

2. The Reformers

If conditions in the early nineteenth-century asylums provided a

[1] John Conolly, *The Treatment of the Insane Without Mechanical Restraints*, London, 1856, p. 143.

promising arena for reformist action, there was no shortage of men
interested in the subject. During this period, certain upper-middle-
class gentlemen began to interest themselves in projects of social
reform of every description. Indeed, for a brief period (1811–17),
these self-styled philanthropists were sufficiently numerous to
support a periodical all their own. Lunacy reform was soon one of
their favourite causes. Of equal or perhaps greater importance for
the emergence of a reform movement was the activity of several
energetic local magistrates – an involvement which is scarcely
surprising, for the Justice of the Peace was the primary instrument
of local government at the time, and hence faced on a daily basis all
the problems created by the decay of the traditional social structure.
Their duties, moreover, which included inspection of the gaols and
workhouses, were apt to bring them into contact with the most
troublesome, and on the whole most ill-treated, sections of the
pauper lunatic population. For a more specific conjunctural reason,
magistrates at the turn of the century became still more acutely
conscious of the problems created by the violent insane. In the
wake of an unsuccessful attempt on the life of George III, the
would-be assassin was acquitted on the grounds of insanity. Under
existing law, there was no provision for detaining someone acquitted
in this fashion. Reluctant to allow Hatfield his freedom, Parliament
rushed through a piece of retroactive legislation, directing that such
lunatics would be detained 'in strict custody' in the County Gaol
or other suitable receptacle during the King's pleasure. In the first
five years of its operation, thirty-seven people were detained under
this act, provoking complaints that 'to confine such persons in a
common Gaol, is equally destructive of the recovery of the insane
and of the security and comfort of the other prisoners'.[1] More than
that, some magistrates, at least, were troubled by the irrationality of
acquitting someone of a criminal charge on grounds of insanity, and
then imprisoning him anyway.

Both strands of the emerging lunacy reform movement, like
almost all Victorian social reforms, were heavily influenced by two
competing philosophical systems which were, in effect, social move-
ments: Evangelicalism and Benthamism. The lunacy reformers'

[1] *Report of the Select Committee on Criminal and Pauper Lunatics*, 1807, p. 4.

ranks included leading adherents of both factions,[1] and the final shape of lunacy legislation in England clearly owes much to the Evangelicals' humanitarianism and paternalism, and to the Benthamite emphasis on expertise and efficiency. Evangelicalism may be thought of as a Methodism of the upper middle classes which nevertheless managed to remain firmly within the Anglican tradition. A group of proselytizing religious reformers, the Evangelicals sought to convert a whole society to the advantages of discipline and regularity over disorder and vice. In many ways, they present us with an ideal-typical example of the type of belief system which Howard Becker suggests produces the moral entrepreneur. Their mission (and how appropriate that word is) was perceived as a holy one, the conditions they chose to combat as transparently evil. They insisted that they were not merely imposing their views on others, but, in a profoundly humanitarian fashion, rescuing the lower classes from the sin and social degradation which threatened them. The Evangelical commitment to a kind of moral imperialism was perhaps most clearly exemplified by the name of one of Wilberforce's favourite associations, 'The Society for the Suppression of Vice'; which, as Sydney Smith caustically commented, was 'a society for suppressing the vices of persons whose income does not exceed £500 per annum'.

The moral self-righteousness implicit in their whole perspective is classically that adopted by a dominant class towards those less favourably situated in the social structure. Their simplified view of the world and their immense moral fervour provided them with both innumerable targets for reform, and the fortitude to pursue their goals in the face of ridicule from the wider society as eccentric moralizers. The religious indifference of the new industrial classes,

---

[1] Among the Evangelicals, William Wilberforce, Lord Robert Seymour, and William Smith all served on one or more of the Parliamentary committees on the lunacy question, while the leading Evangelical of a later generation, Lord Ashley (later Lord Shaftesbury) was heavily involved in lunacy reform from 1827 until his death in 1885. Benthamites who took an active part in the reform process included Sir Samuel Romilly and Samuel Whitbread among M.P.s, and provincial magistrates like Sir George Onesiphorus Paul. Bentham himself wrote on the treatment of the insane, and even in the case of those whose commitment to lunacy reform had different sources, such as the Quaker land agent, Edward Wakefield, the influence of his ideas was strong.

the immorality of the slave trade, widespread cruelty to children and to animals, and, of course, the treatment of the insane were all aspects of contemporary society which they deplored, and problems which they attacked with vigour and determination. Evengelicalism was at its core a conservative movement, concerned to shore up a disintegrating social structure and a paternalistic morality against the threats posed by an undisciplined lower-class rabble, and by a purely materialistic entrepreneurial class. To achieve its ends, however, it was forced into the paradoxical position of helping to create a rash of new social rules. Ironically, too, its emphasis on discipline and order, rooted in the desire to see the old patterns of deference and dependence re-established, readily formed the basis for the entirely different morality required by the radically new industrial society.

If Evangelicalism drew its adherents from among those with a profound distaste for certain aspects of the newly emerging society, Benthamism was the creed of a class of administrators virtually created by that new society. Committed to the need for a 'science of government' and emphasizing the replacement of the amateur by the expert, Benthamism's natural appeal was to this growing class. Providing an intellectually powerful and wide-ranging ideology in support of their claims, it proved an important weapon in their fight against the aristocratic dilettante and the dispersal of power to the periphery. The principle of utility, a kind of primitive cost-benefit analysis, provided a 'rational' method for deciding between alternative courses of action; and since the policy thus arrived at was by definition productive of the greatest happiness of the greatest number, the remaining problem was merely to ensure efficient and uniform implementation of its provisions. Both at the level of policy formation and at the level of practical implementation, such an approach inevitably emphasized the desirability, even the necessity, of centralized professional administration, so that with scarcely a need for qualification, Benthamism may be termed 'the apotheosis of the professional ideal'.[1]

For adherents to a philosophy which claimed to have reduced the problem of choice between competing moral alternatives to a

[1] Harold Perkin, *The Origins of Modern English Society 1780–1880*, London, Routledge & Kegan Paul, 1969, p. 269.

rationalistic, almost mechanical, process of weighing the conse-
squences of each, the Benthamites pursued their ideals in a curiously
passionate way. The Evangelicals were content merely to try to
moralize the individual within the existing social framework. The
Utilitarians sought to moralize the social framework itself. The
fusing of moral and practical considerations implicit in the decision
'to attach honour to actions solely in proportion to their tendency to
increase the sum of happiness, lessen the sum of misery . . .', should
not be taken as requiring an abandonment of moral fervour to the
dictates of expediency. Rather, it implied a shift in the means by
which the good was to be sought, away from the individual and
towards an emphasis on the centrality of social rules and policy. The
Benthamite, with his emphasis on providing institutional mechanisms to uncover as well as to eliminate social evils, was in many ways
a more effective moral entrepreneur than his equally self-righteous
Evangelical contemporary. The Benthamite formula – inquiry,
legislation, execution, inspection, and report – proved a fertile
source of new laws and institutions throughout the nineteenth
century, nowhere more so than in the area of lunacy reform.

The attraction of lunacy reform for both these groups is not
difficult to understand. For the Evangelicals, the desire to ensure
that those who had lost their reason should not also lose their souls
inspired sometimes grotesque efforts to bring the lunatic the consolation of organized religion. Few groups besides the insane
offered such a powerful appeal to the essentially paternalistic
instincts of the Low Churchmen; and after the revelations of the
1815–16 House of Commons Select Committee, few could so
readily claim the pity of the pious for their misery and degradation.
Most important of all, unlike the sufferings of the new urban
proletariat, reform of the conditions under which poor lunatics
were kept provided a cause which could salve the consciences of the
devout upper classes without posing a threat to existing social
arrangements. For the Utilitarians, on the other hand, the conditions
of the insane were a powerful argument against the haphazard,
amateurish social policies of the past, and in favour of the rational,
centralized approach they advocated. Their distrust of local
discretion and of the 'wisdom' of the Common Law was for them
confirmed and justified by the patent anomalies and absurdities

produced by the law as it stood; and by the revelations of appalling cruelty, filth, and neglect produced by the series of Parliamentary inquiries into the treatment of lunatics. In the face of apparently overwhelming evidence that the existing lack of a policy was responsible for gross inhumanity and yet perpetuated a threat to the social order in the form of madmen left at large in the community, the Benthamite insistence on the need for a coherent national policy, and Bentham's own emphasis on the value of disciplining the insane within a special institution, had a natural attraction for those confronted with the problem of what to do with the insane. Not so coincidentally, of course, a centralized, bureaucratically-run system also advanced the interests of the emerging administrative class from which so many of Bentham's supporters came.

3. The Cultural Meaning of Madness

Efforts to secure national legislation on the lunacy question came first from one of these Benthamite administrators, Sir George Onesiphorus Paul, a Gloucestershire magistrate who was also heavily involved in prison reform. Frustrated in his efforts to secure the establishment of a charity asylum at Gloucester in association with the local infirmary, he bombarded the Home Office with complaints concerning the anomalies in existing laws dealing with lunatics and urged the establishment of a system of tax-supported asylums for their 'relief and comfort'. Eventually, in 1807, he secured the appointment of a Select Committee of the House of Commons charged with investigating 'the State of the Criminal and Pauper Lunatics in England and Wales'.

Despite the presence on this Committee of a number of the most active social reformers of the age – such men as Romilly, Whitbread, and Wilberforce – what seems most striking in retrospect is the narrow limits of its inquiries and recommendations. Over the next half century, much of the energy and public support the lunacy reformers mustered for their project was generated by the 'scandals' uncovered by successive legislative inquiries. But in contrast to these later reports, with their volumes of evidence and their impassioned calls for central intervention and direction, the 1807 Committee's activities seem curiously tame. Few witnesses testified before it, and the Committee accepted without further inquiry the testimony of madhouse keepers that 'their [clients'] treatment in general appears to be extremely proper . . .' Claims that existing charity asylums were 'a great success' were accepted with a similar credulousness, and the House of Commons was informed, with considerable confidence, but on the basis of no real evidence, that 'the Measure which appears to Your Committee most adequate to enforce the proper care and management of these unfortunate persons and the most likely to conduce to their perfect cure, is the erection of Asylums for their reception in the different parts of the kingdom'.[1] However dubious the antecedents of this recommendation, it was accepted by Parliament and in the following year a permissive act was passed, authorizing but not compelling magistrates to erect asylums in each county at public expense.

If the 1807 Committee had adopted the asylum solution with little prior investigation of its merits, it also provided the magistrates who were charged with building the asylums with few clear guidelines about what to build. Their report had simply urged that asylums be as large as possible in order to save expense, but 'not exceeding three hundred [inmates]'. The 1808 Act instructed that a site be secured in 'an airy and healthy situation, with a good supply of water, and which may afford the probability of the vicinity of constant medical assistance'. But apart from this, and the provisions concerning finance, admissions, and discharges, the justices were left largely to their own devices.

Faced with the problems of what kind of institution to construct and how to administer it, those local magistrates who chose to build an asylum (and most Quarter-Sessions did not) solved it in the most obvious fashion, by using existing asylums as models. Some appointed a superintendent and sent him to an older asylum to observe its procedures. Others obtained the information they needed through correspondence with those running existing charity hospitals, or accepted the help offered by madhouse keepers. County asylums built from the late 1820s on were able to draw on the experience of their predecessors as an additional source of information. The magistrates' committee in charge of the Middlesex asylum at Hanwell, for example, corresponded frequently with a

[1] *Report of the Select Committee on Criminal and Pauper Lunatics*, 1807, p. 6.

number of other county asylums, seeking both architectural plans and information on the day-to-day administration of an asylum. Eventually, too, it recruited William Ellis, the Superintendent of the West Riding County Asylum, to fill the same position at Hanwell.

To some extent, the treatment the patients in these new asylums received depended on which older institution their asylum was modelled after. But for the most part, the over-riding concern with security and the preservation of order within the institution, coupled with magistrates' demands for economy, ensured a fundamental similarity of approach. Nowhere was the emphasis on custodialism more evident than in the architecture of such places. John Conolly, speaking during the brief period of therapeutic optimism that marked the 1840s, commented that the architects of this period 'appear to have had regard solely to the safe-keeping of the inmates, and the buildings resemble prisons rather than hospitals for the cure of insanity'. As another observer commented,

> Were we to draw out opinions on the treatment of insanity from the construction of the buildings designed for the reception of the patients, we should conclude that the great principle adopted in recovering the faculties of the mind was to immure the demented in gloomy and iron-bound fastnesses; that these were the means best adapted for restoring the wandering intellect, correcting its illusions, or quickening its torpidity: that the depraved or lost social affections were to be corrected or removed by coldness and monotony.[1]

As the experience of these early county asylums demonstrates, even those most heavily involved in lunacy reform lacked at the outset any clear idea of what sort of institution they ought to set up, how it was to be run, or why it would ameliorate the condition of the insane. Hence the new asylums' tendency to be modelled on the very places the reformers were within a few years to denounce so vehemently. A concern with protecting society from the disorder threatened by the raving, a desire to simplify life for those charged with administering the local poorhouses and gaols, and an equally unfocused and unsystematic feeling that the insane themselves deserved to be treated in a more 'humane' fashion; all these were

[1] J. Conolly, op. cit., p. 7; *Westminster Review*, 43, 1845, p. 167.

shared in varying degrees by the earliest reformers. But they did not amount to a coherent alternative vision of what could, and should, be done.

This lack of a plausible alternative conception of how the insane might be managed was a severe handicap to the reformers. They remained trapped within the conventional assumptions of their society, and continued to defer to the 'expertise' of the mad-doctors. By so doing, they accepted practices which they themselves were later to condemn as needless cruelty. Widespread use of mechanical restraint, for instance, was made necessary by the structural deficiencies of existing asylums and by the inadequacies of available management techniques; but it did not lack for sophisticated ideological justifications. Paul's frequent laudatory references to the York Asylum, where chains and other means of restraint were extensively employed, make it clear that he, at least, accepted these doctrines; just as he accepted the contention that fear was the best method of managing maniacs. Over a period of years, he repeatedly praised the Asylum as 'the institution at York under the excellent management of Dr Hunter' and urged it as a model which those building public asylums should strive to emulate. Yet within less than a decade, the York Asylum came to symbolize all that the reformers sought to abolish.

As this should suggest, the perception that the traditional ways of coping with lunatics in madhouses (even such things as the use of whips and chains to maintain a semblance of order) were inherently cruel and inhumane is by no means as simple and self-evident a judgement as both the reformers and later generations came to believe. The practices of eighteenth-century madhouse keepers seem so transparently callous and brutal that we tend to take this judgement as unproblematic, as immediately given to any and all who have occasion to view such actions. The value of Paul's case is that it demonstrates so clearly the shallowness and fallacy of such an assumption. The reformers were eager to portray their activities as motivated by a kind of disinterested moral superiority, and to picture their opponents as moral lepers, devoid of common decency and humanity. However useful such an outlook may be as support for one's own sense of self-righteousness, it remains without analytical utility. Indeed, it has been our readiness to take such claims at face value that has blinded us to a central feature of the reform process, which is that it both reflected and helped to produce a transformation in the moral boundaries of the community.

Cruelty, like deviance, 'is not a quality which lies in behavior itself, but in the interaction between the person who commits an act and those who respond to it'.[1] Consequently, whether or not a set of practices is perceived as inhumane depends, in large part, on the world view of the person who is doing the perceiving. Practices from which we now recoil in horror were once advocated by the most eminent physicians and cultured men of their day. That madmen were chained and whipped in asylums in the eighteenth century was well known at the time. How could it be otherwise when, throughout the century, the doors of Bethlem were open to the public, and the inmates exhibited before the 'impertinent curiosity of sightseers at a mere penny a time . . .', and where every treatise on the management of the mad advocated such treatment? Certainly such practices were not something of which magistrates only became aware at the turn of the century. Yet it was only then that protests began to be heard that such treatment was cruel and inhumane.

To be sure, some of the treatment meted out to lunatics in private madhouses was the natural product of an unregulated free market in madness – the consequence of the unchecked cupidity of the least scrupulous, of the incentives to half-starve and neglect pauper inmates, of the temptation to rely on force as the least troublesome form of control. But there is more to it than that. Even in situations where such factors were obviously inapplicable, lunatics were treated in ways which later generations were to condemn as barbaric and counter-productive – in ways which they (and we) find virtually incomprehensible and almost by default attribute to an under-developed moral sensibility, if not outright inhumanity. The treatment of George III during his recurrent bouts of 'mania' makes this point most dramatically and unambiguously. As Bynum has pointed out,

A great deal was at stake with this patient, and there is every reason to believe that Francis Willis, his sons, and other assistants treated the king

[1] Howard Becker, *Outsiders*, Glencoe, Illinois, 1963, p. 14.

in a manner which (in Willis's considered opinion) would most likely result in the royal patient's recovery. Yet, as the Countess Harcourt described the situation, 'The unhappy patient . . . was no longer treated as a human being. His body was immediately encased in a machine which left no liberty of motion. He was sometimes chained to a stake. He was frequently beaten and starved, and at best he was kept in subjection by menacing and violent language.'[1]

Such treatment would have been unthinkable only a decade or two later.

One is inescapably led to the conclusion that a necessary condition for the emergence of the moral outrage which animated the lunacy reformers was a transformation of the cultural meaning of madness. Such a change can indeed be shown to have occurred. In seventeenth- and eighteenth-century practice, the madman in confinement was treated no better than a beast; for that was precisely what, according to the prevailing paradigm of insanity, he was. In becoming crazy, the lunatic had lost the essence of his humanity, his reason. Pascal's view was typical: 'I can easily conceive of a man without hands, feet, head (for it is only experience which teaches us that the head is more necessary than the feet). But I cannot conceive of a man without thought; that would be a stone or a brute.'[2] Eminent mad-doctors of the early nineteenth century continued to adhere to this position, arguing that 'If the possession of reason be the proud attribute of humanity, its diseases must be ranked among our greatest afflictions, since they sink us from our pre-eminence to a level with the animal creatures.'[3]

The resort to fear, force, and coercion is a tactic entirely appropriate to the management of 'brutes'. Thus, when we look at the treatment of the insane prior to 'reform', we must realize that

the negative fact that the madman is not treated like a 'human being' has a very positive content . . . For classicism, madness in its ultimate form is man in immediate relation to his animality, without other reference, without any recourse. The day would come when from an evolutionary

[1] William Bynum, 'Rationales for Therapy in British Psychiatry', *Medical History*, 18, 1974, p. 319.

[2] Pascal, *Œuvres Complètes*, Paris, 1954, p. 1156.

[3] Joseph Cox, *Practical Observations on Insanity*, 3rd edn, London, 1813, p. ix.

perspective this presence of animality in madness would be considered as the sign – indeed as the very essence – of disease. In the classical period, on the contrary, it manifested the very fact that *the madman was not a sick man*. Animality, in fact, protected the lunatic from whatever might be fragile, precarious, or sickly in man . . . This is why . . . madness was less than ever linked to medicine; nor could it be linked to the domain of correction. Unchained animality could be mastered only by *discipline* and *brutalizing*.[1]

It was this world view which the nineteenth-century reformers, and, indeed, society as a whole, were in the process of abandoning. Much of the reformers' revulsion on being exposed to conditions in contemporary madhouses derived from this changed perspective. For them, the lunatic was no longer an animal, stripped of all remnants of humanity. On the contrary, he remained in essence a man; a man lacking in self-restraint and order, but a man for all that. Moreover, the qualities he lacked might and must be restored to him, so that he could once more function as a sober, rational citizen.

Of course, the replacement of the traditional perspective did not come all at once. 'Unenlightened' circles clung to it long after it had been displaced as the dominant orthodoxy; by which time actions based on it were incomprehensible, and its adherents drew upon themselves the stigma of inhumanity. Paul's continuing attachment in the early years of the century to the doctrine that chains and the inculcation of fear were the best means of managing madness demonstrates that even the reformers did not succeed at a stroke in freeing themselves from the past (though this peculiarity has been overlooked by earlier historians since it conflicts with their notion of a simple humanitarianism as the well-spring of reform). Furthermore, once it is recognized that to a large extent what divided the reformers and their opponents was not the morality of one group and the immorality of the other, but rather the existence of two mutually contradictory paradigms of the essence of insanity, certain otherwise incomprehensible incidents in the history of reform begin to lose their air of paradox.

For example, one of the situations which the reformers were able

[1] Michel Foucault, *Madness and Civilization*, New York, Mentor Books, 1965, pp. 68–9. (London, Tavistock Publications, 1971.)

3

to exploit to greatest advantage was their discovery of the conditions under which a Bethlem inmate, William (or James) Norris, had been kept, night and day, for somewhere between nine and fourteen years. Norris was found to be restrained by a specially constructed piece of apparatus; an iron cage encased his body from the neck down, and this in turn was attached by a short chain to an iron bar running from the floor to the ceiling of the cell. The degree of confinement was such that he could lie only on his back, and could advance no more than twelve inches away from the bar to which he was attached. The most curious aspect of all this was not that a man should be found confined in such a fashion – for there can be no doubt that numerous analogous situations existed at the time. Rather it lies in the response of the hospital authorities. Compelled to institute an official inquiry, the Governors conceded that the facts were as the reformers had stated them, but contended that the confinement was kind and merciful rather than cruel and brutal, and expressed their undiminished confidence in the asylum's medical officers.

One can place two possible interpretations on this bizarre state of affairs. Either the Governors shared the callousness of their subordinates and were ingenuous enough to let this show. Or their protestations were sincere, and they genuinely saw nothing wrong with treating a lunatic in such a fashion. The latter is surely the more plausible; and it is precisely what one would expect of men who still looked at madness in terms of the earlier paradigm – of which conditions in Bethlem were almost an exact reflection. Such 'backward' attitudes persisted even longer in provincial settings. In 1843, for example, the Metropolitan Commissioners in Lunacy, as part of a national survey of conditions in madhouses, visited the West Auckland Licensed House a matter of hours after the local magistrates had inspected it. The former pronounced it 'utterly unfit'; the latter reported 'everything in good order'. The sheer perverseness of this judgement from the reformers' perspective is the clearest evidence that their standards were not universally shared, even by the middle of the century; and these different criteria of evaluation were one reason local power centres resisted efforts to set up a system of nationally supervised, publicly supported asylums.

At the outset, those who denied the legitimacy of the treatment meted out by traditional madhouse keepers and who sought to establish a paradigm which would declare such conduct to be purposively illegitimate, faced the difficult task of overcoming the charge that their ideas were no more than the Utopian schemes of an abstract benevolence, unschooled by contact with the realities of day-to-day management of lunatics. As Samuel Tuke remarked, 'Benevolent persons in various places had long been dissatisfied with the system of management generally pursued, but benevolent theory was powerless when opposed by practical experience.'[1] Fortunately for the reformers, a number of madhouse keepers were by now groping towards methods of managing and 'treating' patients which showed that it was indeed possible to eliminate most of the 'barbarous' and 'objectionable' features of the contemporary asylum. Men like John Ferriar at the Manchester Lunatic Asylum and Edward Long Fox at his madhouse for aristocrats, Brislington House, were becoming convinced that 'the first salutary operation in the mind of a lunatic' lay in 'creating a habit of self-restraint . . .', a goal which might be reached by 'the management of hope and apprehension . . ., small favours, the show of confidence, and apparent distinction . . .', rather than by coercion.[2] In the event, though, it was the fundamentally similar notions developed by the Tuke family at the York Retreat which became nationally known and, under the name 'moral treatment', virtually synonymous with the very idea of reform.

The proximate cause of the establishment of the Retreat in 1792 had been a purely local scandal, involving the death under mysterious circumstances of a Quaker patient at the local charity institution, the York Asylum. Following the repeated urgings of William Tuke, a local tea and coffee merchant, the Quaker community was stimulated by this to construct an asylum of their own for those Friends 'deprived of the use of their reason'. Notwithstanding the apparent obscurity of its provincial, sectarian origins, the Retreat, from a quite early date in its history, attracted the

[1] Cited in R. Hunter and I. MacAlpine, introduction to Samuel Tuke, *Description of the Retreat*, facsimile edn, London, 1964, p. 5.
[2] John Ferriar, *Medical Histories and Reflections*, Vol. II, London, 1795, pp. 111–12.

attention of an occasional visitor concerned with the plight of the insane. The first tribute to its achievements came from a French physician, de la Rive, within two years of its opening, though this attracted more attention on the Continent than in England. Twelve years later, the Glasgow architect, William Stark, publicized the Tukes' activities rather more successfully. Stark's pamphlet, *Remarks on the Construction of Public Hospitals for the Cure of Mental Derangement*, attracted considerable attention among those interested in lunacy reform, and in the problems of designing and running asylums. In consequence, his long eulogy to the practices at the Retreat led to a spate of inquiries and visits by the philanthropically inclined. Thus encouraged, the founder's grandson, Samuel Tuke, decided to publish an account of the institution and of the methods of treatment pursued in it. The appearance of this book in 1813, and the subsequent favourable notice by Sidney Smith in the *Edinburgh Review*, brought the Retreat national attention.

One cannot readily summarize in a phrase or two what moral treatment consisted of, nor reduce it to a few standard formulae, for it was emphatically not a specific technique. Rather it was a general, pragmatic approach, making use of anything which appeared to work and aiming at minimizing external, physical coercion; and it has therefore usually been interpreted as unproblematically 'kind' and 'humane'. Restraint might be necessary to prevent bodily injury, but it ought to be a last resort, and was never to be imposed solely for the convenience of the attendants. While Tuke did not think that restraint could be entirely done away with, he did insist on doing away with its most objectionable forms – gyves, chains, and manacles – and his refusal to employ it as a routine measure was a marked departure from prevailing practice. It made a profound impact on contemporary reformers, who saw his success as proof that the insane could be managed without what were now seen as harshness and cruelty.

This was no 'kindness for kindness' sake'. From its architecture to its domestic arrangements, the Retreat was designed to encourage the individual's own efforts to reassert his powers of self-control. For instead of merely resting content with controlling those who were no longer quite human, which had been the dominant concern of traditional responses to the mad, moral treatment actively sought to *transform* the lunatic, to remodel him into something approximating the bourgeois ideal of the rational individual. The problem with external coercion was that it could force outward conformity, but never the essential internalization of moral standards. Only by 'treating the patient as much in the manner of a rational being, as the state of mind will possibly allow', could one hope to re-educate him to discipline himself. By acting as though 'patients are considered capable of rational and honourable induce-ment . . .', and by making use of the vital weapon of man's '*desire for esteem*', inmates could be induced to collaborate in their own recapture by the forces of reason. 'When properly cultivated', the desire to look well in others' eyes 'leads many to struggle to conceal and overcome their morbid propensities; and, at least, materially assists them in confining their deviations within such bounds, as do not make them obnoxious to the family'.

The staff played a vital role in the re-education process: they must 'treat the patients on the fundamental principles of . . . kind-ness and consideration'. Again, this was not because these were good in themselves, but because 'whatever tends to promote the happiness of the patient, is found to increase his desire to restrain himself, by exciting the wish not to forfeit his enjoyments; and lessening the irritation of mind which too frequently accompanies mental derangement . . . The comfort of the patients is therefore considered of the highest importance in a curative point of view.' Here too lay the value of work, the other major cornerstone of moral treatment: since 'of all the modes by which the patients may be induced to restrain themselves, regular employment is perhaps the most generally efficacious'.

By all reasonable standards, the Retreat was an outstandingly successful experiment. It had demonstrated, to the reformers' satisfaction at least, that the supposedly continuous danger and frenzy to be anticipated from maniacs were the consequence of, rather than the justification for, harsh and misguided methods of management and restraint; indeed, that this reputation was in large part the self-serving creation of the madhouse keepers. It apparently showed that the asylum could provide a comfortable and forgiving environment, where those who could not cope with the world could find respite, and where, in a familial atmosphere, they might be spared the neglect that would otherwise have been their lot. Perhaps even more impressive than this was the fact that, despite a conservative outlook which classified as cured no one who had to be re-admitted to an asylum, the statistics collected during the Retreat's first fifteen years of operation seemed to show that moral treatment could restore a large proportion of cases to sanity.[1]

4. Sources of the Changing Conception of Insanity

One must grant the importance of the changing conceptions of insanity and its appropriate treatment as an intervening cause in the rise of the lunacy reform movement. But of course ideas and conceptions of human nature do not change in a vacuum. They arise from a concrete basis in actual social relations. Put slightly differently, the ways men look at the world are conditioned by their activity in it. The question which we must therefore address is what changes in the conditions of social existence lie behind the changes we have just examined.

In a society still dominated by subsistence forms of agriculture, nature rather than man is the source of activity. Just as man's role in actively remaking the world is underdeveloped and scarcely perceived – favouring theological and supernatural rather than anthropocentric accounts of the physical and social environment – so too the possibilities for transforming man himself go largely unrecognized and the techniques for doing so remain strikingly primitive. In a world not humanly but divinely authored, 'to attempt reform was not only to change men, but even more awesome, to change a universe responding to and reflecting God's will' – to embark on a course akin to sacrilege.[2] And where the rationalizing impact of the marketplace is still weak, structures of domination tend to remain *extensive* rather than intensive – that is, the quality and character of the workforce are taken as given rather than as plastic and amenable to improvement through appropriate management and training.

[1] Samuel Tuke, *Description of the Retreat*, York, 1813.
[2] Howard Solomon, *Public Welfare, Science, and Propaganda in Seventeenth Century France*, Princeton, 1972, pp. 29–30.

But under the rationalization forced by competition, man's *active* role in the process presents itself ever more insistently to people's consciousness. This development is further accelerated and confirmed by the rise of manufacturing – a form of human activity in which nature is relegated simply to a source of raw materials, to be worked on and transformed via active *human* intervention. More than that, economic competition and the factory system are the forcing house for a thorough-going transformation in the relation of man to man. For industrial capitalism demands 'a reform of "character" on the part of every single workman, since their previous character did not fit the new industrial system'.[1] Entrepreneurs concerned to 'make such machines of men as cannot err'[2] soon discover that physical threat and economic coercion will not suffice: men have to be taught to *internalize* the new attitudes and responses, to discipline themselves. More than that, force under capitalism becomes an anachronism (perhaps even an anathema) save as a last resort. For one of the central achievements of the new economic system, one of its major advantages as a system of domination, is that it brings forth 'a peculiar and mystifying . . . form of compulsion to labor for another that is purely economic and "objective".'[3]

The insistence on the importance of the internalization of norms, the conception of how this was to be done, and even the nature of the norms which were to be internalized – in all these respects we can now see how the emerging attitude towards the insane paralleled contemporaneous shifts in the treatment of the 'normal' populace. The new practices, which had their origins in the wider transformation of English society, were shared, developed further, and given a somewhat different theoretical articulation in the context of the lunatic asylum. In a society where self-interest was elevated to a universal law of human nature and where all men were subjected in a superficially equal fashion to the pressures of the marketplace, the notion that all men shared a common humanity

---

[1] Sidney Pollard, op. cit., p. 297.

[2] Josiah Wedgwood, cited in Neil McKendrick, 'Josiah Wedgwood and Factory Discipline', *Historical Journal*, 4, 1961, p. 46.

[3] Maurice Dobb, *Studies in the Development of Capitalism*, New York, 1963, p. 7.

possessed an obvious appeal. By extension, the insane were now drawn into this community of mankind.

As in the wider world, so too in the lunatic asylum: one could no longer be content with the old emphasis on an externally imposed and alien order, which ensured that madness was controlled, yet which could never produce self-restraint. Control must now come from within, which meant that physical violence, now dysfunctional, became abhorrent. Abstracting from the barely conscious activities of their fellow-capitalists, a few of the more perspicacious employers grasped the wider implications of what they were collectively doing: they were providing a practical demonstration of the proposition that 'Any general character, from the most ignorant to the most enlightened, may be given to any community, even to the world at large, by the application of proper means: which means are to a great extent at the command and under the control of those who have influence in the affairs of men.'[1] This realization of the power which was latent in the ability to manipulate the environment and of the possibility of radically transforming the individual's 'nature' was translated in the context of madness into a wholly new stress on the importance of cure. It represents a major structural support of the new ethic of rehabilitation. As the market made the individual 'responsible' for his success or failure, so the environment in the lunatic asylum was designed to create a synthetic link between action and consequences, such that the madman could not escape the recognition that he alone was responsible for the punishment he received. The insane were to be restored to reason by a system of rewards and punishments not essentially different from those used to teach a young child to obey the dictates of 'civilized' morality. Just as the peasantry who formed the new industrial workforce were to be taught the 'rational' self-interest essential for the market system to work, the lunatics, too, were to be made over in the image of bourgeois rationality: defective human mechanisms were to be repaired so that they could once more compete in the marketplace. And finally, just as hard work and self-discipline were the keys to the success of the urban bourgeoisie from whose ranks Tuke came, so his moral treatment

[1] Robert Owen, *A New View of Society*, London, 1813, p. 99.

propounded these same qualities as the means of reclaiming the insane.[1]

5. Private Investigations at the York Asylum and at Bethlem

The gradual emergence in the late eighteenth and early nineteenth centuries of new responses to madness is thus scarcely fortuitous. From the reformers' viewpoint, the importance of the York Retreat was as a practical realization of their own half-formulated ideals. The value of the alternative model it provided quickly became apparent.

Some months before the publication of Tuke's book, Godfrey Higgins, a Yorkshire magistrate, had become aware of the mistreatment of a pauper whom he had ordered to be committed to the York Asylum. At the time, his own efforts to secure an investigation by the institution's governors had proved unavailing. Higgins now renewed his attempts to expose the abuses there. Joining forces with the Tukes, and with several of his fellow magistrates, each of whom subscribed the £20 necessary to become an asylum governor, he forced an official investigation of the institution. On another front, he proceeded with his own inquiry into conditions there. Together, these investigations provided evidence of wrongdoing on a massive scale: maltreatment of patients extending to rape and murder; forging of records to hide deaths among inmates; an extraordinarily widespread use of chains and other forms of mechanical restraint; massive embezzlement of funds; and conditions of utter filth and neglect. Higgins discovered a series of cells whose entrance had been deliberately hidden from view. Conditions here were particularly bad; the cells themselves were

in a very horrid and filthy condition . . . the walls were daubed with excrement; the airholes, of which there was one in each cell, were partly filled with it . . . I then went upstairs . . . into a room . . . twelve feet by seven feet ten inches, in which there were thirteen women who . . . had all come out of those cells that morning . . . I became very sick, and could not remain any longer in the room. I vomited.[2]

[1] I owe this last point to Michael Fears.
[2] *Report of the Select Committee on Madhouses*, 1815.

3*

The reformers could not have asked for a better example of the practices they were hoping to eliminate. The value of the events at York to the cause they were seeking to promote was enhanced by the reluctance of some of the original governors, and particularly of the asylum physician, Dr Best, to concede defeat. Despite the variety and volume of the evidence that reformers produced, for a period of almost a year Best and his supporters among the governors refused to give way. A furious press and pamphlet war took place during the whole of this time, keeping the case continuously before the public, and providing a highly effective forum for the dissemination of the reformers' ideas to an ever wider audience. Inevitably, Best was ultimately forced to resign, and the asylum was reorganized under Tuke's direction.

By a curious coincidence, the publication of Samuel Tuke's *Description of the Retreat* provoked the revelation of similar abuses at Bethlem. Edward Wakefield, who was also a Quaker, had for some years been interested in providing asylums for the insane. In the *Medical and Physical Journal* for April 1814 he announced an effort to set up a 'London Asylum', to be run on the lines of the York Retreat. A committee was formed to further the project, and as part of its preparations, an investigation was undertaken of existing provisions for London's insane at Guy's Hospital, St Luke's, and Bethlem. The conditions they discovered at the latter institution prompted an effort to reopen the issue of lunacy reform at the national level.

The name of Bethlem, or its corrupted form, 'Bedlam', had for centuries been virtually synonymous with the very idea of a separate institution for the insane. Notwithstanding occasional hints of scandal, it had remained a favourite upper-class charity. Its respectability was attested to by the presence of a Board of Governors who were almost exclusively of aristocratic background; and its physician, Thomas Monro, was himself something of a society figure. Despite these upper-class trappings, however, Bethlem contained few patients from wealthy backgrounds; indeed, most of the patients were paupers. Crammed together in a decaying structure which was acknowledged to be in need of replacement, these unfortunates were still managed along traditional lines. With only four keepers employed to supervise 120 inmates, the inspecting party found that many patients continued, for weeks and months at a time, to be chained to the walls of their cells. (Among these, of course, was James Norris in his iron cage.) A number of inmates were left naked, or covered with only a blanket. There was no effort to classify the patients; the furious, violent, and frenetic were distributed indiscriminately among the mild and convalescent cases.

In other respects, too, the inmates were largely abandoned to their fate. Extraordinarily, for an institution which could nominally call on the services of a physician and a surgeon, as well as a resident apothecary, not even the physical ills and ailments of the patients received prompt attention. Several cases were found of inmates who had lost toes or even feet from frostbite. To the efforts of the apothecary to attribute this to the greater susceptibility of the insane to 'mortified extremities', the reformers countered that not a single such incident had occurred in the twenty years of the Retreat's existence. In any event, questioning of the staff brought to light the information that the 'resident' apothecary visited the hospital for only half an hour each day, and on many occasions did not bother to appear for days at a time. Monro, the physician, was seen still more infrequently; evidently his time was too valuable to waste on such unremunerative patients.

Appalled by what he had found, and convinced by now of the need for a more ambitious and thorough-going reform than would be achieved merely by setting up a competing asylum run on the lines of the York Retreat, Wakefield contacted a group of sympathetic M.P.s and revisited Bethlem with them. Armed with this first-hand experience, and with the publicity the scandals at York and Bethlem had received, these M.P.s pressed for a Parliamentary investigation of conditions in madhouses and charity asylums. In April 1815, a Select Committee was authorized and the inquiry began.

Chapter Three

The Chimera of the Curative Asylum

Madmen appear to have been employed to torment other madmen, in most of the places intended for their relief.

(Samuel Tuke, *Description of the Retreat*)

Tenderness is better than torture, kindness more effectual than constraint . . . Nothing has a more favourable and controlling influence over one who is disposed to or actually affected with melancholy or mania, than an exhibition of friendship or philanthropy.

(John Reid, *Essays on Hypochondriasis and Other Nervous Affections*)

I wish to stir up an intelligent and active sympathy, in behalf of the most wretched, the most oppressed, the only helpless of mankind, by proving with how much needless tyranny they are treated – and this in mockery – by men who pretend indeed their cure, but who are, in reality, their tormentors and destroyers.

(John Perceval, *Perceval's Narrative*)

1. The 1815–16 Parliamentary Inquiry

The new Committee included several of those who had been members of the short-lived 1807 investigation, but the inquiry which ensued was quite unlike its predecessor. Lasting almost two years and encompassing a whole series of detailed reports and minutes of evidence, the inquiry surveyed treatment in charity hospitals (Bethlem, York Asylum, St Luke's); in the new county asylums (Nottingham, one of only three open at this time); in private madhouses (a number, ranging from Warburton's houses at

Bethnal Green and Spencer's house at Fonthill Gifford at one extreme, to Brislington House and Laverstock at the other); and in workhouses. The reformers were now sure of what they wanted to achieve. The focus throughout their inquiry was on the conditions endured by those insane confined in institutions, with no effort being made to gather comparable data on lunatics in the community. Yet although abuses and maltreatment of patients were found to be prevalent in virtually every type of institution they examined, both the Committee itself and those who disseminated its findings to a wider public interpreted these revelations as proof of the need for more institutions (albeit under direct public control), as well as justifying (indeed, making imperative) an improved system of inspection and supervision of all receptacles within which lunatics were confined.

The early meetings of the Committee were largely taken up by an investigation of the recent events at the York Asylum and at Bethlem. The reformers realized that this material provided some of their most powerful ammunition against the existing system. Accordingly, they were careful to avoid all appearances of bias, offering those criticized the opportunity to rebut the testimony given against them, while making sure that the abuses and depredations earlier investigations had uncovered received a thorough airing. The reformers' case was overwhelming. At York, as we have seen, they had already succeeded in forcing the resignation of the asylum physician, Dr Best, had dismissed his staff, and had undertaken a total reorganization of the entire institution. Higgins, who had played such a prominent role in these affairs, was the Committee's first witness. He placed on record an extensive narrative of events prior to reform, including the frantic efforts of the asylum staff to conceal their wrongdoing by the destruction of records and, in all probability, by deliberately burning down a large part of the asylum building itself – a fire in which at least four patients were acknowledged to have died. His old adversary, Dr Best, was, therefore, already discredited by the time he appeared before the Committee, and the mixture of bluster and outright denial he exhibited on the witness stand failed to rescue his reputation.

The situation at Bethlem was rather different. In the aftermath of Wakefield's first visit, and his return with a party of M.P.s, the governors had felt compelled to institute their own inquiry into the conduct of their officers and the condition of the asylum. Incredibly, from the reformers' perspective, they had convinced themselves that the charges were without foundation, that the institution was as good, if not better, than any in England, and that the conduct of the physician and apothecary deserved praise rather than opprobrium. Indicative of their attitude was their conclusion on the case of Norris: his confinement, they solemnly averred, had been 'upon the whole, rather a merciful and a humane than a rigorous and severe imposition'.

Consequently, the reformers were here concerned not merely with placing on the public record an account of past mismanagement, but also with provoking a more suitable response from the governors. Wakefield's evidence itself provided a damning indictment of the asylum's administration; but, in addition, several of the M.P.s had themselves witnessed the abuses he complained of on their own tour of Bethlem. When the apothecary and the physician, Haslam and Monro, appeared before the Committee, their position, following their recent vindication by their employers, was ostensibly secure. The hostile cross-examination which they now faced, however, forced both of them, first into evasion and denial, and then into self-contradiction and damaging admissions about their own conduct in office. Finally, in desperation, each man resorted to blaming the other, or the surgeon, Bryan Crowther, who had conveniently died earlier that year. As soon as their first report was printed, the Committee ordered copies to be sent to every governor of Bethlem, a scarcely veiled suggestion that the latter should reconsider their earlier action. In the face of this pressure, the governors convened a special meeting and called the physician and apothecary before them for a second time. Each arrived with an air of injured innocence and presented the governors with a written defence of his conduct, pointing out that the charges against them were the very same ones the governors themselves had concluded were baseless a few months previously. The governors proved no less adept than their employees at contradicting themselves. Haslam was dismissed and within six weeks Monro's resignation was accepted.

In the meantime, the Committee's inquiries had moved from a

concern with conditions in the principal charity hospitals of the period to a consideration of the treatment meted out to those confined in workhouses and in a number of private institutions avowedly operated for profit. Much of the testimony on these places came from a handful of reformers who appear to have made an almost full-time vocation of inspecting the conditions under which lunatics were kept. Wakefield, for example, in his travels as a land-agent, had inspected a number of provincial madhouses. A few, such as Brislington House and Laverstock House, were exceptions to the general trend, and failed to add to the catalogue of abuses the Committee was now uncovering. At Langworthy's House at Box in Wiltshire, however, the pattern was more typical: he was refused permission to see male patients on the grounds that this was one of the days they were not allowed up. Among the women, he found two lying naked on straw pallets, and four others left entirely naked in total darkness: 'in the course of my visiting these places, I never recollect to have seen four living persons in so wretched a place'.[1]

The most extensive evidence on the treatment of the insane confined in workhouses was provided by Henry Alexander, a banker who had developed an interest in lunacy reform. Like Wakefield, he had taken advantage of the travelling he had to do for business purposes to undertake a series of unofficial inquiries into the conditions of the insane. Some he had found in rooms 'no better than dungeons . . .'; elsewhere the cells were 'like pig-styes'. His description of the conditions at the Tavistock Workhouse was particularly graphic. He was refused permission to see the lunatics themselves, and when he persisted, the master reluctantly showed him the quarters they were usually housed in, first warning him that he would find them unfit to enter even though they had been washed out earlier that morning:

I never smelt such a stench in my life, and it was so bad, that a friend who went with me [into the first cell] said he could not enter the other. After having entered one, I said I would go into the other; that if they could survive the night, I could at least inspect them . . . The stench was so great I almost suffocated; and for hours after, if I ate anything, I still retained the same smell; I could not get rid of it; and it should be

[1] *Report of the Select Committee on Madhouses*, 1815, p. 21.

remembered that these cells had been washed out that morning, and had been opened some hours previous.[1]

The Committee next sought evidence on the operations of the system for inspecting Metropolitan madhouses under the 1774 Act, a task which had been delegated to members of the Royal College of Physicians. Dr Richard Powell, who had acted as the secretary to the Commissioners since 1808, was their principal witness. There were thirty-four madhouses under the Commissioners' direct jurisdiction, and Powell testified that on their tours of inspection they visited 'some days, perhaps two; other days six or eight' houses within the space of a few hours. Though they suspected some houses of concealing the actual number of patients crammed into their overcrowded rooms, they made no effort to see that the legal requirement that all inmates be reported to them was observed, or to inquire into the disposition of individual cases. Given the brief duration of the average inspection, such procedures were totally impracticable. At the most recent visit to Miles' establishment at Hoxton, for example, the inspection of the whole structure and the condition of its 486 inmates had been completed within two and a half hours. The lunacy reformers on the Committee were naturally aware that even had the Commissioners bothered to uncover evidence of systematic brutality and neglect, the latter lacked any legal power to intervene. But, of course, this only strengthened their resolve to replace the existing system altogether.

At the close of the inquiries in 1815, therefore, the Committee had uncovered evidence that neglect and maltreatment of lunatics was endemic in all the various types of institutions in which they were incarcerated, and its members were convinced that legislative intervention was urgent. Fearful perhaps that others might not be so readily convinced, they continued their investigations into the following session, uncovering evidence which suggested massive irregularities in two of the largest and best-known private madhouses in London, Warburton's Red and White Houses at Bethnal Green. John Rogers, the apothecary at the White House, gave evidence which suggested a state of affairs at least as sordid as that revealed at Bethlem and the York Asylum. The houses themselves,

[1] ibid.

he alleged, were infested with rats and fleas, and were so cold and damp that many patients suffered from gangrene and tuberculosis. At least one patient had had to have both feet amputated when mortification set in, and as many as a hundred patients had died during the winter of 1810-11 from typhus. Instances of gross brutality inflicted on patients by the keepers went unpunished even where they caused a patient's death. Female patients were liable to be raped. Beating and whipping were common punishments and prolonged restraint was employed as a routine means of managing patients.

Rogers reiterated these and other allegations in a pamphlet he had published at his own expense. The detailed nature of the evidence he gave and his willingness to cite the names and dates of actual cases made him an impressive witness. His testimony was, quite naturally, vigorously contested by Warburton and his minions. Matthew Talbot, superintendent of the White House, accused Rogers of deliberate falsification, and Warburton himself appeared before the Committee to issue a blanket denial of all the charges: 'I never knew of an instance of an injury so much as any boy has received at school from a chilblain, or not more.' Unfortunately, the Committee's failure to investigate conditions at first hand left the issue of who was telling the truth unresolved, though the mere suspicion that such events might have occurred was enough for many of the reformers.

By the time the 1815-16 Committee submitted its final report, there was a wealth of documentation to support the reformers' contention that what they perceived as appalling degradation and inhuman treatment were the lot of madmen in every sort of institution in which they were confined. Future investigations might (and did) add further examples of these self-same abuses inflicted on other madmen in other asylums; but the fundamental picture was already clear, and the evidence sufficiently abundant to convince most observers of the justice of the reformers' claims about conditions in existing asylums, if not the correctness of their prescription for reform. Likewise, the reformers were already convinced that they knew what had to be done to cure the 'intolerable' evils they had exposed. There were two central elements in their plan: the provision of a system of asylums at public expense to take at least all of the pauper lunatics ought to be made compulsory, in order to eliminate the inducements to maltreatment inherent in keeping lunatics for profit; and a vigorous system of inspection by outsiders with no ties to the asylum administration should be implemented, to provide a check against the tendency of all institutions to fall away from their initial ideals and against the temptations for the keepers to neglect and maltreat their helpless 'clients', the mad. These two proposals remained the fundamental features of the reform plan until its eventual implementation. Yet despite the obvious propaganda value of the Committee's revelations in producing converts to the reformers' cause, it took the latter thirty years to attain their objectives.

2. The Fate of the First Reform Bills

In the aftermath of the Committee's findings, the reformers sought, in the first instance, to replace the existing moribund provisions for the inspection of madhouses with the kind of efficient national inspectorate which they considered an essential prerequisite for reform. Three times between 1816 and 1819, members of the Select Committee presented bills to introduce such a provision. Each bill proposed a permanent commission of eight, to be appointed by the Home Office, with power not merely to inspect private madhouses, but also to lay down and enforce standards for the management of these institutions and the treatment of patients. On each occasion, the Parliamentary reformers were able to make use of the massive evidence of abuse which they had uncovered, and the manifest inadequacies of the existing system of inspection, to secure majorities in the House of Commons for the bill's passage; on each occasion the measure was rejected in the Lords.

What accounts for these failures? In the first place, it is clear that the reformers made some tactical errors which hurt their cause. For example, in 1816, when the revelations of their Committee were still fresh in the public mind, the reformers made the error of including in their bill a provision for the stringent inspection of 'single lunatics'. This was a measure known to offend the aristocratic sensibilities of their Lordships, who were concerned to protect the privacy of upper-class families with a lunatic in the closet, and it undoubtedly contributed to the bill's defeat. Subsequently, this provision was so watered down in the 1817 bill as to be almost meaningless, but by then the reform movement was losing its momentum. The *Edinburgh Review* sought to rally support for the measure, urging that while 'many of the evils have already ceased to exist in some of the principal institutions for the insane . . . they were the offspring of circumstances that, without a radical change of system in the control of madhouses, cannot fail to produce again the same deplorable effects'. By now, however, opponents of the bill were exerting pressure in the opposite direction.

Such opposition had a number of sources. Most obviously, it came from those whose interests in the mad business were directly threatened by the new schemes. Madhouse proprietors complained that though the Committee's findings had 'excited a very high degree of public feeling', the testimony it had heard was not given on oath, 'and, whilst it exaggerates praise in a few instances, bestows much undeserved censure in many others'. The publication of such evidence was 'likely to be productive of positive injury in various ways, both to society and to individuals. Society at large must suffer if insane persons are allowed to range uncontrolled, whilst they are not regulated by reason in their conduct, and are morally irresponsible as they should therefore be, for their actions.' In consequence of the prejudice against madhouses the reformers had stirred up, 'it does indeed so suffer at present, and crimes which are referrable to insanity are largely increased'.[1] In a more subtle kind of special pleading, which we will discuss at greater length in Chapter 4, the reformers' proposals were pictured as an assault on medicine's professional prerogatives, as encouraging lay interference in technical decisions about the proper treatment of the insane, and hence as productive of serious damage to the patient's best interests.[2]

---

[1] George Man Burrows, *Cursory Remarks on a Bill now in the House of Peers for Regulating Madhouses*, London, Harding, 1817, p. 1; Anon., *Insanity*, London, 1817, p. 5.

[2] An earlier effort to strengthen the system for inspecting madhouses had also been stifled, in part at least, by medical opposition; see *Medical and Physical Journal*, 1814, pp. 1–2.

One doubts, though, whether such self-interested sophistry would have carried the day but for the existence of a much more broadly-based and politically powerful source of opposition to the reformers' plans. The critical strength of the resistance movement came from its links with the localist bias characteristic of English society until well into the nineteenth century. This aversion to the concentration of power at the national level was extraordinarily widespread and well-entrenched on both the structural and ideological levels. Undoubtedly, its origins lay in the gentry's successful resistance to Stuart attempts to impose an indigenous English form of absolutism (though such convictions concerning the threat which centralized state power offered to the liberties and freedom of a propertied class had received more recent and dramatic confirmation in the French Revolution and its aftermath). The English upper class had secured its power by ensuring that administration remained locally based, and by convincing the common people (as well as themselves) that an increase in the authority of the state threatened to produce an engine of despotism, 'a system of tyranny . . ., the destruction of all public liberty, and the disturbance of all private happiness'.[1] The hegemony of these local landed élites, astutely legitimized through the legal system and finding practical expression in the powers of the magistrate and innumerable autonomous local authorities, did not simply melt away at the first demands for a more rational system. On the contrary, in the first decades of the nineteenth century these administrative units jealously defended their independence against the Benthamites and the rising class of professional administrators.

The effort to rewrite the legal rules concerning insanity and the treatment of the insane was necessarily productive of opposition on this score, since it involved interference with the 15,000 or so local poor law administrations which had previously possessed untrammelled authority to dispose of the insane (along with other types of indigent) with virtually total freedom from central supervision and control. The reformers' proposals for a system of inspection by paid officials dependent upon the central government – officials who would have had the power to enforce centrally determined

---

[1] J. P. Smith (1812), cited in E. P. Thompson, *The Making of the English Working Class*, New York, 1963, p. 82. (London, Penguin, 1970.)

directives and standards – threatened a transformation in political relationships whose importance extended far beyond the narrow sphere of lunacy reform. In securing acceptance of this type of administrative apparatus, the central government would have obtained far greater power than it had hitherto possessed to ensure compliance with its wishes – with a corresponding setback to the power of the landowning class.

The political leverage of the rural aristocracy – locked in a losing battle with the rising manufacturing and commercial bourgeoisie – was by now clearly on the wane. As economic life – indeed, life in general – became increasingly oriented towards and dictated by conditions in national and international markets, so the significance of the purely local and personal dependencies to which the authority of the traditional élites was bound steadily declined in significance. Ever more aware of the advantages of impersonal forms of coercion – most especially the invisible hand of the marketplace – the bourgeoisie were in consequence ever less disposed to rely on the visible and personal authority of an earlier era. And yet, while capitalism dissolved traditional social restraints, capitalists as a class sought a previously unknown degree of stability and predictability in social relationships, for the market was extraordinarily sensitive to disorder and uncertainty. In the long run, only a greatly strengthened state apparatus could provide such guarantees, particularly on a national basis.

In the short run, however, the position of the gentry remained sufficiently entrenched to ensure that the old habits of thought and existing systems of political organization would be defended with much of their old vigour. Two additional factors stiffened resistance to the lunacy reformers' proposals. The plan to make construction of county asylums compulsory threatened local authorities with heavy capital expenditures which they were reluctant to incur, particularly since they faced simultaneous pressures to provide new gaols and workhouses, and to develop a communications network adequate for the emerging industrial society. Then, too, the uneven spread of the new outlook on the insane left many sceptical of the need for change. Local magistrates continued to accept the traditional paradigm of insanity, along with its emphasis on the demonological, almost bestial character of madness. Consequently, they were frequently unable to comprehend why the reformers saw the treatment of lunatics within their jurisdiction as brutal and inhumane; why conditions they saw as unexceptionable produced shock and outrage in others. Not surprisingly, then, it was only after the manufacturing and commercial bourgeoisie had secured a substantial increase in their political power and influence through the 1832 reform of Parliament that the obstacles to central administration and direction were confronted and dealt a decisive defeat; and the issue was fought out, not over the marginal issue of lunacy reform, but over the crucially important matter of Poor Law policy – the Old Poor Law being the single most important remaining limitation on the free market in labour.

3. Renewed Parliamentary Investigation

The defeat of the 1819 bill led to a brief hiatus in the effort to secure legislative implementation of the lunacy reformers' plans. Several leading parliamentary supporters had died, while others had retired. In 1827, however, yet another parliamentary inquiry re-awakened interest in the issue. Between that date and 1845, when the major elements of the reform programme were enacted into law, the reformers' efforts to overcome their opposition proceeded on two fronts. The first and most visible of these was the political: they made use of astute parliamentary manoeuvring and a further series of official inquiries to keep the issue before the public and eventually to wear down their opponents. As we shall see, the success of this first tactic was intimately tied to activity of a rather different sort – the development over the second quarter of the nineteenth century of an increasingly elaborate pro-institutional ideology designed to rally public support for the reformers' plans.

The revival of parliamentary interest in lunacy reform came about through the persistence of Lord Robert Seymour, a member of the 1815–16 Committee who had subsequently given up his seat in Parliament. In his remaining public capacity, as a magistrate for the county of Middlesex, he had sought for years to persuade his reluctant fellow-magistrates of the need for a county asylum. Finally, in 1827, they were prevailed upon to set up a committee of magistrates to inquire into conditions in the private madhouses in the county. Armed with the evidence produced by a visit of the overseers of the poor for St George's parish to one of Warburton's houses, Seymour also approached those interested in lunacy reform in the Commons and pressed for a renewed inquiry into conditions in Metropolitan madhouses. Here again he was success-ful: on 13 June 1827, Robert Gordon, a fellow magistrate and M.P. for Dorset, secured the establishment of a new Select Committee charged with this task.

For the most part, the Committee confined its attention to a detailed inquiry into conditions at Warburton's White House in Bethnal Green, taking extensive testimony from magistrates and parish poor law officers who had visited it to inspect the condition of the pauper patients, from members of the Royal College of Physicians who had inspected it under the provisions of the 1774 Madhouse Act, and also from a number of ex-patients. Almost without exception, their evidence revealed a pattern of systematic abuse, maltreatment, and neglect of the inmates. A large number of the inmates were kept confined in 'crib-rooms', places where

there are nothing but wooden cribs or bedsteads; cases, in fact, filled with straw and covered with a blanket, in which these unfortunate beings are placed at night; and they sleep most of them naked on the straw, covered with a blanket . . . they are mere boxes of the depth of about eighteen inches, where the person lies in; they are all fastened; some all fours, some one, some two, and some three [limbs].

Fifteen of these cribs were crammed into a single room, twenty-nine feet by fifteen. Each day patients were locked into their cribs 'about three o'clock in the afternoon, and . . . did not get up until nine in the morning'. To allow the keepers a day off once a week (and there were only two attendants for 164 male pauper lunatics),

on Saturday evenings, they were locked down in the same state, and kept till Monday morning, without being unchained or allowed to get up to relieve themselves in any way whatever . . . On Monday morning, like the other mornings, when they got up, they were many of them in a very filthy state, and I have seen them, when the snow has been upon the ground, put into a tub of cold water and washed down with a mop; there was a man who came from Northamptonshire, who was treated in that way; I have seen that man brought up from the door of the room, and from the heat of the faeces that were lying upon him, his back has been completely bare for many inches up, and he was treated in the same way by being washed in the way I have stated.

The cribs themselves were generally in a filthy state: 'I turned the straw out of some of the cribs and there were maggots at the bottom of them where sick men had laid.'[1]

As the Committee took pains to document, such conditions were scarcely atypical of those Metropolitan madhouses which concentrated on the pauper lunatic trade, and the reformers now made use of this ostensibly local investigation to reopen the issue of legislation to give effect to at least some of the changes they considered necessary. This time the bills were framed to avoid offending the local gentry and magistrates, and to reduce the most obvious manifestations of central control to a minimum, so as to eliminate the most important source of opposition to the earlier bills. The bill which eventually became the County Asylums Act (9 George IV c. 40) on the surface added little to previous acts regulating these establishments. It did, however, establish a precedent for some central government interest in the internal affairs of county asylums through the apparently trivial provisions that magistrates were to send annual returns of admissions, discharges, and deaths to the Home Office, and that the Secretary of State could, if he so chose, send a visitor to any county asylum – though such a visitor had no legal power to intervene in asylum administration. A second bill, which passed as the Madhouse Act (9 George IV c. 41), marked another partial success for the reformers. The 1827 inquiry had again shown that inspection on a part-time basis by the College of Physicians under the 1774 Madhouse Act was little more than a cosmetic measure with no practical force, and with this new act they finally secured its abolition and replacement. To achieve this, however, they were forced to engage in a temporary tactical retreat from the proposals for a full-time national 'Board of Inspection' which had been so prominent a feature of the 1816, 1817, and 1819 bills, and which remained the solution they ultimately wanted to implement.

[1] *Report of the Select Committee on Pauper Lunatics in Middlesex*, 1827, pp. 156–8.

The 1828 Act did provide for the establishment of a new Commission to license and supervise lunatic asylums. Its activities were, however, to be confined to the Metropolitan area. Moreover, the Commissioners were to be appointed on a purely part-time basis, with the five physician Commissioners receiving token payment, and the rest giving their services gratuitously. In this respect it represented a reversion to the amateur system of the past, an apparent abandonment of the earlier insistence on the Benthamite ideal of full-time, expert administrators. Meanwhile, in the provinces, in what was basically but a minor departure from the provisions of the 1774 Act, the duties of visitation and licensing remained in the hands of the magistrates – three Justices and a medical attendant were to be appointed at the General Quarter Sessions and charged with visiting all houses licensed to receive lunatics at least three times a year. Finally, the Act's provisions for inspection applied only to private madhouses, not to county asylums, or to the charity or 'subscription' asylums.

In all these respects, the bill to regulate madhouses presented in 1828 seemed a weak measure, particularly when compared with the earlier bills the reformers had presented. But it had the decisive merit of conciliating the opposition sufficiently to secure its passage, not entirely unscathed, through the Lords. By allowing the magistrates to continue to perform the duties of visitors in the provinces, it avoided giving offence to the country gentry; the provision exempting the county asylums, which were run by the local magistrates, had the same effect; while the parallel exemption of the charity hospitals circumvented the possibility that the powerful lobby formed by their aristocratic boards of governors would be ranged against the bill: and the provision for the Metropolitan Commissioners to be amateurs stilled fears that the measure would produce a further increase in the powers of the executive.

In practice, the Metropolitan Commission proved to be an extremely effective pressure group on behalf of the expansion of its own activities, and for the establishment of the full-time national inspectorate which the reformers had long sought. All the leading members of the Parliamentary group of lunacy reformers secured appointments to the Commission – eleven of the fifteen Commissioners were M.P.s or former M.P.s, and their ranks included

Robert Gordon, Anthony Ashley Cooper (later Lord Shaftesbury), and Lord Granville Somerset. Such a small and politically influential group was well placed to use their reports as propaganda for their own solution to the problems of insanity and to produce evidence which would convince others of the correctness of their case. Moreover, they could confidently anticipate that while they vigorously enforced the provisions of the 1828 Act, and thus eliminated at least the grosser forms of abuse, a majority of the provincial magistrates would continue to ignore or laxly carry out their responsibilities. Given time, the opponents of the centralized system could be relied upon to produce evidence which would damn their cause.

4. The Elaboration of a Pro-institutional Ideology

The Commissioners were not alone in seeking to revise and extend the reforms of 1828. The more respectable asylum doctors, who were attempting to monopolize the mad business and to transform it into an arena for professional practice, were consequently interested in excluding the more disreputable elements engaging in the madhouse trade. The members of this proto-profession produced large numbers of books and pamphlets which served to bolster their claims to possess a specific expertise in the treatment of the insane; but many of these writers were also concerned 'to condense, in a plain, practical, and still popular form, the results of observation in the treatment of insanity, for the specific purpose of demanding from the public an amelioration of the condition of the insane'.[1] Over the next two decades, this emerging class of professional asylum administrators, acting in concert with a number of lay reformers, developed an increasingly elaborate account of the merits and advantages of the asylum as a response to insanity. Emphasis was placed on the contrast between conditions in traditional madhouses and the possibilities of the new approach based on moral treatment – both as providing more humane care than would otherwise have been possible, and as producing cures in a large number of cases. The growing volume of literature discussing what

[1] W. A. F. Browne, *What Asylums Were, Are, and Ought to Be*, Edinburgh, 1837, p. 1.

an asylum could do and what it should be like was matched by a growing optimism about the likely results of the new system. More and more the asylum was presented as a technical, objective, scientific response to the patient's condition, an environment which provided the best possible conditions for his recovery.

In the absence of public asylums, many pauper lunatics who were 'not so violent as to be perfectly unmanageable' were frequently abandoned, and left to 'linger out their existence in a workhouse'. Here, the reformers objected, 'they are under the care of persons totally and entirely ignorant of the proper treatment of lunatics . . . the rooms in which they are kept are ill-adapted to the confinement of such persons, and . . . from those causes, those unfortunate persons have been constantly confined in strait waistcoats, frequently kept in bed night and day.' But though the maniac was here reduced to the status of an inconvenient object, whose condition required no more than that minimal efforts be made to ensure his physical survival, yet his presence was still a burden upon the workhouse administrators, and on the lives of the sane inmates. If nothing worse, the latter were forced to tolerate the disruptions and unpleasantnesses brought about by the lunatics' refusal to conform to ordinary social conventions, so that under even the most brutal and unfeeling management, 'lunatics in workhouses' unavoidably remained 'an extreme annoyance to the other inhabitants of those houses'.[1]

From this perspective, 'the propriety and necessity of a separate establishment for the care of lunaticks, must be obvious' to even the meanest intelligence. The mental hospital would be an asylum in a dual sense: to the workhouse it would afford relief from the disorder always at least latent in the presence of madmen; and for the maniac himself it would provide a sanctuary, a refuge from the world with which he could no longer cope. Here he would be cared for by those who had a greater practical experience in the management of insanity, in surroundings specifically designed to avoid the structural deficiencies which, in the workhouse, made harsh treatment of the lunatic almost inescapable.

The promise of the specialized institution lay in its ability to create a forgiving environment in which humane care on a mass

[1] *Report of the Select Committee on Madhouses*, 1815, p. 11.

basis was possible; and in the probability that the efforts of those running the asylums would restore a significant number of lunatics to sanity. In the aftermath of the publicity moral treatment had received, even those who did not entirely share the reformers' optimistic faith in the virtues of the asylum found it hard to resist the notion that the grim custodial routines by which the workhouse accommodated itself to the lunatic could be transformed. And since it was assumed that the insane in workhouses were only there because they lacked either the personal resources or the sort of supportive kinship network they needed to survive outside an institution, to advocate the continued segregation of such derelicts behind the walls of a different institution was scarcely controversial. If one could overlook the powerful deterrent factor of the cost of building and maintaining asylums (as parish officials were reluctant and reformers were prone to do), then on most other grounds it was plausible (and probably correct) to assert that at least those lunatics who had formerly starved and rotted in workhouse cellars would be better off in asylums.

But the reformers were not content just to bring these benefits to those who had hitherto been confined in sub-standard institutions. The asylum possessed advantages which even those whose families were still willing and able to care for them should share in. And the reformers and the asylum doctors were determined that they should do so. The idea of confining sick or helpless members of one's family in an institution was not yet a popular one, particularly among the more respectable elements of society. Even the poorest families amongst the working classes made strenuous efforts to avoid bringing the disgrace of the workhouse upon themselves. Similarly, the hospitals of the period still tended to be patronized by a clientele composed of the indigent sick and the friendless traveller far from home. The enormous mortality rates, uncompensated for by greatly increased chances of recovery, together with the lingering stigma of their charity origins, led most of those who could afford it to shun them in favour of treatment at home. As for the deranged, given the mass of unfavourable publicity the reformers themselves had generated about conditions in most existing madhouses, their contention that everyone becoming insane ought to be promptly removed to an institution had an obviously paradoxical air. A family concerned with the welfare of a member afflicted by mental disturbance must surely conclude that 'no person who can keep such a sufferer out, ought to place him in an asylum . . .'[1]

If the asylum superintendents and their reformist mentors were to obtain a population consisting of much more than just chronic pauper derelicts, if the asylum was to amount to more than just a convenient dumping ground for confining the most troublesome flotsam and jetsam of society, then families who could exercise some choice in the matter had somehow to be convinced that the institution should be the place of first rather than last resort. Unless this effort succeeded, asylums would surely remain starved of funds. Moreover, without a significant proportion of upper-class patients, the newly emerging psychiatric profession could look forward to no more than a dubious status as a barely legitimate branch of medicine. For close and unremitting contact with the stigmatized and powerless carries its own peculiar reward – a share of their stigma and marginality.

Yet the conclusion that institutional care was preferable to even the best and most solicitous domestic arrangements was by no means self-evident. Hence it required elaborate ideological justi-fication. Only by emphasizing the expertise of those who ran the asylums and the positive benefits of asylum treatment could the institution's advocates make a presumptive case for extending those 'benefits' to those not compelled to use the asylum's services.

The emerging profession was not above implying that any mad-man, even an apparently placid and harmless case of dementia, was capable of sudden and unprovoked acts of violence, which were peculiarly liable to be directed against members of his immediate family. This element of unpredictability carried with it the clear implication that 'both for their own safety, and that of others, it is necessary that they should be placed in a state of confinement, differing, of course, in degree as the symptoms are violent'. But for all its functionality, the traditional argument, based on the threat a lunatic might pose to the security of the community, was more readily used to justify custody than efforts at cure; so that asylum superintendents were reluctant to employ it as their major argument

[1] Anon., *On the Present State of Lunatic Asylums*, London, 1839, p. 11

for committal. Instead, they preferred to develop an alternative thesis, stressing that the management of insanity 'is an art of itself' and that in its successful treatment, the requisite 'means and advantages can rarely, if ever, be united in the private habitations even of the opulent'.[1]

The much greater experience of asylum personnel with the shapes and forms of mental disturbance was reflected in the ease and skill with which they managed and handled their patients. By contrast, the deranged frequently suffered from the well-meaning but misconceived interventions of devoted relatives. Not surprisingly, then, 'they submit more patiently to discipline from strangers, who are experienced in their treatment, than from relatives and dependents, who are timid, unskilled, and frequently the objects of irritation'. 'A private dwelling is ill-adapted to the wants and requirements of such an unfortunate being', since in addition to there being a specific expertise attached to treating the insane, there were also buildings which were particularly adapted and suited to the condition of insanity. Only a purpose-built asylum could provide the requisite conditions for 'moral and physical management . . . as well as the means of preventing personal injury and inconvenience to the Patient'.[2]

Besides the fact that it lacked most of the basic necessities for the effective treatment of mental illness, the home suffered from a fatal flaw, one which made it the least suitable place of all to keep a lunatic. Quite simply, it was the environment which had nurtured the disturbance in the first place. Lunatics ought not to be treated at home, 'not only on account of the distress and confusion they there produce, but because there circumstances that excite a maniacal paroxysm frequently exist'.[3]

If any families were concerned with the welfare of their insane members, it was surely those who, rather than simply abdicating all responsibility by handing them over to strangers, were prepared to

---

[1] Rev. J. T. Becher, *An Address to the Public on . . . the General Lunatic Asylum near Nottingham*, Newark, 1811, pp. iv–v; William Ellis, *A Letter to Thomas Thompson, M.P.*, Hull, 1815, p. 8.

[2] R. G. Hill, *A Lecture on the Management of Lunatic Asylums*, London, 1839, p. 6; *Brislington House: An Asylum for Lunatics*, n.p., 1806, p. 1.

[3] *Brislington House: An Asylum for Lunatics*, p. 1.

suffer the inconvenience produced by keeping such people at home. But if the asylum doctors were to be believed, such generous and self-sacrificing instincts were fraught with potentially disastrous consequences for the patient himself. After all, 'experience . . . proves that few are cured at home, but many more when removed'.[1] The overwhelming consensus of the experts in the field testified to

the improbability (I had almost said moral impossibility) of an insane person's regaining the use of his reason, except by removing him early to some Institution for that purpose. If such a result is ever to be obtained without the adoption of this plan, it is either a very rare occurrence indeed, or it has ensued from a change of residence, of scene, and of persons around, combined with a mode of treatment in some measure resembling that which can be fully adopted only in a Building constructed for the purpose.[2]

The need for reassurance that 'those we exile to madhouses are receiving treatment, not punishment' seems to have emerged early in the history of the asylum, and to have been offered and accepted on the basis of very little evidence. Perhaps this should not surprise us; after all, it serves important functions for both the madhouse keepers and their true clients, the 'patient's' family. For the former, it provides the necessary material from which the self-image of expertise can be constructed. For the latter, it eases the guilt which must inevitably be attached to the prospect of confining a loved one in an institution which has never managed to obtain a very salubrious reputation. Accordingly, both groups could find comfort in the assurance that 'the treatment of insanity is now so well understood, and the requisites for forming a perfect asylum, or hospital, for the reception of insane patients so fully ascertained by experience that they admit of very little discussion'.[3]

5. The Asylum's Critics

By and large, the reformers and the asylum doctors were extremely

---

[1] *Westminster Review*, 18, 1833, p. 134. This was a safe generalization, since nobody possessed (or was likely to possess) the information necessary to disprove it.

[2] R. G. Hill, op. cit., pp. 4–5.

[3] Andrew Halliday, *A Letter to the Magistrates of Middlesex on . . . Erecting an Asylum for Pauper Lunatics*, London, 1826, p. 13.

effective in proselytizing the asylum's virtues and the need to insulate the insane from the world. From time to time, the wisdom accumulated by the experts was condensed and summarized for popular consumption in one or another of the leading reviews of the period. And laymen could always be impressed by references to a veritable pantheon of names famous for their humanity and/or their skill in treating mental disorder – Cullen, Tuke, Pinel, Esquirol – all of whom were staunch advocates of the seclusion of the insane.

Occasionally, though, a few isolated figures refused to bend to the weight of professional and informed opinion, and raised their voices against the tendency to incarcerate all those labelled as mad. As John Conolly pointed out, it was seldom hard to isolate particular features of someone's behaviour which would lend credence to the idea that he was crazy. To send such a person to an asylum was practically to ensure that the designation would stick: 'Once confined, the very confinement is admitted as the strongest of all proofs that a man must be mad.' Hence to create more institutions would guarantee the discovery of more madmen to fill them. Already, 'the crowd of most of our asylums is made up of odd but harmless individuals, not much more absurd than numbers who are at large'.[1] Moreover, even for those who were manifestly mad, the asylum was more likely to prove harmful than otherwise. After all,

what would be the consequence, if we were to take a sane person, who had been accustomed to enjoy society, and . . . were to lock him up in a small house with a keeper for his only associate, and no place for exercise but a miserable garden? We should certainly not look for any improvement in his moral and intellectual condition. Can we then reasonably expect that *a treatment which would be injurious to a sane mind, should tend to restore a diseased one*?[2]

The most vital deficiencies of the asylum as a curative institution were inherent in its very structure, and hence could not possibly be removed by any conceivable reform. No matter that asylum directors were 'men of great intelligence and humanity'; no matter that

[1] John Conolly, *An Inquiry Concerning the Indications of Insanity*, London, 1830, pp. 4–5, 17.
[2] Anon., *On the Present State of Lunatic Asylums*, p. 39, emphasis in the original.

they may point to the spaciousness of their grounds, to the variety of occupations and amusements prepared for their patients; to the excellence of their food and the convenience of their lodging; and urge that as little restraint is employed as is compatible with their safety: but the fault of the association of lunatics with each other, and the infrequency of any communication between the patient and persons of sound mind mars the whole design.

For those forced to remain within the walls of an asylum, 'the effect of living constantly among mad men or mad women is a loss of all sensibility and self-respect or care; or, not infrequently, a perverse pleasure in adding to the confusion and diversifying the eccentricity of those about them . . . In both cases the disease grows inveterate.' Such a pathological environment thus encourages the very be-haviours which are then used to justify its existence: 'Paroxysms of violence alternate with fits of sullenness; both are considered further proofs of the hopelessness of the case.' The peculiar routines of the asylum are quite unlike those of the outside world. Never-theless, some inmates manage to adjust to them and it is one of the ironies of institutional existence that those who manage this transition most effectively are at the same time reducing their ability to function in the outside world. 'After many hopeless years, such patients become so much accustomed to the routine of the house, as to be mere children; and are content to remain there as they commonly do, until they die.' Equally pathetic were the 'numerous examples . . . in which it was evident that although the patients were not yet sufficiently recovered to be restored to their families without superintendence, [but where] a continued residence in the asylum was gradually ruining the body and the mind'.[1]

The clear implication of these arguments was that the whole effort to reform the treatment of the insane by isolating them in hospitals was a venture which was misconceived from the start. Resting their case on a faulty and incomplete analysis of what was wrong with traditional madhouses, the reformers were committing themselves to 'solutions' which, in the nature of things, could not produce a lasting improvement in the condition of the insane. Yet,

[1] John Conolly, *An Inquiry Concerning the Indications of Insanity*, 1830, pp. 20–22, 31.

4

despite the force and relevance of the critique, it drew no intellectually adequate response from the asylum's proponents. Quite clearly, the critics of the asylum suffered from their lack of organization and numbers, which inhibited their ability to get their opponents to take them seriously. They were, after all, attempting to overturn the conventional wisdom of the overwhelming majority of experts in the field. Those experts had a considerable intellectual investment of their own in the asylum; over many years they had spent considerable time and effort trying to educate the public in the necessity of building asylums. Indeed, they had already persuaded the community to make a sizeable investment of material resources in just such a programme. These were not the sort of commitments which would be easily abandoned.

As I shall show later in this chapter, the proponents of institutionalization were by now so convinced of the superiority of a carefully supervised asylum system that they were prepared to overlook, or rationalize away, not merely plausible *arguments* that they were wrong, but also a mass of empirical evidence which indicated that the strategy which they had chosen would, from the outset, fall far short of the goals they had set for it. This blindness or tunnel vision derived not merely from the normal reluctance of most human beings to concede that they may be mistaken, but also from a specific trait which one must possess to be a successful reformer. It is plainly the case that awareness of the complexity of the world and the moral ambiguity of existing patterns of behaviour is something which always threatens to paralyse action; so that all of us are forced to resort to some degree of cognitive simplification of the world, to take for granted the 'routine grounds of everyday action', if the world is not to overwhelm us. The reformer, though, the man who seeks to alter certain aspects of this socially constructed reality, must characteristically carry such cognitive simplification to an extreme. The ability to reduce the ambiguous to the certain, to order the world in an often grossly stereotypical fashion, is generally a necessary precondition if one is to be a successful moral crusader. If the reformer is to remain dedicated to his task in the face of the ridicule and opposition he is sure to encounter, he must possess abundant confidence in the validity of his chosen alternative; and if he is to convince others of the urgent necessity to change existing arrangements, he must provide convincing, and therefore one-sided, 'proof' of his contention.

Quite apart from the single-mindedness of the reformers, and their consequent lack of receptivity to counter-arguments, certain structural factors made their solution more attractive to the élite than its competitor. It was all very well to suggest that the reformers' cure was worse than the disease, but what was the alternative? What were the likely implications of leaving the insane in the community? There was no systematic evidence available to answer the latter question. Assuming that all those who would later find their way into an asylum and be labelled insane could have been readily identified while still in the community (a large assumption), an adequate assessment of how they were treated would have been a complex and time-consuming task. It was never attempted. The reformers, at least, were here content to rely on a small number of what Goffman has called 'exemplary tales' to demonstrate their contention that leaving the insane in the community invited the grossest forms of abuse. Little or no effort was made to determine whether such stories were in fact representative. Instead, isolated reports of individual cases of maltreatment were elevated to the status of definitive proof of the barbarity of existing conditions.

It is, of course, likely that by the standards of the typical middle-class reformer, the living conditions of the pauper insane would seem appalling. One may doubt, though, whether the reasons for this lay simply in the tendency of the ignorant to maltreat the mad. Living conditions of even the sane members of the lower classes, particularly those crowded together in the new urban slums, were quite sufficient to provoke expressions of horror and disgust in those of their betters who came into contact with them. Where the sane were forced to live in squalor, disease, and misery, on the very edge of starvation, the treatment of a dependent and often troublesome group like the lunatics was unlikely to correspond with middle-class ideals.

This would remain true even if the lunatic fared no worse than other members of his community. Few of those concerned with the plight of the insane could contemplate with equanimity the prospect of leaving them in the sorts of conditions which commonly prevailed in the larger towns:

It will scarcely appear credible, though it is precisely true, that persons
of the lowest class do not put clean sheets on their beds three times a year;
that even where no sheets are used, they never wash or scour their
blankets or coverlets, nor renew them until they are no longer tenable;
that curtains, if unfortunately there should be any, are never cleansed,
but are suffered to continue in the same state until they fall to pieces;
lastly, that from three to eight individuals of different ages often sleep in
the same bed; there being but one room and one bed for each family . . .
The room occupied is either a deep cellar, almost inaccessible to the light
and admitting of no change of air; or a garret with a low roof and small
windows, the passage to which is close, kept dark, and filled not only
with bad air, but with putrid excremental effluvia from a vault at the
bottom of the staircase . . . the cumbrous furniture or utensils of trade
with which the apartments are clogged, prevent the salutary operations
of a broom . . . and favour the accumulation of a heterogeneous filth.[1]

Millions of English men, women and children were virtually living in
shit. The immediate question seems to have been whether they weren't
drowning in it . . . Large numbers of people lived in cellars, below the
level of the street and below the water line. Thus generations of human
beings, out of whose lives the wealth of England was produced, were
compelled to live in wealth's symbolic counterpart. And that substance
which suffused their lives was also a virtual objectification of their social
condition, their place in society: that was what they were.[2]

In such a situation, those who sought to improve the lot of the
pauper insane but who were dubious about the merits of the
asylum were in an impossible bind. Improving the conditions of
existence for lunatics living in the community would have entailed
the provision of relatively generous pension or welfare payments to
provide for their support, implying that the living standards of
families with an insane member would have been raised above those
of the working class generally. Moreover, under this system, the
insane alone would have been beneficiaries of something approximating a modern social welfare system, whilst their sane brethren
were subjected to the rigours of a Poor Law based on the principle
of less eligibility. Such an approach would clearly have been

[1] R. Willan (1801), cited in M. D. George, *London Life in the Eighteenth
Century*, London, 1965, p. 95.
[2] Steven Marcus, *Engels, Manchester and the Working Class*, New York, 1974,
pp. 184–5.

administratively unworkable, not least because of the labile nature of lunacy itself, and the consequent ever-present possibility that given sufficient incentive (or rather desperation) the poorer classes would resort to feigning insanity. In any event, a programme of this sort had absolutely no political appeal to the upper classes as a whole. Engraved deeply into bourgeois consciousness in this period was an abhorrence of all forms of outdoor relief. On the one hand, this abhorrence reflected the lessons they had learned concerning the evils of such relief from the disastrous impact of the Speenhamland system – a system which had undermined the wage labour system while pauperizing, demoralizing, and degrading 'the people it was [allegedly] designed to succor'.[1] On the other hand, the determination to avoid payment of relief to those in the community was at once reflected and strengthened on the ideological level by the hegemony of classical liberalism. For the logical consequence of that doctrine's insistence that each man was to be free to pursue his fortune and at the same time was to be responsible for his own success or failure, coupled with its dogmatic certainty that interference with the dictates of the free market could only be counterproductive in the long run (a proposition that could even be proved theoretically), was to render the notion of social protectionism – in any form – an anathema.

These obstacles presented an absolute barrier to the adoption of any alternative scheme. Only the asylum plan offered the advantage of allowing scope for the exercise of humanitarian impulses, without requiring any fundamental changes in the structure of society. Bowing to the inevitable, the anti-institutional mavericks fell into line. Within a few years, we find that Conolly became a leading and zealous advocate of county asylums for pauper lunatics. He had been anticipated by one of his (anonymous) fellow-critics, who, for all the evils he saw in asylums, thought from the outset that they were quite suitable for paupers: 'As . . . the county or public asylums will soon become general . . . no fear need be entertained for the future fate and condition of pauper lunatics in this country.'[2] Even its staunchest opponents now conceded the asylum's inevitability.

[1] Karl Polanyi, *The Great Transformation*, Boston, Beacon, 1957, p. 81.
[2] Anon., *On the Present State of Lunatic Asylums*, p. 52.

6. The Model Institution

Given their basic commitment to the asylum as the solution to the problem of what to do with lunatics, the reformers laboured hard to translate their ideals into reality. They tried to provide detailed blueprints of how an asylum should be organized and what its principal features ought to be. Throughout, it is quite clear that the dominant influence on their minds, and the model they strove constantly to keep before them, was the York Retreat; and the writings of Samuel Tuke remained their constant guide.

The asylum was to be a home, where the patient was to be known and treated as an individual, where his mind was to be constantly stimulated and encouraged to return to its natural state. Mental patients required dedicated and unremitting care, which could not be administered on a mass basis, but rather must be flexible and adapted to the needs and progress of each case. Such a régime demanded kindness and an unusual degree of forbearance on the part of the staff. If this ideal were to be successfully realized, the attendants would have to be taught to keep constantly in mind the idea 'that the patient is really under the influence of a disease, which deprives him of responsibility, and frequently leads him into expressions and conduct the most opposite to his character and natural dispositions'. For this teaching to be successful, and since the attendant was the person who had the most extensive and intimate contact with the patient, attendants should be selected for their intelligence and upright moral character.[1]

Even these precautions would probably not suffice, though. They recognized that 'the business of an attendant, requires him to counteract some of the strongest principles of our common nature'.[2] Samuel Tuke himself had pointed out that the practice of moral treatment required a degree of altruism only present in those with a true vocation. After all, 'to consider them [the insane] at the same time both as brothers, and as mere automata; to applaud all they do right; and pity, without censuring, whatever they do wrong, requires such a habit of philosophical reflection, and Christian charity, as is certainly difficult to attain'.[3] It was not considered

[1] Samuel Tuke, *Description of the Retreat*, York, 1813, p. 175.
[2] Samuel Tuke, *A Letter on Pauper Lunatic Asylums*, New York, 1815, p. 27.
[3] Samuel Tuke, *Description of the Retreat*, p. 176.

impossible, however. The influence of the superintendent could be a powerful force for good here. In a properly run asylum, the patients must be seen daily, sometimes hourly, by the man who had charge of the institution. By paying 'minute attention' to all aspects of the day-to-day conduct of the institution, by always setting, through his own example, a high standard for subordinates to emulate in their dealings with the inmates, he could foster the kind of intimate and benevolent familial environment in which acts of violence would naturally become rare. From their own experience, though, the reformers knew that 'education and talent are but imperfect securities against the seductions of interest and indolence', so they tried to provide a further barrier to history repeating itself: in the last analysis, they concluded, the best, even 'the only security for the good conduct of the attendants [and medical officers] is the most frequent inspection'.[1]

The emphasis on intimacy, on patients and staff alike being members of an extended 'family', was, at the outset at least, not confined to a mere rhetorical flourish. The propagandists for the asylum vigorously promoted this idea and sought to ensure that it would be carried into effect. Hence, above all else, they emphasized the virtues of small size. Without it, 'the attempt to introduce anything approaching to domestic comfort, is altogether futile; and it becomes necessary for the attendant to rule with an iron hand, to keep in order such a formidable body of malcontents'.[2] 'It is evident,' said Ellis,

. . . that for the patients to have all the care they require, there should never be more than can, with comfort, be attended to; from 100 to 120, are as many as ought to be in any one house; where they are beyond that the individual cases cease to excite the attention they ought; and if once that is the case, not one half the good can be expected to result.

Others thought that the number might be raised to 200, or even to 250; but all the major authorities agreed that it should not rise beyond this point.[3]

The concern with small size, and with recreating the family in the

[1] Samuel Tuke, *A Letter on Pauper Lunatic Asylums*, pp. 27–8.
[2] ibid., p. 15.
[3] William Ellis, *A Treatise on the Nature . . . of Insanity*, London, 1838, p. 17.

institution, did not end here. An institution of fewer than a hundred could dissipate all the advantages which that gave it, if it neglected to classify the patients according to the severity of their disorder, and if the wards themselves grew too large. The ideal size was not more than ten people, and Tuke warned of the consequences of breaking that rule:

> During the last year, I had frequent occasion to visit two Institutions for the insane, in which very opposite plans . . . were adopted. In one, I frequently found upwards of thirty patients in a single apartment; in the other, the number in each room rarely, if ever, exceeded ten. Here I generally found several of the inmates engaged in some useful or amusing employment. Every class seemed to form a little family; they observed each other's eccentricities with amusement or pity; they were interested in each other's welfare, and contracted attachments or aversions. In the large society, the difference of character was very striking. I could perceive no attachments, and very little observation of each other. In the midst of society, everyone seemed in solitude; conversation or amusement was rarely to be observed – employment never. Each individual appeared to be pursuing his own busy cogitations; pacing with restless step from one end of the enclosure to another, or lolling in slothful apathy on the benches. It was evident that society could not exist in such a crowd.[1]

Even the architecture and the physical setting of the asylum could make vital contributions to its success. It should be sited where the patients could enjoy the benefits of fresh, bracing country air, and where there was an extensive and pleasing view of the surrounding countryside to divert the mind from its morbid fantasies. The building itself should emphasize as little as possible the idea of imprisonment or confinement. The insane were very sensitive to their surroundings, and it was not extravagance to design and build institutions which emphasized cheerfulness by being aesthetically pleasing. Asylums should avoid a dull uniformity and their internal arrangements should be such as to allow a maximum of organizational flexibility. Patients, for instance, ought to be able to change rooms in the course of the day to get a change of scenery.

For essentially the same reasons, provision ought always to be made for extensive grounds to be attached to an asylum. These

[1] Samuel Tuke, *A Letter on Pauper Lunatic Asylums*, pp. 14–15.

would allow scope for recreation and harmless diversion, the kinds of mental and physical stimulation which would counter the tendency of insanity to degenerate into outright fatuity. 'The leading principle here is to prevent idleness, to preserve every power of mind and body constantly occupied, and never to allow it to flag or to retire upon itself.'[1] And one of the best ways of putting that principle into practice was to encourage the patients to employ themselves in some useful work. Attaching a farm to every hospital would provide admirable opportunities for the kind of regular employment which greatly helped to restore men's minds.

The advocates of the asylum, then, plainly saw that there were obstacles to the successful realization of their ideal. But they were infinitely remote from the view which saw the proposed cure as worse than the disease, or even as tending only to spread the disease. Rather they were confident that no difficulty was insurmountable, that all the problems they and others had identified could be overcome – indeed, that they already had the answers to most of them. The note of almost unbounded optimism, which they so successfully communicated to their lay audience, was articulated in its purest form in Browne's vision of the asylum of the future:

In place of multiplying individual examples of excellence, let me conclude by describing the aspect of an asylum as it ought to be. Conceive a spacious building resembling the palace of a peer, airy, and elevated, and elegant, surrounded by extensive and swelling grounds and gardens. The interior is fitted up with galleries, and workshops, and music rooms. The sun and the air are allowed to enter at every window, the view of the shrubberies and fields, and groups of labourers is unobstructed by shutters or bars; all is clean, quiet and attractive. The inmates all seem to be activated by the common impulse of enjoyment, all are busy, and delighted by being so. The house and all around appears to be a hive of industry. When you pass the lodge, it is as if you had entered the precincts of some vast emporium of manufacture; labour is divided, so that it may be easy and well performed, and so apportioned, that it may suit the tastes and powers of each labourer. You meet the gardener, the common agriculturist, the mower, the weeder, all intent on their several occupations, and loud in their merriment. The flowers are

[1] William Nisbet, *Two Letters to George Rose M.P. on the . . . State of the Madhouses*, London, 1815, p. 26.

4*

tended, and trained, and watered by one, the humbler task of preparing the vegetables for table, is committed to another. Some of the inhabitants act as domestic servants, some as artizans, some rise to the rank of overseers. The bakehouse, the laundry, the kitchens, are all well supplied with indefatigable workers. In one part of the edifice are companies of straw plaiters, basket-makers, knitters, spinners, among the women; in another, weavers, tailors, saddlers, and shoemakers, among the men. For those who are ignorant of these gentle crafts, but strong and steady, there are loads to carry, water to draw, wood to cut, and for those who are both ignorant and weakly, there is oakum to tease and yarn to wind. The curious thing is, that all are anxious to be engaged, toil incessantly, and in general without any recompense other than being kept from disagreeable thoughts and the pains of illness. They literally work in order to please themselves, and having once experienced the possibility of doing this, and of earning peace, self-applause, and the approbation of all around, sound sleep, and it may be some small remuneration, a difficulty is found in restraining their eagerness, and moderating their exertions. There is in this community no compulsion, no chains, no whips, no corporal chastisement, simply because these are proved to be less effectual means of carrying any point than persuasion, emulation, and the desire of obtaining gratification. But there are gradations of employment. You may visit rooms where there are ladies reading, or at the harp, or piano, or flowering muslin, or engaged in some of those thousand ornamental productions in which female taste and ingenuity are displayed. You will encounter them going to church or to market, or returning from walking, riding and driving in the country. You will see them ministering at the bedside some sick companions. Another wing contains those gentlemen who can engage in intellectual pursuits, or in the amusements and accomplishments of the station to which they belong. The billiard room will, in all probability, present an animated scene. Adjoining apartments are used as news-rooms, the politicians will be there. You will pass those who are fond of reading, drawing, music scattered throughout handsome suites of rooms, finished chastely, but beautifully and looking down upon such fair and fertile scenes as harmonize with the tranquillity which reigns within, and tend to conjure up images of beauty and serenity in the mind which are akin to happiness. But these persons have pursuits, their time is not wholly occupied in the agreeable trifling of conning a debate, or gaining so many points. One acts as an amanuensis, another is engaged in landscape painting, a third devolves to himself a course of historical reading, and submits to examination on the subject of his studies, a fourth seeks consolation from binding the books which he does not read. In short, all are so busy as to overlook, or all are so contented as to forget their misery.

Such is a faithful picture of what may be seen in many institutions, and of what might be seen in all, were asylums conducted as they ought to be.[1]

7. The Reformers Triumphant

Driven forward by such Utopian reveries, and inspired with a limitless confidence in the merits of their chosen solution, the lunacy reformers now embarked upon the final and decisive phase of their campaign. Their aims remained those they had sought in 1815: the establishment on a compulsory basis of a network of public asylums for all pauper lunatics; and the creation of a full-time national inspectorate to supervise the whole system. By the early 1840s, however, the chances of accomplishing these changes were greatly improved. The proponents of localism had fought the attempt to establish a similar measure of central control and direction over Poor Relief and lost. In the course of the 1830s, recalcitrant parishes had been brought around, frequently by the use of government patronage to bribe local élites. Having established the principle with reference to the paupers as a whole, it was difficult to resist the conclusion that the treatment of a much smaller group like the insane ought to be subject to a similar authority, particularly since the parish was clearly too small a unit to deal with them on a specialized basis. Furthermore, the 1832 reform of Parliament had helped to weaken the power the entrenched local landed élites had hitherto enjoyed in the legislature, shifting the balance of political power towards the bourgeoisie – whose interests were best served by uniform national policies.

Meanwhile, as we have seen, the literate public had been provided with a surfeit of tracts arguing the superior merits of the asylum as a solution to the problems of insanity. The Metropolitan Commissioners had made use of their periodic reports to stress the improvements which could be brought about by assiduous and frequent inspection; and to contrast the marked amelioration of conditions in the metropolis with the stagnation or retrogression in

[1] W. A. F. Browne, op. cit., pp. 229–31.

the provinces, where 'the salutary provisions of the Act by which it is required that all houses . . . shall be annually licensed and periodically visited and reported by the Visiting Magistrates, have been in great degree neglected or violated . . .'[1] Finally, the discovery at the Lincoln Asylum that the insane could be managed without resort to any form of mechanical restraint whatsoever, and the successful implementation of such a policy at Hanwell, the largest of all public asylums, had been promoted as a dramatic demonstration of the reformers' contention that the establishment of public asylums would eliminate the horrors of the old madhouse régime. When the *Westminster Review* sought to advance the cause of reform, it simply summarized the content of a number of asylum reports, and concluded triumphantly that evidences of success 'crowd the pages of the Reports before us, and they contain not the prospective theories of an imaginary philanthropy, but the practical results of a tested system'.[2]

With the ground so well prepared in advance, the Metropolitan Commissioners now went beyond mere complaints of the ineffectiveness of provincial inspection. On 17 March 1842, Lord Granville Somerset, the chairman of the Commission, introduced a bill into the Commons to extend its powers for three years to allow it to carry out a comprehensive inspection of all asylums and madhouses in the country. The inspections which followed the bill's passage in early August were extremely extensive and detailed: asylum records were checked for accuracy and conformity to the legal requirements of the various lunacy statutes; close attention was paid to the condition of the building in which the patients were housed; questions were asked about the origins of each asylum and its current sources of financial support; inquiries were made into the role of the medical attendants, and the general administration of the asylum; patients were questioned about the treatment they received; and so on. Two years later, the findings were embodied in a comprehensive report, detailing the condition of every asylum in England, with sections on the nature of insanity and its proper classification, consideration of the arguments for and against the non-restraint system, and a discussion of the admission of pauper

[1] *Annual Report of the Metropolitan Commissioners in Lunacy*, 1838, p. 6.
[2] *Westminster Review*, 37, 1842, p. 310.

lunatics from workhouses, concluding with detailed recommendations about the direction reform should take.

The Commission found that 'the asylums thus brought before
our view exhibit instances of about every degree of merit and
defect'. Institutions in several categories were found to be reasonably satisfactory, but in a number of instances there were 'Asylums
and Licensed Houses which deserve almost unqualified censure'. It
was these extreme cases which provided the best argument for
change, and which were widely cited in summaries of the Report
written for popular consumption and in the Parliamentary debates
on the legislation the reformers introduced. The types of abuses
uncovered differed little from those found by Parliamentary
inquiries earlier in the century: At West Auckland,

each sex had only one sitting room, with windows that did not admit of
any prospect from them, and the violent and the quiet, and the dirty and
the clean were shut up together. There was only one small walled yard,
and when one sex was in it, the other was locked up . . . In the small,
cheerless day-room of the males, with only one (unglazed) window, five
men were restrained, by leg-locks . . . and two more were wearing, in
addition, iron hand-cuffs and fetters from the wrist to the ankle: they
were all tranquil. The reason assigned for this coercion was, that without
it they would escape . . . Chains were fastened to the floor in many places,
and to many of the bedsteads. The males slept two to a bed . . .

– something which shocked Victorian sensibilities. At a house in
Derby,

the straw in the paupers' beds was found filthy, and some of the bedding
was in a disgusting condition from running sores, and was of the worst
materials, and insufficient. Two cells, in which three sick epileptic
paupers slept, were damp, unhealthy, and unfit for habitation. The beds
of some of the private patients were in an equally bad state.

Another house was described as

deficient in every comfort and almost every convenience. The refractory
patients were confined to strong chairs, their arms being also fastened to
the chair. One of these – a woman – was entirely naked on both the days
the Commissioners visited the asylum, and without doubt during the
night. The stench was so offensive that it was almost impossible to
remain there.

A major theme of the Report was that only the creation of a powerful national inspectorate on a permanent basis would ensure the elimination of such abuses. Local inspection by magistrates was simply inadequate. All the asylums the Commissioners termed 'utterly unfit' were private establishments in the provinces receiving paupers, licensed by the local magistrates and hitherto visited only by them. No house in the London area, where the Commissioners themselves had had complete control for a decade and a half, exhibited comparable defects. Warburton's, for instance, which in 1828 was as bad as any of the provincial houses, was now apparently transformed:

We have visited few, if any, receptacles for the insane in which the patients are more kindly or more judiciously treated . . . the abuses which existed previously to the year 1828 led to the introduction of a system of visitation by commissioners in the metropolitan district. The houses at Bethnal Green, which were among the worst, now rank with the best receptacles for the insane.

Only continued vigilant inspection could assure such results: 'we . . . are convinced that some of these very houses of which we now speak in terms of commendation, would soon become the scenes of great abuses were it not for the checks interposed by constant and watchful visitation to which they are subjected.'

In emphasizing the gains inspection could produce, as they had to in order to convince others of the necessity for a national inspectorate, the Metropolitan Commissioners threatened to undermine their own case for the other major reform they sought to introduce. For if effective supervision alone could raise an institution from the ranks of the worst to among the best, why was it not sufficient by itself? Why was it necessary to introduce a measure to compel the counties to make a large capital investment in the erection of sufficient public asylums to accommodate every pauper patient? After all, their own description of existing county asylums had been a lukewarm endorsement at best:

It is apparent . . . that although a few . . . are well adapted to their purpose, and a very large proportion of them are extremely well conducted; yet some are quite unfit for the reception of the insane, some are placed in ineligible sites, some are deficient in the necessary means of

providing outdoor employment for paupers, some are ill-contrived and
defective in their internal accommodations, some are cheerless and confined in their yards and airing grounds, and some are larger than seems
consistent with the good management of their establishments and the
proper health and care of their inmates.

But county asylums offered a decisive advantage over the private
system – the judgement and conduct of those running them could
not be perverted by considerations of personal profit. The defects
of existing institutions of this sort were largely the product of
inexperience and could readily be eliminated by more expert
guidance on the part of the central authorities. Consequently, after
Ashley had summarized the worst abuses the Report had uncovered for the House of Commons, he assured his listeners that
'to correct these evils there was no remedy but the multiplication of
county asylums'. Experience showed that many counties were
deterred from performing their manifest duty by considerations of
expense, so providing adequate accommodation for pauper lunatics
at public expense ought henceforth to be made compulsory.

Throughout the nineteenth century, it was an article of faith
among those who dealt with lunatics that the deranged were more
easily restored in the early stages of the disorder, so that delay in
seeking help could prove disastrous. Whatever its scientific merits,
as ideology such a belief was of great assistance to the asylum
doctors. It helped, of course, to explain the low proportion of their
patients they managed to restore to sanity. More important than
that, it did so in a way which demonstrated that the failure lay, not
with the asylum, but with the public. If asylums did not cure, it
was because the public did not send lunatics to them fast enough;
and since existing asylums were already flooded with chronic cases,
the situation could only be remedied by building still more asylums;
and since the supply of asylum beds could never catch up with the
demand, which appeared to expand in proportion with the number
of available beds, the proposition would never be tested.

Here was the Commission's final and decisive argument for more
public asylums:

At the Retreat, York, at the Asylums of Lincoln and Northampton,
and at the Asylum for the County of Suffolk, tables are published,

exhibiting the large proportion of cures effected in cases where patients are admitted within three months of their attacks, the less proportion when admitted after three months, and the almost hopelessness of cure when persons are permitted to remain in Workhouses or elsewhere, and are not sent into proper asylums until after a lapse of a year from the period when they have been first subject to insanity.

At the same time, the testimony from county asylum super-intendents exhibited their virtually 'unanimous opinion that pauper lunatics are sent there at so late a period of their disease as to impede or prevent their ultimate recovery'. The problem was that 'even if there did exist on the part of the guardians and overseers of the poor a full knowledge of the importance of early treatment, and the most earnest desire to avail themselves of its advantages, throughout almost the whole of England, and in the whole of Wales, there is so great a want of accommodation for the reception of the insane that they could not carry their views into effect'.

The Report was completed just before the close of the 1844 session of Parliament. On 23 July, Ashley, in a long speech, out-lined its major conclusions and urged legislative enactment of its major recommendations. Though action was postponed until the following year, this speech did help to draw attention to the Report's findings. Later the same year, the Tory *Quarterly Review* published a long article on the subject, endorsing all the Com-mission's suggestions and calling for their swift passage into law. Early in 1845, its Benthamite counterpart, the *Westminster Review*, followed suit. Both pieces dwelt at length on the intolerable condi-tions which had been found, and concluded that even on strictly economic grounds, the Commission's proposals deserved support. For 'the very great probability of cure in the early stages of insanity', provided lunatics received prompt asylum treatment, suggested that making proper provision for the insane population of the country would ultimately reduce the numbers needing support at public expense. By the time Ashley introduced legislation to give effect to the Report's recommendations, in June 1845, informed opinion had moved decisively in his favour. The two bills he proposed both received government backing and passed swiftly through both Houses of Parliament, becoming law on 4 and 8 August 1845.

The first, the Lunatics Act of 1845 (8 & 9 Vict. c. 100) established a permanent national Lunacy Commission, with power to make detailed and frequent inspections of all types of asylums – whether public, private, or charity foundations. The second Act (8 & 9 Vict. c. 126) made the erection of county and borough asylums to house pauper lunatics compulsory. In keeping with the recommendations of the Metropolitan Commissioners, and to ensure that the presence of large numbers of chronic cases would not interfere with the asylum doctors' ability to produce the cures they had promised, counties were authorized, though not instructed, to erect separate, less costly, buildings for chronic lunatics. And to ensure that accommodation was not overcrowded or insufficient, counties which failed of their own volition to make adequate provision for their insane population could be compelled to do so.

8. The Ideal and the Reality

By 1845, therefore, the reformers had been successful in securing the enactment of both the key elements in their plan to remedy the condition and treatment of the insane. The insane had been sharply distinguished from other types of indigent and troublesome people and the asylum had been officially recognized as the most suitable place for them. A whole network of such institutions was now to be created at public expense, within whose walls all cases of lunacy were to be treated by members of the medical profession who had made or would make the treatment of mental disturbance their speciality. Most cases would now be cured. It was, the reformers agreed, a triumph for science and humanity.

Experience, however, was already suggesting that this optimism about the future was misplaced. As early as 1845, under the multiple and reinforcing pressures which derived from the difficulties associated with the routinization of reform, the economies imposed by cost-conscious local authorities, and the impact of an overwhelming lower-class clientele, there were clear signs of the collapse of the very things the reformers thought were indispensable to the success of the whole enterprise. The asylum doctors themselves contributed to this process. Bowing to political and social realities, the medical superintendents of county asylums began to compromise and water down their requirements, always consoling themselves with the thought that 'the worst asylum that can at this day by possibility be conceived, will still afford great protection' to the poor lunatic, compared to the treatment he would get elsewhere.[1]

County asylums had proved expensive to build and expensive to operate. In 1843, the average weekly cost of caring for a pauper lunatic in a public asylum was 7s. 6¾d., a sum which did not include any provision for the capital cost of the building itself. By contrast, lunatics were maintained in the community for only 2s. 7¼d., roughly what it cost to keep a pauper in an ordinary workhouse. Hostile Poor Law officials alleged that 'a vast sum of money has been thrown away in the erection of [asylums]', and that running them more nearly along the lines of workhouses would enable lunatics to 'be kept at one half or a third or a fourth of the expense at which they are now kept'.[2]

By way of justification of their 'excessive' expenditures on paupers, the asylum's proponents produced a number of counterarguments. To begin with, the inmates they had to deal with were far more difficult and intractable as a class than the average workhouse inmate, and required closer and more continuous supervision, all of which raised costs. Then again, the workhouse was specifically designed to deter the able-bodied, undeserving poor from seeking public relief, so that within its walls the strictest regard for economy was highly functional. Not only was it unfair to subject those who were not responsible for their own condition to such treatment, it was also likely to be counterproductive, making permanent what skilful attention might cure. The false economy of the Poor Law officials overlooked the fact that it was cheaper in the long run to pay a higher sum for a few months, and have the patients restored to sanity and productivity, than to provide 'inexpensive' custodial care for a lifetime.

Many magistrates and parish officials remained stubbornly unconvinced, with the result that, before the 1845 Act made their

---

[1] John Thurnam, *Observations and Essays on the Statistics of Insanity*, London, 1845, p. 104.

[2] *Select Committee on the Poor Law Amendment Act*, 1838, cited in Kathleen Jones, *Lunacy, Law and Conscience, 1744–1845*, London, Routledge & Kegan Paul, 1955, pp. 165–6.

erection compulsory, the majority of counties failed to build their own asylums. The magistrates were reluctant to impose extra local taxes which would fall heavily on their own class, and were strengthened in their resolve by the parish Guardians of the poor. Where asylums *were* erected, these men sought to keep costs to a minimum and to pare down the 'frills and luxuries' the reformers wanted, arguing that paupers could not appreciate them anyway. Even those who agreed that 'nothing [should] be neglected which may tend to facilitate the recovery of the patients' were inclined to view the more costly aspects of moral treatment with a somewhat jaundiced eye. They insisted that 'when this accommodation is to be produced for the poor and paid for out of Poor Rates, it is imperative that it should be done with the strictest eye to economy'.[1]

Realizing that 'the main impediment in the way of constructing county asylums has been . . . and at present is, the fear of the enormous expense supposed to be necessarily attendant upon such undertakings',[2] the reformers now discovered that some of the things they had formerly insisted on could be safely discarded. It was conceded that 'the first object that should be kept in view, after providing for the comfort and health of the patients, is economy; for, after all that can be said of the feelings of humanity towards this unfortunate class of our fellow-creatures, their sufferings are too much out of sight to create that sympathy for them'.[3] William Ellis, now superintendent at Hanwell, showed a keen awareness of the consequences of this concession for those who, like him, sought to extend the benefits of asylum treatment to all of the insane. As he revealingly put it, 'It becomes necessary to show that to render them efficient assistance need cost very little more than to neglect them'[4] – a necessity which did not disappear because it unavoidably meant that the fundamental principles of moral treatment would have to be compromised in the process.

The Metropolitan Commissioners had found grave defects in the siting, construction, architecture, and facilities of existing county

---

[1] *Memorial from the Parish of Brighthelmston, Sussex, Concerning the Proposed County Asylum*, 1845.

[2] Ashley, in *Hansard* 81, Third Series, 1845, column 190.

[3] William Ellis, op. cit., p. 267.

[4] ibid.

asylums. Apparently all these deficiencies could be overcome while making radical economies in the construction of future asylums, for Ashley now asserted that while the buildings at Hanwell and the Surrey Asylum had cost £160 and £245 a head respectively, perfectly adequate accommodation for curable cases could be built for £80. For chronic cases, the cost could be even less. The 1844 Report provides us with some notion of how this was to be achieved: 'Although we have no wish to advocate the erection of unsightly buildings, we think that no unnecessary cost should be incurred for architectural decoration; especially as these Asylums are erected for persons who, when in health, are accustomed to dwell in cottages.' Ellis provides us with an indication of what dispensing with surplus architectural decoration would mean in practice: 'In asylums designated for paupers only, it is unnecessary to have any plaster on the walls; limewash on the bricks is all that is required.'[1] The cheerful and pleasing architecture, which in initial formulations of moral treatment played such an important role in creating and sustaining the optimistic and familial atmosphere so essential to success, was now, with the blessing of the asylum doctors, transformed into an 'unnecessary cost'. Asylum buildings became increasingly monotonous, drearily functional, prison-like.

If the reformers had collaborated, with little apparent discomfort, in this departure from their earlier ideals, they were somewhat less willing to accept some of the other changes the magistrates insisted on. One of the most important of these, symbolically and actually, was the question of asylum size. Tuke and his followers had made a powerful case for the contention that small asylums were a necessary, even if not a sufficient, condition for individualized care of patients. Several of the earliest county asylums had conformed quite closely to these designs and to the model provided by the York Retreat. Lincoln was built for sixty patients, Nottingham for eighty, Gloucester for 120. Even those erected in highly urbanized counties were originally quite modest in size – the West Riding Asylum at Wakefield had space for 150, and that at Lancaster for 170.

The small intimate institution did not survive for long. The influx of a horde of derelict paupers brought the demise of the

[1] ibid., p. 275.

notion that the asylum should be a substitute household. Instead, local magistrates insisted on taking advantage of presumed economies of scale. Until well into the twentieth century, the average size of county asylums grew almost yearly. While the trend towards larger asylums became well-nigh universal after 1845, it was already well-marked by then. Five of the fifteen county asylums built by 1844 contained well over the recommended maximum of 200 patients: the Kent Asylum contained 300; Surrey 360; Wakefield 420; Lancaster 611; and Hanwell as many as 975, with a nominal capacity of 1,000. The profession relaxed its standards somewhat, but not sufficiently. When the Metropolitan Commissioners censured the Middlesex magistrates, alleging that their policies were directly responsible for the 'evils and inconveniences which have been experienced at Hanwell owing to its extreme size', they were merely providing a faithful reflection of the best professional opinion. They had no effect. As Conolly put it, 'the magistrates go on adding wing to wing and story to story, contrary to the opinion of the profession and to common sense, rendering the institution most unfavourable to the treatment of patients, and their management most harassing and unsatisfactory to the medical superintendent'.[1] All the powers of persuasion the asylum doctors could muster, all their elaborate statistical proofs that it was cheaper to cure in a small asylum than to immure in a vast custodial warehouse, were in vain. The magistrates who employed them remained unconvinced, and given the choice between hypothetical cures and concrete savings, they consistently chose the latter.

'[Hanwell] was designed for three hundred patients; but, with greatly economizing the room, and making use of a part of the basement, it has been fitted to accommodate six hundred and fifteen.'[2] Whatever the consequences of this for the patients' daily existence, the magistrates were clearly delighted, for during this same period, the weekly cost of each patient's maintenance fell from 9s. a week to only 5s. 10d. In similar fashion, the buildings at the Wakefield Asylum, originally intended for 150 patients, were made to accommodate 296. It was not until well into the second half of the

---

[1] Letter from John Conolly to Sir James Clark, cited in the *Edinburgh Review*, 131, 1871, p. 221.
[2] Ellis, op. cit., p. 283.

nineteenth century that these 'monstrous asylums' became general, but the larger asylums of the 1830s and 1840s already exhibited many of the features which would later be typical of the asylum system as a whole.[1] Large numbers from the outset required the development of an orderly bureaucratic routine. Prior to the opening of Hanwell, for example, the magistrates drew up a detailed and elaborate code of rules. The duties and qualifications of each of the officers, keepers, and servants were carefully specified, and lines of authority drawn. Efforts were made to provide for every contingency: there were rules covering how dead patients were to be buried; regulations about when patients were to get up and go to bed, and when they were to eat ('Patients will breakfast at eight, dine at one, and sup at seven'); the diet tables were so detailed, they even included instructions as to how the ingredients used in the gruel given out at breakfast and supper were to be prepared.

This system of fixed rules was enforced by a discipline based on solitary confinement and deprivation of privileges, rather than whips and chains. At first these were supplemented by the use of the shower bath as a punishment, by mild mechanical restraint, or by 'the terror . . . of the electrifying machine'. As superintendents became accustomed to managing such large numbers, however, they began to realize that they could do without mechanical restraint. They discovered in a pragmatic way what Goffman has so elegantly shown the rest of us, that in the context of life in a total institution, manipulation of small rewards and privileges, seclusion, or the threat of removal to a 'worse' ward have such profound implications for the self that more overtly punitive strategies are seldom required.

The degree of regimentation needed to administer an institution of 600 or 1,000 inmates ensured that such asylums would be the virtual antithesis of their supposed inspiration, the York Retreat. To Tuke, moral treatment had meant the creation of a stimulating environment where routine could be sacrificed to the needs of the individual. Here the same term disguised a monotonous reality in which the needs of the patients were necessarily subordinated to

[1] The increasing size of asylum populations and the reasons for the apparent rise in the number of mad people in the course of the nineteenth century are examined at some length in Chapter 7 below.

those of the institution; indeed, where a patient's needs were unlikely even to find expression.

9. Controlling the Uncontrollable

All of this suggests that the county asylums were an aberrant development, a deviation from the ideals of moral treatment, as, in a sense, they were. But in an ironic way they also embodied some of the core principles of the new approach. They showed, more clearly than did the Retreat, the true character of the 'reform' Tuke had unwittingly fostered.

The central fact about moral treatment, after all, and the reason for its immediate appeal, was the way it demonstrated that the most repellent features of existing madhouses were actually unnecessary cruelties. One of Tuke's proudest claims was that 'neither chains nor corporal punishment are tolerated, on any pretext in this establishment'. Instead, the patient's desire for esteem could often be exploited to induce good behaviour. Where this did not produce the desired result, 'the general comfort of the patients ought to be considered; and those who are violent require to be separated from the more tranquil, and to be prevented, by some means, from offensive conduct towards their fellow-sufferers'. This could be achieved when 'the patients are arranged into classes, as much as may be, according to the degree in which they approach to rational or orderly conduct'. Such a system had the crucial additional advantage of providing patients with a powerful incentive to exercise self-restraint: the insane 'quickly perceive, or if not, they are informed on the first occasion, that their treatment depends, in great measure on their conduct'.[1]

One of the questions which has puzzled historians of psychiatry (and which also puzzled some of the reformers themselves) was why it took so long to realize that brutal methods of managing the mad were counter-productive, and to discover that lunatics responded better to 'humane' treatment. What was involved here was, I suggest, something more than just the development of a more refined conscience about the conditions the insane were forced to endure. So long as there existed no alternative methods of

[1] Tuke, *Description of the Retreat*, pp. 141, 157.

managing those who would otherwise fail to conform to the rules required for the smooth functioning of an institution, the cruelties of the madhouse keeper were, in fact, functionally necessary. In the absence of better techniques, chains and fear – though crude – were the only mechanisms which could guarantee at least a minimum of order.

Concentration on the humanitarian aspect of moral treatment has blinded us to the fact that, from a different perspective, it was precisely such a superior way of *managing* patients. For two of what I have just shown were crucial elements in moral treatment, the ward system and the creation of an intimate tie between the patient's position in this classificatory system and his behaviour, are still the fundamental weapons which mental hospitals use to control the uncontrollable. As Goffman puts it,

since mental patients are persons who on the outside decline to respond to efforts at social control, there is a question of how social control can be achieved on the inside. I believe that it is achieved largely through the 'ward system', the means of control that has slowly evolved in modern mental hospitals. The key, I feel, is a system of wards graded for the degree of allowable misbehaviour and the degree of discomfort and deprivation prevalent in them. Whatever the level of the new patient's misbehaviour, then, a ward can be found for him in which this conduct is routinely dealt with and to a degree allowed. In effect, by accepting the life conditions on these wards, the patient is allowed to continue his misbehaviour, except that now he does not particularly bother anyone by it, since it is routinely handled, if not accepted, on the ward. When he requests some improvement in his lot he is then, in effect, made to say 'uncle', made to state verbally that he is ready to mend his ways. When he gives in verbally he is likely to be allowed an improvement in life conditions. Should he then again misbehave in the old way, and persist in this, he is lectured and returned to his previous conditions. If instead of backsliding he states his willingness to behave even better, and retains this line for a suitable length of time, he is advanced further within the quick discharge cycle through which most first admissions are moved up and out within a year. A point is then often reached where the patient is entrusted to a kinsman, either for walks in the hospital grounds, or for town expeditions, the kinsman now being transformed into someone who has the incarcerating establishment and the law to reinforce the threat: 'Be good or else I'll send you back.' What we find here (and do not on the outside) is a very model of what psychologists might call a learning situation – all hinged on the process of an admitted giving in.[1]

Tuke's invention of these techniques, then, paralleling those simultaneously being developed for the management of the sane workforce in large industrial establishments, made it possible for the first time to abandon the brutal and overly harsh methods of management which had previously been inescapably connected with the concentration of large numbers of madmen together in an institutional environment. It was the latent strength of moral treatment as a mechanism for enforcing conformity which came to be emphasized in the vast pauper asylums. There, to the extent that moral treatment was an advance, what it did was to place a far more effective and thorough-going means of control in the hands of the custodians, while simultaneously, by removing the necessity for the asylum's crudest features, it made the reality of that imprisonment and control far more difficult to perceive. So that by cruel irony, it was the same central feature of moral treatment which gave it its appeal as a humanitarian reform and which allowed its transformation into a repressive instrument for controlling large numbers of people.

Increasing size inevitably made the doctors more remote, broke the ties which were supposed to unite superintendent and patient. The daily, sometimes hourly, contact between patient and physician, which the proponents of the institution were arguing was such a valuable feature of asylum life, was already disappearing. Ellis might sometimes refer to 900 patients as his 'family', but the term was clearly a matter of rhetoric rather than reality. He was, it is true, required by the rules at Hanwell to visit each ward and each patient at least once daily; but since the rules also stipulated that he was to prepare an annual report, keep day-books and casebooks, a record of the name, age, sex, date of admission, occupation, etc., of every patient, act as steward and treasurer of the institution and keep the accounts, as well as oversee every aspect of the institution, his time for this task was naturally limited. The situation had not changed much when the Metropolitan Commissioners visited in 1844:

[1] Erving Goffman, *Asylums*, Garden City, New York, Doubleday, 1961, pp. 361–2. (London, Penguin, 1970.)

The two resident Medical Officers have between them nearly 1,000 patients to attend, and are required by the rules to see every patient twice a day. Each of these officers has an average of 30 patients on the sick list, and above 50 on the extra diet list. Besides these duties, they are required to mix medicines and to keep the registers and diaries. Some attention is also required to be paid to chronic cases in which the general health and state of mind are often varying.

Given the increasing remoteness of the superintendents from the patients, 'much authority . . . in large asylums is now necessarily placed in the hands of the attendants'.[1] We have seen that Tuke had emphasized how crucial their role was. Moral treatment depended for its success on the extraordinary devotion and patience of those who were called on to administer it. Especially as asylums began to fill up with incurable cases, 'success' could frequently not be measured in conventional terms. Since the incurables could provide little in exchange for the humane care they received except gratitude (and often not even that), maintaining the requisite morale and dedication among the staff was likely to be difficult, at best. Given the low rewards characteristically offered to those who do society's dirty work, aggravated by the unwillingness of any save the least successful elements of such a class-conscious society as Victorian England to tolerate the defiling close daily contact with the derelict, it proved impossible. Asylums were compelled to recruit their attendants from 'the unemployed of other professions . . . if they possess physical strength and a tolerable reputation for sobriety, it is enough; and the latter quality is frequently dispensed with. They enter upon their duties completely ignorant of what insanity is.'[2] Close supervision and carefully designed bureaucratic rules could coerce a measure of conformity from such an ill-suited lot and ensure the mechanical and perfunctory performance of custodial tasks; but they could not provide the dedicated self-sacrifice, the unflagging interest in the patient's welfare, which moral treatment required. As in other respects, moral treatment could not survive the perils of routinization.

[1] *Metropolitan Commissioners in Lunacy, 1844 Report*, p. 24.
[2] W. A. F. Browne (1837), cited in R. A. Hunter and I. MacAlpine, *Three Hundred Years of Psychiatry*, London, Oxford University Press, 1963, p. 868.

While the reformers continued to use the increased likelihood of cure as one of the primary arguments in favour of asylum treatment, there were already signs that the asylums were filling with chronic cases for whom nothing could be done. Like most of its counterparts, Hanwell was originally planned to be for 'the reception of those only whose malady being of recent date is found to be most susceptible of cure'. In order 'not to fill the asylum with incurables . . . all pauper Lunatics of these Parishes should be examined, and those Lunatics having the least inveterate symptoms be selected for the County Asylum'.[1] Despite every precaution, however, within three years of its opening, Ellis drew the attention of the magistrates to the 'melancholy fact of the house being filled with old and incurable cases'; something he attributed 'almost entirely to the neglect of proper remedies in the early stages of the disease'.[2] At Lancaster, too, there were complaints of 'the Asylum being crowded with chronic and almost hopeless cases'. And Pritchard, the superintendent of the Northampton Asylum, strove to make a virtue of necessity, arguing that

to express a regret that these pitiable wrecks of intellectual being should find here an Asylum, that during their brief period of mere vegetative existence they should enjoy through its medium every comfort which their unfortunate situation demands, would be as foreign to the dictates of right feeling as to the benevolent views of those by whom it was founded.[3]

To convince his listeners of the advantages of the asylum, Ashley might engage in elaborate and optimistic calculations of the theoretical savings curative institutions would produce. But to do so, he had to ignore the evidence which demonstrated that existing 'county asylums have . . . become, and the evil is daily increasing, places of security, rather than curative establishments'.[4] For it is one of the many ironies of the English lunacy reform

[1] Middlesex Lunatic Asylum, Minutes of the Visiting Justices, Vol. II, 1830, pp. 323, 412.

[2] Hanwell Lunatic Asylum, Fourth Annual Report, 1849.

[3] Lancaster Lunatic Asylum Annual Report 1845, p. 19; Northampton General Lunatic Asylum Annual Report 1840, p. 12.

[4] *Westminster Review*, 43, 1845, p. 171.

movement that just as it reached its goals, and the optimism it had been so sedulously promoting reached its peak, experience was showing the fragility of the assumptions on which its whole programme rested. There was much truth in the comment made by David Uwins, a London mad-doctor and writer on insanity:

No well regulated mind can for a moment doubt that the recent inquisitions by our statesmen and legislators on the nature of insanity and the economy of lunatic establishments have been prompted by a grandeur of design and a largeness of benevolence; the only room for doubt and distrust is in reference to the complete fulfilment of sanguine expectation. It is in the very spirit and nature of reform to be too condemnatory of what is, and too hopeful of what is to come.[1]

[1] David Uwins, *A Treatise on those Disorders of the Brain and Nervous System, which Are Usually Considered and Called Mental*, London, 1833, p. 235, footnote.

Chapter Four

From Madness to Mental Illness:
Medical Men as Moral Entrepreneurs

'When *I* use a word,' Humpty Dumpty said, in a rather scornful tone, 'it means just what I choose it to mean – neither more nor less.'
'The question is,' said Alice, 'whether you *can* make words mean so many different things.'
'The question is,' said Humpty Dumpty, 'which is to be master – that's all.'
(Lewis Carroll, *Through the Looking Glass, and What Alice Found There*)

---

1. Madness and Medicine

Prior to the segregation of the mad into specialized institutions, medical interest in and concern with the mad was for the most part quite slight. In historical terms, of course, the idea that insanity was a disease was not without precedent. For many centuries, though, the medical approach to lunacy had either been ignored or been forced to compete with theological and demonological perspectives. An occasional medical treatise revived the ancient Greek view that insanity was an illness, but few medical men took any active *practical* interest in the treatment of madmen. Physicians had been placed in charge of the Bethlem Hospital only from the end of the sixteenth century onwards, and since none of those appointed to this position published any books on insanity or made any claims to provide effective therapy, their impact in promoting the medical cause was minimal. As late as the first half of the eighteenth century, James Munro (1680–1752), the physician at Bethlem, was almost the only doctor in and around London who specialized in 'treating' the mentally ill. Thereafter, however, the increasing reliance on private madhouses and charity asylums as a means of coping with insanity prompted a quickening of medical interest and involvement in this area.

Most early madhouses were private speculations run for profit. Given the difficulties others experienced in managing the insane and the lack of legal restrictions on entry into the business or upon the actual conduct of the business, they were generally a very profitable investment. Initially, the traffic in this species of human misery was a trade monopolized by no single occupational group. Speculators from a wide variety of backgrounds looking for easy profits, as well as more 'respectable' groups such as the clergy, all sought to obtain a share of a lucrative market. It was at precisely this stage that the medical profession (or rather, diverse individuals laying claim to possess some sort of medical training and knowledge) first began to assert an interest in lunacy. A number of doctors trying to gain a share of the lucrative new business, and possibly also to improve the treatment of the insane, began opening madhouses of their own or became involved in efforts to set up charity hospitals for the care of lunatics.

The English medical profession at this time was composed of three separate elements – physicians, surgeons, and apothecaries – each of whom catered to a different clientele. The physicians, the upper class's doctors, generally possessed a medical degree, and in London at least were members of the Royal College of Physicians: but an M.D. was no guarantee of more than passing acquaintance with classical authors in the field, with no assurance of clinical experience; and membership of the College depended more on social connections than medical skill. Surgeons had only recently severed their links with the barber's trade; entry into their ranks was usually by apprenticeship and their status was distinctly lower than that of the physicians. Apothecaries catered largely to the middle and lower classes; they too were recruited by apprenticeship and lacked any real control over licensing and entry, so that those calling themselves apothecaries might vary from semi-illiterate quacks to highly competent practitioners by the standards of the time.

The doctors entering the mad business were not drawn exclusively from any one of these three classes; nor, so far as one can judge, did they differ significantly from the rest of the profession in skill or respectability. While 'doctors' with little claim to the title did enter the field, so too did well-known society physicians and those trained at some of the best medical schools of the time. By no means was the mad business a refuge of only the most disreputable elements of the medical profession. On the contrary, it was those drawn from the most educated and literate elements of the profession who were among the most vigorous and effective partisans of medicine's claims in this area.

The earliest lay proprietors of madhouses had often attempted to attract clients by claiming to provide cures as well as care. Indeed, throughout the eighteenth century, a major way of drumming up trade and attracting clients, other than through advertising, was by publishing small books or tracts making considerable claims for the author's success in curing lunatics. In an increasingly rationalized and secularized social and cultural climate, this idea that expert intervention could provide a means of restoring the deranged to reason naturally proved an attractive one; and since recovery seems to occur spontaneously in approximately one third of cases of mental illness, a ready source of cures to 'prove' such claims was available. In the absence of any clear notion of how to subject such claims to empirical scrutiny, madhouse proprietors were frequently successful in deceiving the public (and probably themselves) with arguments based on the *post hoc ergo propter hoc* fallacy. Of all those making these claims, medical madhouse keepers could do so most plausibly. To understand why this should be so, one need only recall certain basic characteristics of eighteenth-century medicine.

Unlike its modern successor, eighteenth-century medicine did not involve identifying specific disease entities and then prescribing specialized treatments directed at them. Rather it possessed a number of things which were regarded as useful weapons against any and all types of bodily dysfunction. No English doctor went quite so far as the American, Benjamin Rush, who reduced all illnesses to one underlying pathology, and prescribed a single remedy, depletion. Nevertheless, adherents of almost every one of the eighteenth-century medical 'systems' exhibited a touching faith in a number of cure-alls – such things as purges, vomits, bleedings, and various mysterious coloured powders, whose secrets were known only to their compounders. These theories and their associated remedies were readily adapted to incorporate the new disease of insanity; it was but a small leap to assert that these things would also cure lunatics.

The doctors, then, had an advantage when it came to justifying their claims to cure insanity, because everybody 'knew' that they possessed powerful remedies whose use demanded special training and expertise, and whose 'efficacy' against a wide range of complaints was generally acknowledged. They exploited this advantage to good effect, arguing that bleedings, vomits, purges, and the like were also efficacious in cases of insanity, which was, after all, a disease of the mind or brain. Respectable institutions must be set up under the control of physicians, for only in this way could the danger of incurability, 'either by the Disorder gaining Strength beyond the Reach of Physick, or by the patient falling into the Hands of Persons utterly unskilled in the Treatment of the Disorder, or who have found their Advantage in neglecting every Method necessary to obtain a Cure',[1] be avoided.

A number of other factors entered into and added weight to the attempt to claim insanity as part of the legitimate domain of medicine. The promoters of the new St Luke's Hospital were partly motivated by the desire to improve the medical knowledge of insanity, and their efforts to raise funds publicized the idea that medicine had something to offer the insane. The involvement of William Battie, a successful society physician later elected President of the Royal College of Physicians, first in promoting the hospital and then in serving as its first resident physician, must have helped to overcome the scruples of many of his colleagues who might otherwise have hesitated to risk their reputations by entering such a positively disreputable, though highly profitable, field. As other charity asylums founded in the eighteenth century were frequently located alongside and associated with existing infirmaries, the link between insanity and medicine was strengthened in the public

[1] St Luke's Hospital, *Considerations upon the usefulness and necessity of establishing an Hospital as a further provision for poor Lunaticks*, in manuscript at St Luke's Woodside, London, 1750.

mind.[1] The appearance of a number of books on the medical treatment of insanity gave further support to the mad-doctors' claims, and such famous medical teachers as William Cullen began to incorporate material on the subject into their lectures, so that some physicians could assert that they had specialized training in this area. Numerically, medical men might still be a minority of those trafficking in madness, but their view of insanity as an illness was an increasingly influential one in upper-class circles, its attractions reinforced by the fortuitous circumstance of George III's illness, with its associated mania; for the King's disorder meant that 'the topic of insanity was widely discussed in a context which excluded the attitude of moral condemnation'.[2] On this basis, therefore, doctors were gradually acquiring a powerful, although very far from an overwhelmingly dominant position in the mad business by the end of the eighteenth century.

2. The Obstacles to a Medical Monopoly

Modern professions are not simply the *dominant* or most important providers of a particular service; instead they effectively *monopolize* a service market, claim to do so on the basis of a unique, scientifically based expertise and training, and make use of their exclusive control of valuable markets to secure for themselves not merely monopoly profits in the monetary sense, but also significant status advantages. During the nineteenth century, mad-doctors manoeuvred to secure such a position for themselves and acceptance of their particular view of the nature of madness, seeking to transform their existing foothold in the marketplace into a cognitive and practical monopoly of the field, and to acquire for those practising this line of work the status prerogatives 'owed' to professionals – most notably autonomous control by the practitioners themselves over the conditions and conduct of their work. The process was,

[1] The medical approach benefited further from the association with charity; for these institutions apparently lacked a motive for keeping sane people confined, and their benevolent status disarmed much of the public hostility then directed against the profit-seeking (mostly non-medical) private madhouses.

[2] Kathleen Jones, *Lunacy, Law and Conscience 1744–1845*, London, Routledge & Kegan Paul, 1955, p. 26.

however, by no means a simple one. Structural weaknesses of both an internal and an external sort posed serious obstacles to the medical capture and reorganization of the 'trade in lunacy', and more specific conjunctural factors for a time threatened even that degree of market control which medical men had already won.

The consequence of the growth of separate institutional provision for the mad was the creation of a guaranteed, albeit initially limited market for a new type of service, which in turn prompted the emergence of competing groups seeking to control this market. For professionalization to occur, one group had to succeed in driving out all its competitors or in subordinating all who persisted in this line of work to its authority. The ordinary operations of the market-place were unlikely to produce such a result. For in the mad business, the criteria of success were somewhat ambiguous, the verification of competing claims was difficult, and the very existence of a cognitive system markedly superior to any other was in doubt. So long as those in competition were forced to produce 'evidence' of their superiority, it was unlikely that a single group would succeed in securing a dominant position and in choking off the entry of potential competitors. And so long as this remained the case, the idea that anyone possessed expertise in this area remained problematic.

In the face of competing claims of apparently equal plausibility, the most rational as well as the most likely public policy was to continue to permit free entry into the trade in lunacy. Yet to allow this was to perpetuate the very conditions standing in the way of the emergence of a distinctive and relatively homogeneous occupational group possessing a plausible claim to be granted a professional monopoly. In the first place, the lack of barriers to entry into the mad business allowed unscrupulous elements to enter the trade, and thus depressed public confidence in all its practitioners. Worse than this, the existence of a number of groups each clamouring to be recognized as *the* experts in the treatment of insanity, each purporting to produce 'evidence' in support of its claims, and each concerned to denigrate and discredit its rivals, was scarcely a situation calculated to promote public belief in the legitimacy of such pretensions on anyone's part. Lack of public confidence was likewise reflected in the low social status accorded to practitioners in the field, and this set in motion a self-fulfilling prophecy through its negative effects on the quality of those attracted to the madhouse trade. All of which meant that those dealing with lunatics had difficulty securing even a modest degree of occupational stability.

Furthermore, efforts to remedy this state of affairs faced severe obstacles of a similar sort. Since entrance into the mad business was not contingent upon having undergone prolonged and probably costly professional training, the ability of those striving to obtain professional status for psychiatry to attract candidates for such training was severely curtailed; a situation made worse by their inability to provide a guaranteed connection between their type of learning and subsequent earnings. A vicious circle seemed to be at work, for lacking *general public belief in [their] competence, in the value of [their] professed knowledge and skill*,[1] mad-doctors were in a poor position to obtain the monopoly they sought. But without it they could scarcely hope to overcome the inherent weaknesses produced by the fluid, unregulated market for the type of services which they offered.

To complicate the situation still further, there were serious internal weaknesses in the mad-doctors' position. Though use was made of therapeutic rhetoric, early medical approaches to the treatment of the insane remained in many ways firmly wedded to the past, and were legitimated more by reference to classical authority than by rational demonstration. While more overtly coercive means of controlling the lunatic (for example, whipping and the use of chains) were given a medical gloss, in practice even the standard medical techniques of the time (such as bleeding and the administration of cathartics) were primarily employed as useful ways of disciplining and restraining 'patients' who were still seen in the animalistic terms of the traditional paradigm of insanity. Temporarily, at least, this commitment rendered the mad-doctors' position a vulnerable one, when changed circumstances made these sorts of responses no longer comprehensible or acceptable.

As I have suggested in the previous chapter, towards the end of the eighteenth century there began to occur, as part of a wider transformation in the cultural boundaries of the community, a

[1] E. Freidson, *Profession of Medicine*, New York, Dodd, Mead, 1970, p. 11, emphasis in the original.

major shift in the cultural meaning of madness, as well as an increased stress on cognitive rationality rather than traditional usage as the basis of an action's legitimacy. These developments threatened to undermine medicine's claims to jurisdiction over the insane. For the growth of a new perspective on insanity, one which viewed the lunatic as essentially human, though lacking in self-restraint and discipline, and which saw the primary task for therapy to be the development of control from within the madman's own psyche rather than concentration upon an externally imposed and alien order, led inexorably to a perception of the practices which formed the core of the medical claim to possess special competence in the treatment of insanity as presumptively inhumane. This was a presumption which might have been overturned had there been demonstrable evidence of either the practices' therapeutic effectiveness or their practical necessity.

In fact there was neither. And the invention by laymen of a new approach, moral treatment, which controlled the insane without resort to these traditional devices, and which convincingly claimed to have demonstrated the therapeutic bankruptcy of standard medical techniques in this area, weakened and ultimately destroyed the plausibility of any such contentions. Under these circumstances, the negotiation of cognitive exclusiveness on the part of mad-doctors, whereby insanity came to be defined as a disease, and hence as a condition within the sole purview of the medical profession, was necessarily a prolonged and complicated process.

3. The Threat Posed by Moral Treatment

English ideas on the moral treatment of the insane were inextricably bound up with the experience of the York Retreat, and that experience constituted 'a rather damning attack on the medical profession's capacity to deal with mental illness'.[1] The Retreat's founder, William Tuke, was a layman with a considerable distrust of the medical profession of his day. But sceptical as he was of the value of medicine, he possessed a sufficiently open mind to investigate its claims to have specific remedies for mental illness.

[1] William Bynum, 'Rationales for Therapy in British Psychiatry: 1780–1835', *Medical History*, 18, 1974, p. 323.

With his encouragement, both the first visiting physician, Dr Fowler, and his successors made a trial of all the various medicines and techniques which members of the profession had suggested: 'bleeding, blister, setons, evacuants, and many other prescriptions which have been highly recommended by writers on insanity'.

The results must have been a disappointment, though perhaps not a surprise. In Samuel Tuke's words, 'the experience of the Retreat . . . will not add much to the honour or extent of medical science. I regret . . . to relate the pharmaceutical means which have failed, rather than to record those which have succeeded.' Fowler found that

the sanguine expectations, which he successively formed of the benefit to be derived from various pharmaceutical remedies, were, in great measure, as successively disappointed; and, although the proportion of cures, in the early part of the Institution, was respectable, yet the medical means were so imperfectly connected with the progress of recovery, that he could not avoid suspecting them, to be rather concomitants than causes. Further experiments and observations confirmed his suspicions; and led him to the painful conclusion (painful alike to our pride and our humanity), 'that medicine, as yet, possesses very inadequate means to relieve the most grievous of human diseases'.

Fowler's death in 1801, and the swift demise of his successor, meant that the Retreat had three visiting physicians within its first five years of operation. Each of the others arrived convinced of medicine's applicability and value. Both were disillusioned:

They have had recourse to various means, suggested either by their own knowledge and ingenuity, or recommended by later writers; but their success has not been such, as to rescue this branch of their profession, from the charge, unjustly exhibited by some against the art of medicine in general, of its being chiefly conjectural.[1]

Numerous trials had shown that all of the various suggestions that had been made, with the possible exception of warm baths for melancholics, were either useless or positively harmful.

Henceforth, the visiting physician confined his attention to treating cases of bodily illness, and it was the lay people who were

[1] Samuel Tuke, *Description of the Retreat*, York, 1813, pp. 110, 111, 115.

in charge of the day-to-day running of the institution – the Tukes and George and Katherine Jepson – who began to develop the alternative response to insanity which became known as moral treatment.

At the Retreat, like the Bicêtre [where Pinel was independently developing his own version of moral treatment], the physician was a shadowy figure, the burden of therapeutic responsibility having fallen on the keepers and other staff whose personal contacts with the patient were so much greater than that of the physician.[1]

By the beginning of the second decade of the nineteenth century, the staff's substitution of moral constraint and kindness for fear and physical restraint in the management of the insane, their insistence on the importance of encouraging the inmate to re-exert his own powers of self control, and their demonstration that many lunatics recovered when treated in this fashion, were being given considerable publicity – both through the efforts of a stream of visitors interested in lunacy reform, and through the writings of William Tuke's grandson, Samuel. Men like William Stark eulogized the Retreat for showing that managing the insane 'requires no aid from the arm of violence, or the exertions of brutal force . . .' and Andrew Duncan, a leading Edinburgh physician, was so impressed by his visit that he commented:

The fraternity denominated Quakers have demonstrated beyond contradiction, the very great advantages resulting from a mode of treatment in cases of Insanity much more mild than was before introduced into any Lunatic Asylum at home or abroad. In the management of this institution, they have set an example which claims the imitation, and deserves the thanks, of every sect and every nation.[2]

But Duncan's attitude was far from representative of his medical colleagues' views. On the contrary, the initial response of most of the medical profession to the claims of moral treatment was one of

[1] W. Bynum, op. cit., p. 324.

[2] William Stark, *Remarks on the Construction of Public Hospitals for the Cure of Mental Derangement*, Glasgow, Hedderwick, 1810, p. 12; *Short Account of the Rise, Progress, and Present State of the Lunatic Asylum at Edinburgh*, Edinburgh, Neill, 1812, p. 15.

hostility. In the face of the evidence, they simply tried to reassert the value of the traditional medical approach. George Nesse Hill, a surgeon from Chester and author of one of the best-known works on the subject published at this time, assured his readers that 'Insanity is as generally curable as any of those violent Diseases most successfully treated by Medicine', and truculently asserted that 'direct medical remedies can never be too early introduced or too readily applied'. William Nisbet, a leading London practitioner who wrote extensively upon a wide range of medical subjects, concurred: 'The disease of insanity in all its shades and varieties, belongs, in point of treatment, to the department of the physician alone . . . the medical treatment . . . is that part on which the whole success of the cure hangs.'[1] And when the 1815 Select Committee asked Dr John Weir, the official inspector of the conditions under which naval maniacs were kept, for his opinion on the value of medical intervention, he qualified his answer only slightly: 'In recent cases, and those unconnected with organic lesions of the brain, malformation of the skull, and hereditary disposition to insanity . . . medical treatment is of the utmost importance.' Nor should this reaction come as a surprise. After all, moral treatment challenged their traditional paradigm of what was suitable as a method of treating illness of any sort. Furthermore, its wholesale rejection of standard medical techniques naturally ran counter to the profession's deep intellectual, emotional, and practical investment in the value of its own theory and practice. As William Bynum has noted, 'if physicians *qua* physician could do nothing for the lunatic except treat his bodily afflictions, then the medical man had no special claim to a unique place in the treatment of mental illness. Their income, prestige, and medical theories were all threatened.'[2]

As a consequence of this initial reluctance to abandon outmoded conceptions and treatments of insanity, the medical profession's continuing status as the most prominent group involved in coping with the insane became, for a time, distinctly problematic. For those

---

[1] George Nesse Hill, *An Essay on the Prevention and Cure of Insanity*, London, Longman *et al.*, 1814, pp. 201, 205; William Nisbet, *Two Letters to . . . George Rose M.P. on the Reports at Present before the House of Commons on the State of Madhouses*, London, Cox, 1815, pp. 7, 21.

[2] W. Bynum, op. cit., p. 325.

outside the profession, of course, lacked its prior commitments, and so were readier converts to the value of the new approach. Furthermore, the evidence of even the medical witnesses before the Select Committee provided support for William Tuke's contention that 'in cases of mental derangement . . . very little can be done [by way of medical treatment]'.

The evidence given by Best and Monro, physicians at York and Bethlem respectively, was particularly damaging. The Monro family had been physicians to Bethlem for almost a century, and prior to the 1815 inquiry, Thomas Monro himself had been thought of as one of the foremost experts in the medical treatment of insanity. Like Best, though, the credibility of his testimony was coloured by the Committee's knowledge of conditions in his asylum, and he was treated as a hostile witness. Under close questioning by the Committee, the extent of his medical treatment was now revealed to the public:

in the months of May, June, July, August, and September, we generally administer medicines; we do not in the winter season, because the house is so excessively cold that it is not thought proper . . . We apply generally bleeding, purging, and vomit; those are the general remedies we apply . . . All the patients who require bleeding are generally bled on a particular day, and they are purged on a particular day.

Later in his testimony, Monro gave a few more details: all the patients under his care, except those manifestly too weak to survive such a heroic régime, 'are ordered to be bled about the latter end of May, or the beginning of May, according to the weather; and after they have been bled they take vomits once a week for a certain number of weeks, after that we purge the patients . . .' Thereafter, of course, patients were kept chained to their beds at least four days out of every seven.

A Committee convinced of the value of moral treatment's emphasis on treating every lunatic as an individual was in principle unlikely to approve of such indiscriminate mass medication. Under the even more hostile questioning he now faced, Monro was forced to make a still more damaging admission. 'Do you think,' he was asked, 'it is within the scope of medical knowledge to discover any other efficacious means of treating Insane persons?'

> With respect to the means used, I really do not depend a vast deal upon medicine; I do not think medicine is the sheet anchor; it is more by management that those patients are cured than by medicine; . . . the disease is not cured by medicine, in my opinion. If I am obliged to make that public I must do so.

The only question which remained was why Monro continued to employ therapies he conceded were useless. He himself had already provided an answer to that: 'That has been the practice invariably for years, long before my time; it was handed down to me by my father, and I do not know any better practice.'[1]

St Luke's Hospital had not come in for the severe criticism directed at Bethlem. Nevertheless, when its physician, Dr Sutherland, was called to give evidence his answers were extremely circumspect, and he sought to be as non-controversial as possible. While he felt that medicines for the stomach might be of some indirect benefit, he conceded that 'moral treatment is of course more especially important in the treatment of mental disorder'. Similarly, when Dr John Harness, a Commissioner of the Transport Board, was asked 'What is your opinion as to the utility of medical treatment of Insanity?' he replied, 'Although much may be effected by medical treatment, I have before stated that I am not sanguine in the expectation of a permanent advantage from it.'[2]

Doctors at this time played another important role *vis-à-vis* the insane. Five Commissioners selected from the members of the Royal College of Physicians were charged with annually inspecting metropolitan madhouses under the 1774 Act. Even conceding the defects of that Act, as the reformers did, the College's record was hardly one to inspire confidence in a system of medical policing of asylums, or in physicians' willingness to judge the work of their colleagues. According to Dr Richard Powell, the secretary to the Royal College, and himself a Commissioner, the visits took no more than six days a year to perform. Often, as many as six or eight madhouses were visited in a single day. No attempt was made to see whether the numbers resident corresponded to those the Commissioners had received notification of. The justification for medical

[1] *House of Commons Select Committee*, 1815, pp. 93, 95, 99.
[2] ibid., pp. 136, 159.

5*

visitation was primarily that no one else was competent to assess the medical treatment administered. Yet Powell conceded that, apart from cursory inquiries as to the condition of the patients, no effort was made to discover what medical treatment the patients received, let alone to find out how effective it was.

The most respectable medical figure to appear before the Committee was Sir Henry Halford, who was already 'indisputably at the head of London practice'. A favourite of George III, he was later physician to George IV and Victoria, and, from 1820 to his death in 1844, President of the Royal College of Physicians. As the official spokesman for the most prestigious branch of the medical profession and an influential figure in upper-class circles, his evidence was obviously presented with a view to making a strong case for the value of the medical approach and in an effort to rectify the damage done by Best's and Monro's testimony. In practice, his evidence was too rambling and confused for that. Having begun by asserting that medical intervention was valuable, at least in the early stages of the disorder, he subsequently conceded that 'our knowledge of insanity has not kept pace with our knowledge of other distempers . . .', a situation he blamed on 'the habit we find established, of transferring patients under this malady, as soon as it has declared itself, to the care of persons who too frequently limit their attention to the mere personal security of their patients, without attempting to assist them by the resources of medicine'. The profession, he acknowledged, had 'much to learn on the subject of mental derangement'. By the end of his testimony, he had given the impression that medicine lacked reliable knowledge in this area, and could offer little by way of effective therapy. In mitigation, he urged that 'we want facts in the history of the disease', coupled with the vague hope that 'if they are carefully recorded, under the observation of enlightened physicians, no doubt, they will sooner or later be collected in sufficient number, to admit of safe and useful inductions'.[1] As a performance, this was scarcely calculated to convince the somewhat sceptical audience which he faced. He had provided neither evidence nor plausible argument to refute the contention of those who favoured moral treatment that 'against mere insanity, unaccompanied by bodily derangement, [medicine]

[1] *House of Commons Select Committee*, 1816, First Report, pp. 13–14.

appears to be almost powerless'. Nor had he succeeded in erasing the unfavourable impression created by earlier medical testimony.

If Monro did not know of any better weapons to use against insanity than the traditional anti-phlogistic system, the laymen who were acquainted at first hand with the results of moral treatment obviously thought that *they* did. Both their testimony before official inquiries and the pamphlets they were busily writing now took on a tone of considerable hostility to medicine's claims to jurisdiction in this area. When Edward Wakefield was asked: 'In consequence of the observations you have made on the state and management of Lunatic Establishments, and the manner of inspecting them, are you of the opinion that medical persons exclusively ought to be Inspectors and Comptrollers of Madhouses?' his response was,

I think they are the most unfit of any class of persons. In the first place, from every enquiry I have made, I am satisfied that medicine has little or no effect on the disease, and the only reason for their selection is the confidence which is placed in their being able to apply a remedy to the malady. They are all persons interested more or less. It is extremely difficult in examining either the public Institutions or private houses, not to have a strong impression upon your mind, that medical men derive a profit in some shape or form from those different establishments . . . The rendering therefore, of any interested class of persons the Inspectors and Comptrollers, I hold to be mischievous in the greatest possible degree.[1]

Higgins, the Yorkshire magistrate who had done much to uncover the scandals at the York Asylum, had witnessed at first hand over many months the practices of one of the most famous medical 'specialists' in the field. His comments were, if anything, still more hostile. He pointed out that in the aftermath of Dr Best's departure from the York Asylum and the establishment of an efficient system of lay visitation there, the number of deaths of patients fell from twenty a year to only four. Furthermore, thirty patients were almost at once found fit for discharge. In his caustic fashion he demanded to know 'who after this will doubt the efficacy of my

[1] *House of Commons Select Committee*, 1815, p. 24. A year later, however, following a visit to William Finch's madhouse, near Salisbury, Wakefield changed his mind, and conceded that insanity was a disease 'which in its incipient state is capable of relief from medicine'.

medicine – visitors and committees? I will warrant it superior even to Dr Hunter's famous secret *insane powders* – either green or grey – or his patent Brazil salts into the bargain.' Higgins was clearly angered by efforts on the part of the medical profession to explain away what he perceived as cruelty as legitimate medical techniques for 'treating' insanity, or to attribute to the progress of the condition itself what he saw as the consequences of neglect. In contemptuous tones, he commented:

Amongst much medical nonsense, published by physicians interested to conceal their neglect, and the abuses of their establishments, it has been said, that persons afflicted with insanity are more liable than others to mortification of their extremities. Nothing of the kind was ever experienced at the institution of the Quakers. If the members of the royal and learned College of Physicians were chained, or shut up naked, on straw saturated with urine and excrement, with a scanty allowance of food, – exposed to the indecency of a northern climate, in cells having windows unglazed – I have no doubt that they would soon exhibit as strong a tendency to mortified extremities, as any of their patients.[1]

William Ellis, though himself medically qualified and in charge of the Refuge, a private madhouse at Hull, by now possessed first-hand acquaintance with Tuke's work at the Retreat, and had absorbed much of the latter's scepticism about the activities of his fellow professionals. His *Letter to Thomas Thompson, M.P.* (a member of the 1815–16 Committee) contained a number of critical remarks directed at them. In particular, he alleged that

the management of the insane has been in too few hands; and many of those who have been engaged in it, finding it a very lucrative concern, have wished to involve it in great mystery, and, in order to prevent institutions for their cure from becoming more general, were desirous

---

[1] Godfrey Higgins, *The Evidence taken before a Committee of the House of Commons respecting the Asylum at York; with observations and notes*, Doncaster, Sheardown, 1816, p. 48 and footnote. Dr Hunter was, until his death, when he was succeeded by his protégé Dr Best, the physician to the York Asylum. In addition to his lucrative trade at the asylum, which included extensive embezzlement of its funds, he energetically promoted his 'powders' as a certain, if expensive, home remedy for insanity for those who could not afford his full-time ministrations.

that it should be thought that there was some secret in the way of medicine for the cure, not easily found out. Some medical men have gone so far as even to condescend to the greatest quackery in the treatment of insanity.

On the contrary, Ellis contended, there were no medical specifics for the successful treatment of insanity, and the acceptance of the idea that the care of the insane was best left to experts, medical or otherwise, was the surest guarantee of abuse. In his own proposals for reform, therefore, he advocated constant lay supervision of all asylums by local magistrates.

4. The Weaknesses of Moral Treatment as a Professional Ideology

The propagation of the notion that 'very little dependence is to be placed on medicine alone for the cure of insanity' posed a clear threat to the professional dominance of this field. Given that those most convinced of the truth of this proposition were also the prime movers in trying to obtain lunacy reform, the doctors interested in insanity were unable any longer to ignore or depreciate moral treatment. They had to find some way to accommodate to it.

At first sight, moral treatment seemed to be an unpromising basis for any profession trying to assert special competence in the treatment of the insane. In Freidson's words, 'one of the things that marks off professions from occupations is the professions' claims to schooling in knowledge of an especially esoteric, scientific, or abstract character that is markedly superior to the mere experience of suffering from the illness or of having attempted pragmatically to heal a procession of sufferers from the illness'.[1] Moral treatment had begun by rejecting existing 'scientific' responses as worse than useless; and the remedies proposed in their place – warm baths and kindness – hardly provided much of a foundation for claims to possess the kinds of expertise and special skills which ordinarily form the basis for the grant of professional autonomy.

In practice, however, this feature of moral treatment proved an advantage to those bent on re-asserting medicine's jurisdiction in this area. The very difficulty of erecting professional claims on such

[1] E. Freidson, *Professional Dominance*, New York, Atherton, 1970, p. 106.

a flimsy basis largely precluded the emergence of an organized group of competitors – lay therapists. Moreover, Tuke had explicitly *not* sought to create or train a group of experts in moral treatment. He and his followers were deeply suspicious of any plan to hand the treatment of lunatics over to experts. In the words of William Ellis, 'Of the abuses that have existed, the cause of a great proportion of them may be traced to the mystery with which many of those who have had the management of the insane have constantly endeavoured to envelop it.' Those who had developed moral treatment claimed that the new approach was little more than an application of common sense and humanity; and these were scarcely qualities monopolized by experts. Indeed, the grant of a measure of autonomy which accompanied the acceptance of someone as an expert threatened to remove the surest guarantee of humane treatment for the insane – searching inquiry and oversight by outsiders.

Interestingly enough, the earliest recruits to moral treatment were primarily those who were interested in the cause of lunacy reform, but who were unlikely, given their social status, to undertake themselves the task of administering an asylum – magistrates and upper-middle-class philanthropists. The major exception to this generalization, William Ellis, was a doctor rather than just an expert in moral treatment. In the absence of any rival helping group, medicine set about assimilating moral treatment within its own sphere of competence.

Even while specifically denying medical claims to expertise in the area of insanity, the promoters of moral treatment had continued to employ a vocabulary laden with terms borrowed from medicine: 'patient', 'mental illness', 'moral *treatment*', and so on. This failure to develop an alternative technical jargon itself made the re-assertion of medical control somewhat easier, inasmuch as one of the most important connotations of the label 'illness' and its associated array of concepts is the idea that the syndrome to which it is applied is essentially a medical one. Given the critical role of language in shaping the social construction of reality, to employ terms which imply that something is a medical problem, and yet to deny that doctors are those most competent to deal with it, seems perverse.

The lack of an alternative model of insanity in the form of a coherent, well-articulated theory had this further consequence: that the denial of the applicability of medicinal remedies implied a view of insanity as essentially irremediable ('incurable'), or as remediable ('curable') only by accident or through the operation of spontaneous tendencies towards recovery. Tuke himself seems to have adhered to the latter view. Thus, in his efforts to secure the establishment of asylums for the insane poor, he urged that 'though we can do but little by the aid of medicine towards the cure of insanity, it is surely not the less our duty to use every means in our power to alleviate the complaint, or at least place the poor sufferer in a situation where nature may take her own course, and not be obstructed in the relief which she herself would probably bring to him'. And his discussion of the Retreat's success in restoring patients to sanity concludes: 'As we have not discovered any anti-maniacal specific, and profess to do little more than assist Nature, in the performance of her own cure, the term *recovered*, is adopted in preference to that of *cured*.'[1] Such modesty may well have been warranted; yet it was scarcely as appealing as the claim that one could actively influence the outcome in the desired direction. Practically speaking, it left moral treatment vulnerable to assimilation by a medical profession less scrupulously modest in its claims.

The challenge moral treatment posed to the medical dominance of the treatment of insanity was thus not as clear-cut as it might have been. Furthermore, the medical profession possessed certain initial advantages as it sought to re-assert its jurisdiction, advantages which could, however, have proved purely ephemeral. After all, there were, as yet, no legal barriers to the development of an organized rival group of therapists, and language is not immutable. The interested segments of the medical profession now moved to secure what they rightly perceived to be their imperilled position.

The potential consequences of taking Tuke seriously were most clearly articulated by Browne a half century later:

If therapeutic agents are cast aside or degraded from their legitimate rank, it will become the duty of the physician to give place to the divine or

[1] Samuel Tuke, 'Essay on the State of the Insane Poor', *The Philanthropist*, I, 1811, p. 357; Samuel Tuke, *Description of the Retreat*, pp. 216–17.

moralist, whose chosen mission it is to minister to the mind diseased; and of the heads of establishments like this [lunatic asylum] to depute their authority to the well-educated man of the world, who could, I feel assured, conduct an asylum fiscally, and as an intellectual boarding house, a great deal better than any of us.

Earlier he had complained that

a want of power or inclination to discriminate between the inutility of medicine from its being inapplicable, and from its being injudiciously applied, had led to the adoption of the absurd opinion that the insane ought not to be committed to the charge of medical men. A manager of a large and excellent institution, entertaining this view, has declared that the exhibition of medicine in insanity was useless, and that the disease was to be cured by moral treatment only.[1]

The pernicious doctrine that traditional medical remedies were useless had spread dangerously far, even among those who continued to insist that doctors were the most qualified to treat lunatics. 'We must confess,' said Spurzheim, one of the founders of phrenology and a prolific writer on insanity, 'that hitherto medical art has acquired very little merit in the cure of insanity; nature alone does almost everything.' When the *Quarterly Review*'s correspondent argued for medical control, he simultaneously made the dangerous concession that

the powers of medicine, merely upon mental hallucination are exceedingly circumscribed and feeble . . . we want principles on which to form any satisfactory indications of treatment . . . Almost the whole of . . . what may be called the strict medical treatment of madness must be regarded, at present, at least, as empirical, and the most extensive experience proves that very little is to be done.

Casting about for justifications for his insistence on medicine's entitlement to pre-eminence, he found remarkably few. The administration of warm baths now became something which could only be done under careful professional supervision. After all, the use of such a powerful technique had to be guided by an expert

---

[1] W. A. F. Browne, *The Moral Treatment of the Insane: A Lecture*, London, Adlard, 1864, p. 5; W. A. F. Browne, *What Asylums Were, Are, and Ought to Be*, Edinburgh, 1837, p. 178.

1. The second Bethlem, built in 1675-6, prior to the addition of wings for incurables. By 1815, when the treatment of its inmates provided lunacy reformers with much of their most potent ammunition, it was on the point of physical collapse, and it was replaced by a third asylum in St George's Fields. The third Bethlem is now the Imperial War Museum.

2. The second St Luke's Hospital, London, opened in 1787. George Dance, the architect, also designed Newgate Prison. Neither Bethlem nor St Luke's possessed a chapel for its inmates. This differentiates them sharply from the general hospitals built in the eighteenth century. Perhaps it is not too fanciful to link this omission to the lunatics' ontological status in this period: deprived of the divine attribute of reason, the God-given quality which distinguished man from the brutes, the insane were presumably incapable of communion with the Deity. By contrast, the prominent place occupied by the Chapel in nineteenth-century asylum architecture reflects not just the influence of Evangelical reformers, but also the decreasing emphasis on the loss of reason as the defining characteristic of insanity, and the new insistence that the insane had not lost their essential humanity.

3. The original building at the York Retreat. At the front were gardens and only a small fence. The impression of a place of confinement was further diminished by avoiding bars on the windows (instead the frames and partitions were made of iron), and by building the wall around the exercising courts (behind the main building) at the bottom of a slope allowing the inmates unhampered views over the surrounding countryside.

4. Chester County Asylum one of the earliest county asylums, built for 110 patients under the permissive Act of 1808 and opened in 1829. Its relatively modest size contrasts sharply with the vastness of the asylums built only a decade or so later.

5. Brislington House, the first purpose-built private asylum in England. Completed in 1806 for Edward Long Fox, it was designed for an upper-class clientele and was located in the centre of a well-wooded estate some three miles from Bristol. In addition to the central asylum buildings, a brochure of 1836 advertises a number of houses on the estate 'inhabited by members of the nobility, who are accommodated with servants from the institution; and are allowed to pursue any style of living and expense as to carriages, horses, etc. most suitable to their former habits, and not inconsistent with their present situation'.

6. View of a portion of the grounds at Ticehurst Asylum, from a brochure published in 1830, showing the hermitage and bowling green. Even at this early date, the asylum provided an extraordinary range of amenities for its aristocratic clientele.

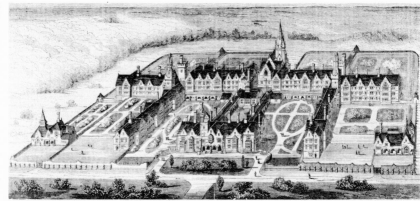

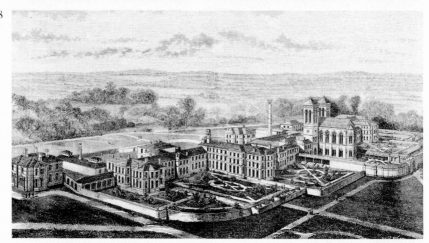

7 and 8. The Essex County Asylum at Brentwood and the City and County Asylum at Hereford. Asylum architects endeavoured to make the running of each institution as self-contained as possible. Their designs commonly made provision for such things as a gasworks, a farm, a chapel for the patients (note its prominence in the examples shown), a mortuary, a graveyard, a laundry, housing for staff on the grounds. Asylums were thus equipped to provide for almost all the wants of their inhabitants, from admission to the grave.

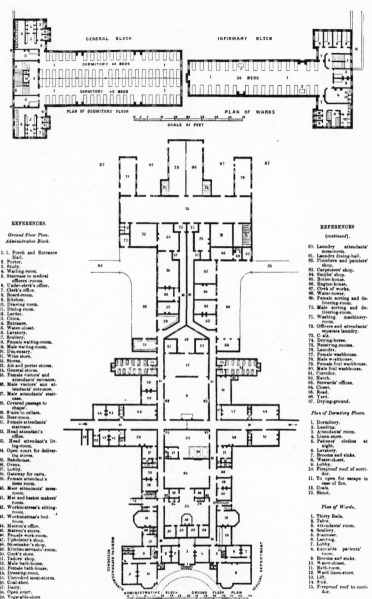

ASYLUM FOR IMBECILE POOR.

9 and 10. General view of the design for the Metropolitan asylums for chronic lunatics at Caterham and Leavesden, and floor plans of a general block and an infirmary block. These institutions were designed to cram as many patients as possible into the available space. The dormitories also served as dayrooms. The inmates' entire existence, with the exception of meals taken in the dining hall and occasional excursions to the exercise yard, was spent contemplating these four walls.

11. On their second visit to Bethlem, Wakefield's party of reformers brought with them an artist, G. Arnald, who sketched a picture of Norris in his iron cage. This picture was mass-produced in the form of cheap engravings and used to great effect by the reformers.

12. Interior of Bethlem in 1745, showing an inmate undergoing the routine 'bleeding' which formed part of the Monro family's standard treatment for lunacy for over a century.

13. Interior of St Luke's Hospital in 1809, drawn by Rowlandson and Pugin, and taken from *The Microcosm of London*. In his notes on a visit to St Luke's Samuel Tuke commented: 'The superintendent . . . thinks confinement or restraint may be imposed as a punishment with some advantage, and, on the whole, thinks fear the most effectual principle by which to reduce the insane to orderly conduct. The building has entirely the appearance of a place of confinement, enclosed by high walls, and there are strong iron gates to the windows.'

14. 'Twelfth Night Entertainments at the Hanwell Lunatic Asylum'. A drawing taken from the *Illustrated London News*, 15 January 1848, demonstrating the happy effects of reform and the success of Conolly's non-restraint system. The entertainments at Hanwell were still segregated by sex – the female patients had had their party on New Year's Eve; the one shown here was for 250 male patients. The long corridor in which the inmates are seated at dinner was one of a number which ordinarily served as dayrooms. The figures in the foreground on the right include some of the asylum officers and Magistrates' Committee, with their wives.

15. A patients' ball, held in the kitchen of the Somerset County Asylum, c. 1847.

16. The dining hall at Prestwich County Asylum, Lancashire, where the inmates gathered in shifts to be fed.

assessment of the condition of the individual patient. Cathartics were somehow rescued from the oblivion into which other medical remedies had been cast, once more with the caution that 'the practice of purging' was by no means 'of so simple and straight-forward a nature as might be at first sight conceived'. Conscious that these contentions might seem less than compelling, he resorted to the argument from experience: 'were it only on account of the frequent opportunities which more strictly medical practitioners have of witnessing aberrations of the intellect, from different sources, these would appear to be the fittest persons for the treatment of lunacy'.[1]

5. Medical Resistance to Reform

The necessity for a more strenuous and convincing defence of professional prerogatives was clear, and was rendered the more urgent as the lunacy reformers sought to give legislative effect to their schemes. As we have seen in the previous chapter, in the aftermath of the findings of the 1815-16 Select Committee, the reformers in the Commons made a sustained effort to devise a system of strict outside supervision and control of madhouse keepers, so as to insure against the repetition of previous abuses. Each of the bills they introduced to give effect to this plan would have empowered boards of laymen to inquire into the treatment and management of patients, to direct discontinuance of practices they considered cruel or unnecessarily harsh, and to order the discharge of any patient they considered restored to sanity. If one follows Freidson in considering autonomy, the right to deny legitimacy to outside criticism of work and its performance, as one of the core characteristics of any profession, such proposals to introduce lay control and evaluation of 'expert' performance must clearly be seen as of enormous strategic importance; and as likely to provoke intense opposition from those threatened by such control. Such opposition was indeed forthcoming from doctors in the mad business.

[1] J. G. Spurzheim, *Observations on the Deranged Manifestations of the Mind, or Insanity*, London, Baldwin, Craddock, & Joy, 1817, p. 197; [David Uwins, M.D.], 'Insanity and Madhouses', *Quarterly Review*, 15, 1816, pp. 402-3.

Burrows, in particular, was scathing in his criticisms of these bills. Somewhat disingenuously, he commented, 'The provision of this [1817] Bill induces me to conclude that I certainly misinterpreted the import of many of the queries of the Members of the Committee of Inquiry; for I was led to think that a conviction had arisen out of the investigation, that all houses for the reception of insane persons ought to be under the superintendence of men of character and ability, and particularly of medical men.' Assuming that this was so (a large assumption, of course), it was simply absurd to allow the judgement of rank amateurs to override the mature judgement of a competent expert. If the legislature was convinced of the necessity of appointing Commissioners to inspect madhouses, these ought, as in the past, to be medical men. One faced a situation in which 'the most experienced will acknowledge the liability of being deceived, even where frequent opportunities of judging of the sanity of the mind have occurred. How then can those who are not only casual but unprofessional visitors pretend to decide on any particular case, or prescribe any alteration, or condemn any mode of treatment?' It made no sense to ask a layman to pass judgement on the curative treatment of a patient, 'for if any difference of opinion were to arise upon a question relative to the management or release of a patient, it were surely most proper that the medical opinion should prevail'. Furthermore, allowing 'country gentlemen' to visit asylums, unaccompanied by medical men, in order to check for possible abuses, threatened the welfare of the patients in the most serious possible degree. The commotion their visits would cause, and the interference their ignorance might lead them to indulge in, would set at naught the asylum doctor's most skilful efforts to cure his patients. Consequently, the reformers would proceed with their plans only at 'the hazard of great injury to the patients'.[1]

Such lobbying met with success. In 1816, in 1817, and again in 1819, the reformers succeeded in steering bills embodying the

[1] George Man Burrows, *Cursory Remarks on a Bill now in the House of Peers for Regulating Madhouses*, London, Harding, 1817, pp. 52, 23–5. Burrows was the proprietor of madhouses in Chelsea and, from 1823, in Clapham. He had previously taken a leading role in efforts to upgrade the status and qualifications of apothecaries, and subsequently wrote two well-known treatises on insanity.

changes they sought through the Commons, only to see them go down to defeat in the Lords. Their Lordships' opposition was undoubtedly motivated by more than just the desire to protect the prerogatives of the medical profession.[1] At the very least, however, the doctors' protests provided them with a convenient ideological cloak for their opposition, and while votes may actually have been swayed by other considerations, they were justified on these neutral, technical grounds.

The Marquess of Lansdowne, who introduced the 1819 bill into the Lords, clearly foresaw the direction the debate would take, and attempted to reassure his audience that, while some systems of visitation and control by outsiders 'might retard the cure of persons so affected', the insane would only benefit from the specific provisions of this bill. Speaking against the bill, Eldon brushed this aside, and reiterated the standard professional line: 'It was of the utmost importance, with a view to the proper care of these unhappy individuals, and with a view to their recovery that they should be under the superintendance [*sic*] of men who had made this branch of medicine their peculiar study, and that the superintendance of physicians should not be interfered with.' Yet this was precisely what the bill before them sought to do, and in consequence, 'he conscientiously believed its regulations would tend to aggravate the malady with which the unfortunate persons were afflicted, or to retard their cure'. One of the most objectionable features of the bill from his (and the medical profession's) perspective was that it

gave a number of penalties, half of which were to go to the informer, and it was evident that informers would be found amongst the attendants and servants in receptacles for lunatics, who would thus be made judges of the conduct of the physicians, and it would be impossible for the latter, under such circumstances, to resort to many of those means which their experience had taught them were most effectual for the cure of their unhappy patients.

Eldon had the authority of the best medical opinion behind him (indeed, he was defending that authority) when he asserted that 'there could not be a more false humanity than an over-humanity

[1] See Chapter 3, Section II above.

with regard to persons afflicted with insanity'.[1] In the division which followed, the bill was rejected 35 to 14.

6. The Defence of Medical Hegemony

Temporarily, at least, the mad-doctors had successfully resisted efforts to restrict their professional autonomy, for with the rejection of the 1819 bill, the reform movement lost its momentum. Their victory was a fragile and uncertain one, however, so long as it rested on a marriage of convenience with political forces whose power was on the wane, and as long as they remained vulnerable to charges from enthusiasts for moral treatment that their expertise had no scientific or practical foundation. If they were to overcome their vulnerability, they had to develop a more sophisticated justification of their privileged position.

As part of this process, from about 1815 onwards, a veritable spate of books and articles purporting to be medical treatises on the treatment of insanity began to appear. Similarly, the claim that instruction in its treatment formed a part of the normal curriculum of medical training, which had been made by an earlier generation of mad-doctors, was reinforced when Dr (later Sir) Alexander Morison, a well-known society physician, began a course of lectures on the topic. These he repeated annually from 1823 to the late 1840s, while the published version simultaneously went through a number of editions. All of this activity was probably stimulated at least in part by the increased attention all members of the educated élite were giving to insanity, in the wake of two major parliamentary inquiries into the subject within the short space of eight years, and in consequence of the revelations of the second of these about conditions in madhouses. But more importantly than that, it represented an effort to reassert the validity of the medical model of mental disturbance, and to ensure a maximum of professional autonomy in the treatment of lunatics.

Dr Francis Willis, grandson of the man who had 'treated' George III's madness, explicitly wrote his treatise to emphasize the medical nature of insanity, an endeavour rendered 'the more necessary, because derangement has been considered by some to be

---

[1] *Hansard*, Vol. 40, First Series, 1819, Col. 1345.

merely and exclusively a mental disease, curable without the aid of medicine, by what are termed moral remedies; such as travelling and various kinds of amusements'. The language used by John and Thomas Mayo was even more revealing. Their announced purpose in publishing their *Remarks on Insanity* was 'to vindicate the rights of [our] profession over Insanity, and to elucidate its medical treatment',[1] two tasks which were obviously closely connected. For the mere existence of a large body of what purported to be technical literature passing on the fruits of scientific knowledge about the management of the insane gave impressive-seeming substance to the claim of expertise, regardless of its practical usefulness or merits. Complicated nosographies like that developed by Prichard[2] bewildered and impressed the average layman. Given such an array of diagnostic categories, recognition of the precise form of mental disease an individual lunatic was labouring under clearly became a matter for expert determination.

When medical ideas about insanity had to be presented to a lay audience, the availability of a large body of specialized 'knowledge' was valuable in a different way. For it enabled writers who wanted to advance medicine's cause to circumvent the ordinary requirement that they produce evidence in support of their contentions. Non-technical discussion of the medical treatment of insanity could be justified on the grounds of the general importance of making the public aware of the potential contribution medicine could make, but any pressures to move beyond vague generalities could now be resisted as being 'more properly the province of journals exclusively devoted to technical science'. To enter upon such 'purely professional' topics would 'only be interesting to a comparatively small number of our readers', and would simply be above the heads of the majority of lay readers, since they lacked the requisite training.[3]

[1] Francis Willis, *A Treatise on Mental Derangement*, London, Longman et al., 1823, p. 2; John and Thomas Mayo, *Remarks on Insanity*, London, Underwood, 1817.

[2] James Cowles Prichard, the author of *A Treatise on Insanity* (London, 1835) and inventor of the term 'moral insanity', later became one of the first Commissioners in Lunacy. He was also an eminent ethnologist.

[3] [David Uwins], 'Burrows' Inquiry into Certain Errors Relative to Insanity', *Quarterly Review*, 24, 1820, p. 169.

Morison's lectures were the most visible sign that members of the medical profession were in fact receiving such training. It scarcely mattered that Morison himself had no practical experience that would have given him justification for claiming expertise in this area; or that his lectures were an unoriginal mélange of ideas uncritically assembled from existing works in the field. Instruction in 'a curriculum that includes some *special* theoretical content (whether scientifically proven or not) may represent a declaration that there is a body of special knowledge and skill necessary for the occupation', which is not otherwise obtainable.[1] Here, the availability of special education, regardless of its specific content or scientific validity, bolstered the medical profession's claims to expertise and esoteric knowledge.

The effort to press these claims proceeded on other fronts as well. The more respectable part of the medical profession used its prestige and ready access to élite circles to promote its cause. As part of this process, medical men running asylums made strenuous and eventually successful efforts to persuade their lay audience that they possessed a more common and/or intense commitment to a service orientation than did their non-medically qualified competitors. At a time when madhouses were acquiring considerable disrepute, Nisbet took pains to emphasize that 'Out of thirty-three licenses for the metropolis, only three are in the hands of medical men. The chief part is in the hands of persons unacquainted with medicine, who take up this branch of medicine as a beneficial pursuit, and whose object is to make the most of it.' Similarly, Conolly urged the importance 'of making medical men as familiar with disorders of the mind as with other disorders; and thus of rescuing lunatics from those whose interest it is to represent such maladies as more obscure, and more difficult to manage than they are'. Burrows's writings and his evidence before the 1828 Select Committee of the House of Lords likewise both reflected and promoted 'the widespread view that lay proprietors were more likely to be corrupt and avaricious than their medically trained colleagues'. So that when the *Quarterly Review* informed its readers that 'the superintendent of a mad-house ought to be a man of

---

[1] E. Freidson, *Professional Dominance*, pp. 134-5.

character and responsibility', it recommended in the same breath that 'he should always be chosen from the medical profession'.[1]

The articles which appeared in the leading literary periodicals of the time were virtually all written by physicians. The profession did not neglect the opportunity to present itself in a favourable light. Those, for instance, who relied on the *Edinburgh Review*'s summary for an account of the findings of the 1815–16 inquiry, learned that 'it is the decided opinion of *all* the most judicious and experienced witnesses examined before the Committee, that the proper employment of medicine, though neglected most deplorably in several public asylums, and in almost all the private establishments, has the best effect in cases of insanity'. Similarly, Burrows informed his readers that 'from a perusal of the replies to the Questions put by the Committee, it is evident that insanity is greatly under the control of medicine – a fact that strictly accounts with my own observations'.[2]

The profession was able to use its representation in Parliament, and its position as one of the three ancient learned professions, to ensure that its views received due consideration. When there was a renewed inquiry into conditions in private madhouses, it could call on the services of eminently respectable society physicians like Sir Anthony Carlisle and Dr John Bright to lend their authority to the contention that this was a medical problem. Medical certification of insanity (for private patients only) had been required by the 1774 Madhouse Act as an additional security against improper confinement of the sane, and the doctors now sought to clarify and extend their authority in this area, so as to develop an officially approved monopoly of the right to define mental health and illness. Further efforts were made to get medicine's special competence *vis-à-vis* the insane recognized and written into the growing volume of lunacy legislation which flowed from the findings of the 1827 Select

[1] William Nisbet, *Two Letters to . . . George Rose M.P. on the Reports at Present before the House of Commons on the State of the Madhouses*, pp. 8–9; J. Conolly, *An Inquiry Concerning the Indications of Insanity*, London, 1830, p. 7; William Parry-Jones, *The Trade in Lunacy*, London, Routledge & Kegan Paul, 1972, p. 82; [David Uwins], 'Burrows' Inquiry into Certain Errors Relative to Insanity', p. 190.

[2] [W. H. Fitton, M.D.], 'Lunatic Asylums', *Edinburgh Review*, 28, 1817, pp. 454–5; G. M. Burrows, op, cit., p. 52.

Committee. While the major bill was pending in the House of
Lords, a special committee of peers sat to hear the views of the
medical profession on the proposed changes. The testimony of men
like E. L. Fox, E. Finch, and W. T. Monro is indicative of considerable resentment of supervision and inspection by magistrates,
particularly when efforts were made by these laymen to meddle with
decisions which were properly the prerogative of the professional,
such as when a patient was ready for discharge. While legislation
was awaiting passage, the Royal College of Physicians appointed a
Committee of its own to (as Parry-Jones delicately puts it) 'enquire
into the expediency of the provisions of the 1828 Bill'. And at the
same time, a rash of pamphlets written by members of the medical
profession appeared, urging that further inspection was 'a useless
inquisition into private concerns, destructive of all that privacy that
is truly desirable for the patient', and that the proposal itself
'betrays a want of confidence in their [mad-doctors'] moral and
medical character'.[1]

Some outside regulation and inspection of asylums was made
inevitable by the continuing revelations of abuses and maltreatment
of patients in its absence. Hence the doctors sought to turn this into
a system of professional self-regulation by obtaining a dominant
role for medical practitioners. Under the 1828 Act in the provinces
only the medical visitor, and not the magistrates who accompanied
him, received payment, while among the newly created Metropolitan Commissioners in Lunacy five out of fifteen were physicians.
This representation was not achieved and maintained without a
struggle. As late as 1842, Ashley expressed considerable scepticism
about any requirement that commissioners to inspect asylums
should be medically qualified, arguing that 'although so far as
health was concerned the opinion of a medical man was of the
greatest importance, yet it having been once established that the
insanity of a patient did not arise from the state of his bodily health,
a man of common sense could give as good an opinion as any
medical man he knew [respecting his treatment and the question of
his sanity]'. Thomas Wakely M.P., the editor of the leading medical
periodical, the *Lancet*, defended his profession's prerogatives,

[1] All cited in R. A. Hunter and I. MacAlpine, *Three Hundred Years of
Psychiatry*, London, Oxford University Press, 1963, p. 791.

terming insanity 'a grievous disease', and stigmatizing any proposal to have lunatic asylums inspected by lawyers alone as 'an insult to the medical profession'.

Such a proposal now formed a part of the Licensed Lunatic Asylums Bill, introduced to expand temporarily the jurisdiction of the Metropolitan Commissioners to allow them to inspect asylums throughout the country, to prepare for a further national reform. When the bill came up again, Wakely renewed his attack:

> He objected to the clause appointing barristers to the office of commissioners of lunatic asylums. What could be more absurd than to select members of the legal profession to sit in judgement on cases of mental derangement? Was not insanity invariably associated with bodily disease? The investigations in which the commissioners would be involved would be purely of a medical character, and therefore barristers, if they were appointed, would be incompetent to perform the duties which would devolve upon them.

On the contrary, observed Lord Granville Somerset, the commissioners were solely concerned with 'whether [the lunatic] was treated properly and with kindness', and this could as well be discovered by a lawyer as a doctor.[1] Both sides had their adherents in the debate which followed, and eventually some sentiment emerged for a compromise, whereby the commissioners would operate in pairs, one with legal and one with medical training. This was the solution eventually adopted, so that the number of Metropolitan Commissioners was expanded to include seven doctors. Since the 1844 Commission Report formed the basis of the 1845 reforms, this expanded medical representation was of considerable importance. When the Report discussed the nature of insanity and its medical and moral treatment, the lay members of the Commission deferred to the specialized knowledge of their medical colleagues, and thus these sections of the Report faithfully reflected the orthodox medical viewpoint. In turn, this official acknowledgement of medicine's legitimate interest in insanity (and Ashley was now one of the converted) helped to shape the legislation and its subsequent implementation.

[1] *Hansard*, Vol. 61, Third Series, 1842, Cols. 806, 804; Vol. 62, Third Series, 1842, Cols. 886, 887.

7. Persuasion at the Local Level

Simultaneously, the profession was active on the local level, where the magistrates who were engaged in setting up the new system of public asylums were an obvious target for these efforts. In some counties the magistrates were already convinced that insanity was a medical province, and hence needed no prompting to place their asylum in the hands of a local doctor. At Nottingham, for instance, Becher, who was the man most responsible for getting the asylum built, was convinced that the management of insanity 'is an art of itself', a disease having its basis in organic lesions of the body which only doctors were competent to treat. In consequence, an apothecary was placed in charge of the day-to-day management of the asylum, subject to the control of a visiting physician 'who shall be entrusted with the medical treatment of the patients'.[1] The magistrates at Hanwell and Wakefield followed a similar plan, except that here ultimate authority rested in the hands of the resident physician. Elsewhere, however, asylum committees chose to place the daily control of the institution in the hands of a lay superintendent, or even tried to run it themselves. The Staffordshire magistrates chose a layman as their chief resident officer. At the Cornwall Asylum at Bodmin, after the first appointment of a surgeon, James Duck, as superintendent proved unsatisfactory, he was replaced by a lay 'Governor and Contractor'.

The magistrates at Bedford initially also chose this latter plan. Among the candidates they considered to head their asylum were a former assistant keeper at St Luke's, and a house painter who had had some experience looking after a lunatic he had come across in the course of his business. They had previously decided that, since the medical care needed by lunatics was slight, and they 'will not require the same species of unremitting attention during the whole of the four and twenty hours as Patients in Hospitals do', that 'Mr Leach, our House Surgeon at the Infirmary who so ably discharges his duties there might from the Contiguity of the Establishments' be induced to attend to the occasional medical needs of the asylum

---

[1] [Rev. J. T. Becher], *An Address to the Public on the Nature, Design, and Constitution of the General Lunatic Asylum near Nottingham*, Newark, Ridge, 1811, pp. iv, xi–xii; *Nottingham Lunatic Asylum Articles of Union*, Newark, Ridge, n.d., pp. 17–19.

patients. At a subsequent meeting held on 27 April 1812, the house painter, William Pether, and his wife were appointed 'the Governor and Matron of the Lunatic Asylum with a Salary of Sixty Guineas per Annum'.[1]

Within less than a year, local physicians were seeking their first foothold in the new institution. A letter was received from a Dr G. O. Yeats offering 'to undertake the office of the Medical Superintendent and Physician of this Institution gratuitously'. He justified the need for such assistance by pointing out that there were 'a considerable number of lunatics whose diseases will require medical aid'. Naturally enough, the offer was accepted. A few more months went by before Yeats tried to convince the magistrates that medicine could be used not merely to cure the patients' physical ailments, but also to help to restore them to sanity. In a second long letter to the managing committee, he argued that

however anxious the legislature has been strictly to confine the inmates of the house and to guard against the possibility of there being restored to the world unfit members of society, yet equal anxiety is exprest that every possible care should be taken by medical means for such restoration . . . It is very desirable, then, in order to render the Asylum, not only a place for incarceration, but one where every facility may be given for the amelioration of the condition and for the cure of the maladies of its unfortunate inmates,

that the medical officer be given broader powers over the treatment of the patients.[2]

The process by which the physician invoked the privileges of his office to subordinate the lay superintendent to medical control, and eventually to squeeze him out altogether, had now begun. Three days later, Pether received his new instructions: 'It was ordered that the Governor in all matters relating to the Health and Distribution of the Patients with a view to their Convalescence or their Medical Treatment, do obey implicitly the instructions of the Physician.' In February of the following year, Yeats was obliged to submit his

[1] *Bedfordshire County Asylum Minutes*, 1812, pp. 4–5, 7, 9.

[2] ibid., 2 January 1813, pp. 39, 41; letter from Dr G. O. Yeats to the Committee of Magistrates on the Asylum, dated 21 April 1813, in miscellaneous papers relating to the founding of the asylum, at Bedfordshire Record Office.

resignation as non-resident Medical Superintendent, as he was moving to London; but his colleague, Dr Thackeray, offered to assume the position in his stead, once more gratuitously.[1]

During Thackeray's term in office, he and various other doctors made efforts to educate the magistrates to the fact that insanity was a disease just like any other disease physicians were called upon to treat, and that there ought therefore to be provision for a full-time resident medical officer to run the asylum. In 1815, he complained in a letter to the magistrates of

the insufficiency of the present Medical Means to fulfil the benevolent designs of the Institution. Their asylum probably affords a solitary example in which a large and important medical establishment is conducted without the assistance of a Resident director in the character of a House apothecary. The defect in its constitution by totally precluding the employment of all the remedies requiring constant attention to their efforts and by preventing the observation and accumulation of Facts for the advancement of the Science of medicine greatly limits its service as a Medical Institution.

Such a state of affairs was rendered the more deplorable because proper classification of the various varieties of mental disease revealed that each major sub-type was almost certainly the consequence of an underlying physical pathology – mania reflected a disorder of the brain; melancholia of the abdominal viscera; and nervousness, a disturbed state of the nervous system.

Thackeray felt that 'if there be any foundation for this classification of mental disease, great encouragement I think is held out in it for placing a Lunatic Asylum on the footing of a Medical Institution'.[2] The magistrates clearly did not agree. Dr Maclean, who had replaced Leach as House Surgeon at the Infirmary, continued to hold that post, and to perform the duties of Secretary and Head Apothecary at the Infirmary, so that his attendance on the asylum patients was a distinctly part-time affair; and Thackeray still contributed his services on a voluntary, unpaid visiting basis. On Maclean's resignation from his various posts in June 1823, the

[1] ibid., 24 April 1813; 5 February and 5 March 1814.
[2] Thackeray to the Magistrates' Committee, 7 August 1815, in miscellaneous papers at the Bedfordshire Record Office.

governors ordered that his successor could perform these same duties, and in September a Mr Harris accepted the appointment.

Further efforts were now made to dislodge the layman, Pether, and to replace him with a resident medical officer. The large proportion of chronic derelicts among the asylum population here posed a problem for those advocating a greater role for medicine, since it was not clear what benefits, if any, the increased expenditure for a full-time medical officer would bring. Thackeray conceded the difficulty, but sought to persuade the magistrates that it was a temporary state of affairs, the consequence of the failure to employ medical treatment while such cases were still curable – a mistake they should take care to avoid in the future:

The present state of the house in which there are but a few subjects under medical treatment may perhaps have led to the idea that little occasion exists for the establishment of such a department. Were this state a *permanent* condition of the house the conclusion would be just; but it should be regarded [as] wholly an *accidental* one, depending on the Infancy of the Institution. The asylum is at present filled chiefly with patients whose disorders from their *long* standing, discourage every hope of benefit from medical exertion. In the progress, however, of time, *recent* cases of derangement will be continually presenting themselves, when much encouragement will be offered for the active interference of Art.[1]

For a while the magistrates still proved recalcitrant. Thackeray and Harris submitted further memoranda in support of their position, and obtained testimonials reinforcing their contentions from other physicians who happened to visit the asylum. Finally, the magistrates bowed to the weight of professional opinion:

Dr Thackeray and Mr Harris having separately called the attention of the magistrates to the expediency of providing regular resident medical aid to the Institution and the Magistrates having noticed a similar suggestion entered in the visitors' journal by the Medical Superintendent of the Bicêtre of Paris and another foreigner and Dr Thompson of the twenty-fifth of July last, and having taken the same into their consideration, Resolved to recommend the subject to the next court of Quarter Sessions.[2]

[1] *Memorandum from Dr Thackeray, M.D.*, at Bedfordshire Record Office.
[2] *Bedfordshire County Asylum Visitors' Book*, 5 February 1827.

Pether's position swiftly became untenable, as he lost almost all his remaining authority. Finally, in 1828 he resigned his position as general manager, and was succeeded by Harris. Paramount authority over all aspects of asylum administration now rested in medical hands.

8. Madness as Mental Illness

The activities, both local and national, which we have just been discussing, all made use of, and owed much of their success to, the arguments which were developed in the medical literature of the time. For it was the contentions advanced here which convinced almost all the educated classes that insanity was indeed a disease and that its treatment ought therefore to be entrusted to doctors. Consequently, I want now to devote some time to a consideration of just what these arguments were.

Moral treatment lacked a well developed ideological rationale for why it should work. Tuke had explicitly eschewed any desire to develop a theoretical account of the nature of mental disturbance, and had refused to elaborate moral treatment into a rigid 'scientific' therapy. In the past, 'the want of facts relative to this subject, and our disposition to hasty generalization, have led to many conclusions equally unfriendly to the progress of knowledge, and the comfort of patients'. He therefore resisted efforts to achieve a premature systematization of knowledge, and encouraged a pragmatic approach: 'I have happily little occasion for theory, since my province is to relate, not only what ought to be done, but also what, in most instances, is actually performed.' He even refused to choose between a psychological and a somatic etiology of insanity, arguing that 'whatever theory we maintain in regard to the remote causes of insanity, we must consider moral treatment of very high importance'. If its origins lay in the mind, 'applications made immediately to it are the most natural, and the most likely to be attended with success'; if in the body, 'we shall still readily admit, from the reciprocal action of the two parts of our system upon each other, that the greatest attention is necessary, to whatever is calculated to affect the mind'.[1]

---

[1] Samuel Tuke, *Description of the Retreat*, pp. viii, xxii, 138, 131–2. This refusal to reduce moral treatment to a set of formulae, and the insistence that it

Undoubtedly, though, the nature of the therapy he advanced, and the manner in which advocates of moral treatment persistently and explicitly denied the value of a medical approach, could, at the very least, be more readily reconciled with a mental rather than a somatic etiology of insanity. Francis Willis was not alone in accusing those favouring moral treatment of propagating the doctrine that 'mental derangement must arise from causes, and be cured by remedies, that solely and exclusively operate on the mind'. Physicians stigmatized this as an 'absurd opinion' but were obviously afraid of the threat it posed to their position.

The single most effective response to an attack on these lines would have been to demonstrate that insanity was in fact caused by biophysical variables. A somatic interpretation of insanity would place it beyond dispute within medicine's recognized sphere of competence, and make plausible the assertion that it responded to medicine's conventional remedies for disease. The trouble was that the doctors could not show the existence of the necessary physical lesions, and this inconvenient fact was already in the public domain.

Unable to produce scientific evidence in support of their personal predilection for a somatic interpretation, the doctors invented an ingenious metaphysical argument which, dressed in the trappings of science, proved an equally satisfactory functional alternative. They began by postulating a Cartesian dualism between mind and body. The mind, which was an immortal, immaterial substance, identical with the Christian doctrine of the soul,[1] was forced in this world to operate through the medium of a material instrument, the brain. This was an apparently innocuous distinction, but once it had been conceded, the doctors had no trouble 'proving' their case. For to argue that the mind was subject to disease, or even, in the case of

---

rested on a commonsense approach to the problem of insanity aimed at eliminating artificial obstacles to recovery, made for a refreshing lack of dogmatism. At the same time, however, they were a crucial factor in weakening its ability to resist takeover and transformation by those espousing a less modest ideal; for by denying that schooled human knowledge and intervention were needed to cope with insanity, they at least delayed the rise of an occupational group claiming training in the new therapy.

[1] As Bynum (*Medical History*, 1974, p. 320) points out, the French even use the same word, l'âme, for the two concepts.

outright idiotism, death, was to contradict the very foundation of
Christianity, the belief in an immortal soul. On the other hand,
adoption of a somatic viewpoint provided a wholly satisfactory
resolution of the dilemma: 'From the admission of this principle,
derangement is no longer considered a disease of the understanding,
but of the centre of the nervous system, upon the unimpaired
condition of which the exercise of the understanding depends. The
brain is at fault and not the mind.' The brain, as a material organ,
was liable to irritation and inflammation, and it was this which
produced insanity. 'But let this oppression [of the brain] be relieved,
this irritation be removed, and the mind rises to its native strength,
clear and calm, uninjured, immutable, immortal. In all cases where
disorder of the mind is detectable, from the faintest peculiarity to
the widest deviation from health, it must and can only be traced
directly or indirectly to the brain.'[1]

The failure to *observe* physical lesions of the brain in most cases
of insanity could now be explained in either of two ways, neither of
which threatened the somatic interpretation. On the one hand, it
might be that existing instruments and techniques were simply too
crude to detect the very subtle changes involved. On the other hand,
it could be that insanity in its early stages was correlated only with

[1] W. A. F. Browne, *What Asylums Were, Are, and Ought to Be*, p. 4. For
elaborations of this entire somatic ideology which most clearly reveal the
ultimately theological grounds on which the explanation was offered (and
accepted), see Sir Alexander Morison, *Outlines of Lectures on . . . Insanity*, 4th
edn, London, Longman *et al.*, 1848, pp. 34–44; and Sir Andrew Halliday, *A
General View of the Present State of Lunatics and Lunatic Asylums*, London,
Underwood, 1828, pp. 2–4: 'the anatomist sought in vain for some visible
derangement of structure, or a diseased state of the parts in many cases where it
was perfectly ascertainable that death had ensued from insanity . . . hence the
common opinion seemed to be confirmed, that it was an incomprehensible and
consequently an incurable malady of the mind. Taking this view of the disease,
it is not at all wonderful that it was considered as beyond the reach of medical
science . . . Besides, we may suppose that many very able men, led away by
what appeared to be the general opinion of mankind, would shrink from the
strict investigation of a subject that seemed to lead to a doubt of the im-
materiality of the mind; a truth so evident to their own feelings, and so expressly
established by divine revelation. If they once admitted that the mind could
become diseased, it would follow as a matter of course, that the mind might die.
They, therefore, refrained from meeting a question which involved such
dangerous consequences, while they were unable to explain it . . .'

functional changes in the brain, which only at a later stage, when the patient became chronic, passed over into structural ones.

The intuitive appeal of this explanation to an audience of convinced Christians was enormous, and suffered scarcely at all from its extra-scientific character.[1] And by 'proving' that insanity was a somatic complaint, it decisively reinforced medical claims to jurisdiction in this area. The obvious achievements of moral treatment could not simply be overlooked – they were too well-established in the public mind for that. However, it could be, and was, just absorbed into the realm of ordinary medical techniques. Moral treatment now became just one weapon among many (even if a particularly valuable one), which the skilful physician used in his battle against mental illness. Texts like Prichard's included a chapter on moral treatment as a matter of course; while those who rejected the conventional medical methods were accused of unnecessarily reducing their chances of curing their patients. In support of this position, certain mad-doctors claimed to have cured a higher percentage of their patients than had the Retreat, and attributed this to their willingness to use *both* moral and medical means. Others claimed to provide proof of the efficacy of medical means in certain cases, proof which took the form of citing instances of insanity known to the author where the patient had recovered at some time after the administration of traditional medical remedies.

A number of doctors now proposed a truce. Extremists on both sides might argue for the unique value of a moral or a medical approach, but all reasonable men could see that a judicious *combination* of these two therapies was likely to be more valuable than either taken by itself. 'To those acquainted with the workings of the malady and its peculiar characteristics,' said Neville, 'it will

[1] Parenthetically, it may well be that scientific theories under some circumstances are not very effective weapons for converting laymen, since they may depart too radically from the lay world view, and/or be too complicated to lend themselves to a convincing simplistic presentation to a lay audience. For propaganda purposes, quasi-theories like this one, which do not really have a scientific status, may be a better way of persuading laymen that one has expertise, simply because they provide a closer fit with the preconceptions of the expert's audience. In this case, there is a rather delightful irony in the fact that the doctors were forced to rely on spiritual assumptions to prove a materialist case.

6

be easy to perceive the errors and partial views of such as profess to apply a medicinal agent only, as a specific, or those who advocate a course of moral treatment only for a cure. There is no doubt that a cooperation of medicinal and moral means is requisite to effect a thorough cure.' Now while from one perspective this represented a concession, particularly when compared with earlier emphases on the exclusive value of medicine, the concession was a harmless one. For it left the physician, as the only person who could legitimately dispense the medical side of the treatment, firmly in control. Thus, Neville thought that moral and medical treatment could only be carried out 'under the guidance of persons of sound professional education, and mature experience of the disease'; while Ellis commented that 'from what has been said on the treatment of the insane in Lunatic Asylums, it will be obvious, that, according to my notions, no-one, except a medical man, and a benevolent one, ought to be entrusted with the management of them'.[1]

And indeed, that was exactly what did happen. By the 1830s almost all the public mental hospitals had a resident medical director. Moreover, the magistrates' committees, which in several instances had been heavily involved in the day-to-day administration of asylums, increasingly left everything to the experts. The Metropolitan Commissioners, not entirely approvingly, commented in 1844 that the pattern at Bedford was being generally emulated, with 'almost the entire control of the County Asylum being delegated to the Medical and General Superintendent'. Similarly, in the private sector, the more reputable institutions acquired either a medical proprietor or a full-time resident medical superintendent. Symptomatic of medicine's gains in this respect was the appointment of a resident physician to run the York Retreat, where moral treatment had originated, and which, for the first forty-two years of its existence, had had a succession of lay superintendents.

As the last step in this process, the asylum doctor solved the problem of restricting access to his clientele, and transforming his

---

[1] William B. Neville, *On Insanity, Its Nature, Causes and Cure*, London, Longman *et al.*, 1836, p. 14; William Ellis, *A Treatise on the Nature, Symptoms, Causes, and Treatment of Insanity*, London, Holdsworth, 1838, p. 314. (Neville was the visiting doctor to Earls Court private madhouse.)

dominance of the treatment of mental illness into a virtual monopoly, in a typically professional manner, by arranging 'to have himself designated as the expert in such a way as to exclude all other claimants, his designation being official and bureaucratic insofar as it is formally established by law'.[1] The Madhouse Act of 1828 introduced the first legal requirements with respect to medical attendance: each asylum had to make arrangements for a doctor to visit the patients at least once a week, and for him to sign a weekly register. Where an asylum contained more than a hundred patients, it had to employ a medical superintendent. These requirements were stiffened by the 1845 Lunatics Act, which required, among other things, that all asylums keep a Medical Visitation Book, and a record of the medical treatment of each patient in a Medical Case Book. And, from 1846 on, the Lunacy Commissioners, who included a large contingent from the medical profession, manifested a steadily growing hostility to non-medically run asylums. With the help of élite sponsorship, the asylum doctors were now able to drive competing lay people out of the same line of work, and to subordinate those who stayed in the field to their authority.

[1] E. Freidson, *Professional Dominance*, p. 116.

Chapter Five

Mad-Doctors and Magistrates: Psychiatry's Struggle for Professional Autonomy

Half the harm that is done in this world
Is due to people who want to feel important.
They don't mean to do harm – but the harm does not interest them
Because they are involved in the endless struggle
To think well of themselves.

(T. S. Eliot, *The Cocktail Party*)

1. Problems for the New Profession

By 1845 the medical profession had secured powerful support for the proposition that insanity was a disease, and thus was naturally something which doctors alone were qualified to treat. For the rest of the century, the asylum doctors were primarily preoccupied with consolidating their position, being particularly concerned to develop and secure a large measure of professional autonomy. One of the first moves towards the establishment of a distinct identity for this new group of 'experts' was the creation of their own professional organization, the Association of Medical Officers of Asylums and Hospitals for the Insane. Founded in 1841, the Association drew its membership from the medical staff of both public and private asylums. This created problems, since there existed a 'distinct line of demarcation between the medical officers of public asylums and the proprietors of private asylums'.[1] The

[1] *Journal of Mental Science*, 6, 1860, p. 22. The division reflected wide differences in the social status of most of the patients treated by the two sets of practitioners, and the inevitable divergences of interest and outlook between salaried public employees and private, fee-dependent entrepreneurs.

division hampered moves to unify the profession and, for much of the nineteenth century, diminished the organization's effectiveness. Temporarily, at least, the Association was further weakened as a weapon in the professionalization process by its failure to publish its own journal – no one being willing to assume the position of editor – for this meant that contacts among the membership were effectively limited to those provided by a single conference once a year. When the first English periodical wholly devoted to the treatment of insanity as a medical speciality appeared, in 1848, it was published completely independently of the Association. Owned and edited by Dr Forbes Winslow, the proprietor of two Metropolitan Licensed Houses, the *Journal of Psychological Medicine and Mental Pathology* not surprisingly exhibited an editorial bias in favour of private asylums. But it was the public sector which was expanding most rapidly by now, and the county asylum superintendents were obtaining a dominant position in the Association. In 1853, the society commenced publication of its own periodical, the *Asylum Journal*, under the editorship of John Charles Bucknill of the Devon County Asylum.

'Any profession bases its claim for its position on the possession of a skill so esoteric or complex that non-members of the profession cannot perform the work safely or satisfactorily and cannot even evaluate the work properly.'[1] Herein lay much of the significance of the appearance of two specialized technical journals on the medical treatment of insanity. For their existence, when coupled with the large number of monographs on the subject which had been published over the previous twenty or thirty years, made it difficult for outsiders to avoid concluding that considerable expertise had already been developed in handling and treating the insane, and that existing knowledge was in the process of being further refined and extended. Both journals lost no opportunity of emphasizing that 'Insanity is purely a disease of the brain. The physician is now the responsible guardian of the lunatic and must ever remain so',[2] a theme which was also prominent in the medical texts which continued to appear on the subject.

In the early part of the century, entry into the ranks of asylum

[1] E. Freidson, *Profession of Medicine*, New York, Dodd, Mead, 1970, p. 45.
[2] *Journal of Mental Science*, 2 October 1858.

superintendents was largely an unstructured process. Even among the medical men entering the field, few could claim to have had any formal training in the care and cure of the insane; though some had presumably attended lectures on the subject given by Cullen or Morison, while others had relatives already in the business, and thus had some practical experience by way of preparation. As most county asylums opened after a considerable expansion of the private madhouse system had already taken place, a number recruited their first superintendent from those who had had prior experience in the private sector. Others simply installed a local doctor who professed an interest in the job.

In later years, the recruitment pattern changed somewhat, and the means of entry into the profession became more stable and formalized. This was particularly marked in the case of the county asylums, where the distinctive system generally employed contributed to the development of an increasingly isolated speciality. As these asylums grew in size, first one, then a number of assistant physicians were employed by each to ease the burden falling on the medical superintendent. The assistants became, in effect, apprentices, superintendents in training, and it was from this pool of experienced men that most senior positions were filled. In some of the largest asylums, a hierarchical structure emerged in the ranks of the assistants, each step up the ladder bringing increased administrative responsibility and less direct contact with patients.

Bucknill and Tuke's claim that by mid-century 'a knowledge of the nature and treatment of Insanity is now expected of every well-educated man' was certainly an exaggeration. Granville was nearer the mark when he asserted that, among most general practitioners of the period, 'The lack of acquaintance with lunacy is extraordinary. The great body of medical men appear to know scarcely more of arrangements and method of treatment adopted in asylums than the general public.'[1] Nevertheless, at least some of those interested in a career as an asylum doctor managed to obtain limited instruction in asylum methods as part of their normal medical training – most commonly through attendance at a course of 'clinical lectures' given

[1] J. C. Bucknill and D. H. Tuke, *A Manual of Psychological Medicine*, Philadelphia, Blanchard & Lee, 1858, p. ix; J. M. Granville, *The Care and Cure of the Insane*, I, London, Hardwicke & Bogue, 1877, p. 328.

annually at St Luke's Hospital in London. Only a handful of medical students bothered to attend. But for all that, the existence of the course allowed at least some of those applying for positions at asylums to claim that they had received some formal training in the speciality; and the asylum authorities themselves promoted this as one of the important 'benefits conferred upon the community by the hospital . . .'[1]

The notion that insanity was caused by organic lesions of the brain remained a vital prop for the asylum doctors' contention that it was fundamentally and incontestably a medical problem. The contrary view that insanity was 'a spiritual malady – a functional disease . . . an affection of the immaterial essence . . . a disorder of the soul and not simply the result of the derangement of the material instrument of the mind interfering with the healthy action of its manifestations . . . naturally led to the conclusion – false in theory and destructive in practice – that for the alleviation and cure of this spiritual malady, spiritual remedies were the most important and essential'. Such contentions were 'at variance with all a priori and a posteriori reasoning', and would suggest 'the clergyman rather than the physician as the logical person to treat insanity'. They gave 'force and longevity to the idea that the administration of physical agents is of little or no avail in the treatment of the disorders of the mind'.[2] Yet on the contrary, the best medical knowledge indicated that 'a system of cerebral pathology' must be built upon '*the physiological principle . . . that mental health is dependent upon the due nutrition, stimulation and repose of the brain; that is, upon the conditions of exhaustion and reparation of its nerve substance being maintained in a healthy and regular state; and that mental disease results from the interruption or disturbance of these conditions*'.[3] Those who refused to acknowledge insanity's somatic basis were chasing 'a phantom of the mind – a pathological enigma, having no actual existence apart from the actual imagination which gave it birth'.[4]

The difficulty which all this strong language was designed to

[1] *St Luke's Hospital Annual Report*, 1886, p. 19.

[2] Forbes Winslow, *On Insanity*, London, Churchill, 1854, pp. 50–51.

[3] J. C. Bucknill and D. H. Tuke, *A Manual of Psychological Medicine*, p. 342, emphasis in the original.

[4] Forbes Winslow, op. cit., p. 51.

gloss over was that no evidence could in fact be produced to show that insanity had a somatic origin. Bucknill and Tuke conceded as much. 'A rational pathology must ever be founded upon the basis of physiology . . . In all the organs of the body, except the brain, great advances have been made in the knowledge of their physiological laws . . . But it is quite otherwise with the noble organ which lords it over the rest of the body.' Here, the most diligent investigation could produce no positive evidence in support of the somatic hypothesis. Nevertheless, this did not prevent confident assertions being made that 'Insanity never exists without a physical cause . . . whence it seems to follow that physical agents ought to be resorted to in the first instance, as the means of restoring the healthy and natural state.' The public was assured that 'Daily experience confirms the opinion that Insanity is a disease, and as such, that it is essential that appropriate remedies should be prescribed for each case, and this is the reason why the duties of dispensing medicines have become more onerous' for asylum superintendents.[1] As this suggests, a corollary of the consistent efforts to emphasize that insanity was produced by a physical pathology was the widespread predilection or bias among asylum doctors in favour of physical treatment or 'remedies'. This is not to imply, though, that there was agreement as to the particular treatment to be adopted in any given case, or even as to the value of any one agent in countering mental disturbance, for there was not.

Both the emphasis on the value of conventional medical treatment and the disagreement as to which particular procedures were in fact effective were evident when the Commissioners in Lunacy sought to obtain a representative sampling of professional opinion on the treatment of insanity for their 1847 Report. There was, it is true, nearly unanimous condemnation of the use of massive general blood-letting in cases of mania; but while some condemned local bleeding with leeches as harmful or useless, many others testified to its great value. Emetics and purgatives were endorsed by practically everyone, though with sharp disagreements as to when they should be employed, and wide variations in the degree of enthusiasm

[1] J. C. Bucknill and D. H. Tuke, *A Manual of Psychological Medicine*, p. 341; *Commissioners in Lunacy Annual Report*, 1847, p. 229; *St Luke's Annual Report*, 1854, p. 9.

displayed. The use of opium had formerly been held to be injurious; 'This is now looked upon as prejudice by many of the most experienced physicians' – though not by others – and it was used to calm excited patients. The profession was similarly unable to reach a consensus over the treatment of melancholia. 'Most of the medical officers who had given us an account of their practices in this form of mental disorder, seem to agree in directing their attention to the state of the alimentary canal, and the organs subservient to the digestive functions, and to be of the opinion that in cases of Melancholia the primary cause is to be sought in some derangement there seated.' Again, however, there were others who dissented, and who alleged that the problem lay with 'the vascular system of the brain'. General paralysis and epilepsy were widely regarded as incurable, but where efforts were made to treat cases, recourse was had to 'the usual physical remedies'. The following is typical: 'Dr Tyerman had tried shaving the head, blisters to the nape or vertex, occasional local depletion, once arteriotomy, calomel followed by purgatives, hot and cold shower baths during severe paroxyms, tonics' – none with particularly happy results.[1]

Indeed, it was on the question of results that the asylum doctors' claims as to the efficacy of medicine proved most difficult to sustain. The enthusiasm of many physicians for the type of remedies they employed against other forms of disease cannot be doubted. At St Luke's, for instance, the superintendent boasted that 'The average number of curable cases . . . has been during the last year 87; the number of prescriptions dispensed has been 6,846 during the year – a proof that our faith in medicine as a most efficient means of treatment has not been shaken.' But the demonstrated inability of a policy of active medical intervention to produce recoveries amounting to more than a fraction of each year's admissions soon forced a more sober assessment of the value of existing somatic treatments. Little more than ten years after the establishment of county asylums on a compulsory basis, the publication of what was to be the standard medical text on insanity contained the admission that

[1] *Commissioners in Lunacy Annual Report*, 1847, pp. 180–86, 189, 204, 213. On the persistent inability of the profession to agree on the relative merits of particular remedies, see D. H. Tuke, *Chapters in the History of the Insane in the British Isles*, London, Kegan Paul & Trench, 1882, pp. 485–7.

'In the chronic stages of insanity active remedies are rarely admissible, except to obviate some intercurrent condition, which produces too much disturbance and danger to be permitted to run a natural course and wear itself out. In recent insanity, with symptoms of physical disturbance of little violence and urgency, active medicinal treatment may oftentimes be dispensed with.' So that in what amounted to the overwhelming majority of cases admitted to asylums, it was conceded that 'any active medicinal interference is more likely to do harm than good'.[1]

For most asylum doctors, the acknowledged failure of this generation of medical treatments to sustain the hopes the profession had originally entertained produced, not an abandonment of their conviction as to medicine's value in curing insanity, but rather a search for new somatic remedies which would give more plausible substance to the claim. The problem, it was concluded, must lie in the administration of the wrong remedies or of the right remedies in the wrong way, and not in the nature of the undertaking itself. In an almost haphazard fashion, a veritable plethora of drugs and medical techniques was enlisted in the battle against insanity. 'Hypodermic injections of morphia, the administration of the bromides, chloral hydrate, hypocymine, physotigma, cannabis indica, amyl nitrate, conium, digitalis, ergot, pilocarpine, the application of electricity, the use of the Turkish bath and the wet pack, and other remedies too numerous to mention, have had their strenuous advocates during late years.'[2]

'Perhaps the fundamental reason for physical treatments, whatever their later rationale, [was that] *without them doctors would have had no lever with which to operate on diseases of the mind* . . .' Given the gap between their claims and their capacities, 'doctors could not afford not to try anything that was ever reported to have achieved results'. Yet although the advocates of conventional medical treatment neglected nothing in their contemporary medical armamentarium, they discovered nothing which worked. Quite clearly, 'If the success of the treatment of insanity bore any considerable proportion to the number of remedies which have been brought

[1] *St Luke's Annual Report*, 1853, p. 11; J. C. Bucknill and D. H. Tuke, *A Manual of Psychological Medicine*, pp. 481-2.

[2] D. H. Tuke, *History of the Insane*, 1882, p. 485.

forward, it would be my easy and agreeable duty to record the triumphs of medicine in the distressing malady which they are employed to combat. But this, unhappily, is not the case . . . each remedy . . . failing to fulfil all the hopes raised on its first trial.' The medical remedies first suggested had proved almost wholly ineffective, and unfortunately, 'there are no new remedies or modes of relief which can be recommended with confidence'.[1] As a practical matter, therefore, asylum superintendents were forced to fall back on their one remaining claim to expertise, their knowledge of moral treatment (which by now meant little more than the efficient management of large numbers of inmates).

2. Managers of the Mad

All this left the asylum doctors in a distinctly vulnerable position. They had originally gained their monopoly in the treatment of insanity without a knowledge base which would have given them a rationally defensible claim to special expertise in this area, though they had convinced others that they possessed one. Such an assertion was precarious from the outset. As practising professionals, their inability to produce the cures their alleged expertise should have helped them provide was swiftly evident. And while it was true that, through being the only people with experience in dealing with large masses of crazy people in an institutional environment, they perforce developed certain empirically derived skills in managing asylums, yet in the last decades of the nineteenth century they remained as far as ever from possessing any genuinely scientifically-based knowledge about how to treat and cure the insane. Certainly large claims to expertise and extraordinary insight here rested upon a slender foundation. But did the failure of the asylum doctors' claim to possess special expertise to produce tangible results in the form of cures result in serious threats to their monopolistic control of asylums, or to their capacity to sustain a viable degree of professional autonomy?

---

[1] R. A. Hunter and I. MacAlpine, *Three Hundred Years of Psychiatry*, London, Oxford University Press, 1963, p. 743; D. H. Tuke, *History of the Insane*, p. 485; J. M. Granville, op. cit., II, p. 112.

By the Acts of 1828 and 1845, the medical profession had acquired a virtually exclusive right to direct the treatment of the insane, and thereafter, its concern became one of maintaining, rather than obtaining, a monopolistic position. The profession's control of asylums, the only legitimate institutions for the treatment of insanity, effectively shut out all potential competitors, for the latter would have had to oppose unsubstantiated claims to demonstrated performance. Furthermore, the asylum doctors' institutional base gave them a powerful leverage for getting the community to utilize their services (thereby indirectly supporting their professional authority), quite apart from whether those doing so were convinced of their competence. For while employment of the asylum by the relatives of 'crazy' people or by local Poor Law authorities did not necessarily reflect acceptance of the superintendent's claims or his esoteric definition of what was 'really' wrong with the troublesome people they sent him, their ready use of his services unavoidably added to the aura of legitimacy surrounding his activities. So long as his services were in such demand, it was difficult to avoid concluding that he was performing a useful and valuable task for the community.

If the attractions of a convenient institution in which to dump the undesirable sufficed to ensure at least the passive acquiescence of the asylum doctors' true clients, the families and parish officials, in their continued existence, their nominal clients, the asylum's inmates, had little choice but to cooperate in sustaining their definition of the situation. Freidson has argued that, for the profession of medicine as a whole, 'a significant monopoly could not occur until a secure and practical technology of work was developed'. In essence this was because doctors could not force clients to come to them, they had to *attract* them. Fortunately for psychiatrists, they formed an exception to this generalization, because of the peculiar structural characteristics of their practice. Once they had secured control over asylums, they no longer had to attract clients – the institution did that for them. And once patients were obtained, they formed literally a captive audience held in a context which gave immense power to their captors. Consequently, psychiatry was able, like the scholarly professions, to 'survive solely by gaining the interest and patronage of a special, powerful sponsor without having to gain general lay confidence'.[1]

Fortunately for the psychiatric profession, their inability to produce significant numbers of cures was of only slight concern to their sponsors. For there had emerged a widespread consensus among local and national élites on the value of a custodial operation, so that the impact of occasional grumbling about the asylum doctors' performance was muted, and the sort of sustained criticism which might have undermined their position simply failed to materialize. Moreover, their ability (or lack of ability) to produce cures by no means exhausted the asylum doctors' usefulness. They were, after all, no worse than anyone else as administrators, and their medical skills were useful in ministering to the numerous physical ailments of the decrepit specimens the asylums were continuously receiving. And by sustaining the illusion that asylums were medical institutions, they placed a humanitarian and scientific gloss on the community's behaviour, legitimizing the removal of difficult and troublesome people whose confinement would have been awkward to justify on other grounds.

However, if there was little reason for the authorities to revoke the monopoly they had originally granted to the asylum doctors, there were also slender grounds for granting them the kind of autonomy which ordinarily goes with professional status. The best medical opinion conceded that 'Ordinary medicines, which are the principal remedies for disease of the body, are only exceptional and accidental agents in the treatment of disease of the mind.'[2] And the low cure rates characteristic of the asylum system as a whole rendered implausible the claim that psychiatrists possessed even non-pharmaceutical remedies with any real efficacy.

In this situation,

magistrates, like other mortals, have had their convictions strengthened, that medical superintendents, considered in their professional capacity, are rather ornamental than essential members of an asylum staff; very well in their way in cases of casual sickness or injury, useful to legalize the exit of the inmates from the world, and not bad scape-goats in

[1] E. Freidson, *Profession of Medicine*, pp. 21–2.
[2] J. M. Granville, op. cit., I, p. 76.

misadventures and unpleasant investigations into the management, and in general not worse administrators . . . than would be members of most other occupations and professions.[1]

The magistrates on asylum committees were in sufficiently close and frequent contact with the routine practices in these institutions that they could scarcely avoid the perception that 'the medical super-intendent of most English asylums is simply an overseer or on-looker, and his place might be filled by a layman of moderate intelligence, did not the law require medical qualifications, and did not accidents and emergencies arise in such establishments for which medical skill is called in requisition'.[2] From quite an early period in the history of the county asylums, there were complaints from the superintendents of their employers' 'forgetfulness that insanity is a disease, and their consequent want of due appreciation of medical science in its treatment'.[3]

Legally speaking, the superintendents of county and borough asylums were merely the salaried employees of individual asylum committees, each of which consisted of a group of magistrates chosen for the task at the local General Quarter Sessions. These laymen could, if they so chose, issue detailed directives as to the conduct of the institution, and could, if necessary, enforce their views by using their power to dismiss a superintendent without further appeal at any time. A few extraordinarily energetic committees actually exercised their enormous discretionary powers, and were heavily involved in the routine governance of 'their' asylums. Most, how-ever, did not go to these lengths, satisfying themselves with laying down general guidelines as to the conduct of the institution. Having control over the key area of finance, they were content to leave the more mundane matters in the hands of their presumably capable subordinate, subject always to his rendering an annual account of his discharge of that trust, and to their own periodic tours of inspection.

Where the conduct of their underlings did not satisfy them, committees did not hesitate to invoke their authority to dismiss

[1] J. T. Arlidge, *On the State of Lunacy and the Legal Provision for the Insane*, London, Churchill, 1859, p. 104.

[2] Sir James Clark, *Memoir of John Conolly*, London, Murray, 1869, p. 233.

[3] *Asylum Journal*, 1, 15 November 1853, p. 6.

them, even over the objections of professional colleagues and of the Commissioners in Lunacy. Not surprisingly, the Association of Medical Officers of Asylums and Hospitals for the Insane proved acutely sensitive about this power of arbitrary dismissal. One case it fought particularly hard was John Millar's dismissal as head of the Buckinghamshire County Asylum in 1856.

Millar was widely regarded as a competent superintendent and possessed a high professional reputation. Even the magistrates who discharged him conceded that in previous years, 'Mr Millar possessed the general confidence of successive committees', and the records for this period show that his skill had frequently been commended both by his employers and by the Commissioners in Lunacy. However, following the emigration of his chief supporter, Mr Carrington, who had served as chairman of the magistrates' committee, he abruptly lost the support of the remaining magistrates, and was dismissed, ostensibly on the grounds of vague charges of maladministration.[1]

Millar refused to concede defeat. He published a pamphlet on his own behalf, and obtained the intervention of the Association of which he was a member. John Hitchman, superintendent of the Derbyshire County Asylum and the Association's president, began by sending a letter in his official capacity inquiring into the Committee's reasons for its decision. The response was a curt note indicating that 'the Committee do not recognize the authority of any such constituted Association to submit to them the questions your letter . . . contained'. In an effort to bring further pressure to bear, the Association drew up a letter and secured the signatures of eighty-six doctors, including the major figures in contemporary English psychiatry – men like Daniel Hack Tuke, John Charles Bucknill, and John Conolly. [2]This was then 'extensively circulated' to all the leading people in the county, the signatories complaining that 'This dismissal has been the occasion of alarm and profound discouragement to the medical men who have charge of fifteen thousand of the insane poor of this kingdom', and deploring the

[1] As we shall see in the next chapter, the real reason was probably pressure from cost-conscious Poor Law officials.

[2] All this correspondence is reproduced in the *Bucks County Asylum Annual Report* for 1857.

likely effects on the quality of men attracted to the field were this 'ignominious dismissal' upheld.

The Commissioners in Lunacy added their regrets 'that the Institution is about to lose the services of Mr Millar to whom the present creditable state of the patients is, in our opinion, mainly due'.[1] But the Committee simply stood its ground, and lacking any sanctions with which to force a change of mind, the Association and Millar himself were forced to concede defeat. In this, as in other similar cases,[2] the asylum doctors were simply unable to establish themselves as '*the prime source of the criteria that qualify a man to work in an acceptable fashion*'.[3] Thus, in an important sense, psychiatry, at least in the public sphere, still lacked one of the crucial appurtenances of a profession. It remained an isolated specialty, with only superficial ties with the rest of the medical enterprise. And while the asylum doctors' class origins and medical training prevented such developments being carried to an extreme, both their salaries and their prestige remained conspicuously low.

The superintendents' working conditions contributed to this isolation. Almost all of them were lodged either in special quarters in the main asylum buildings, or, more typically, in a house built for them in the grounds; and their manifold duties ensured that they ventured beyond the asylum walls scarcely more frequently than their patients. This physical and social segregation was encouraged by (one might almost say enforced by) their employers, who adhered to the recommendation made by the Lunacy Commissioners that the asylum doctor should 'be precluded from private Practice, and should devote his whole time and Energies to the Duties of his Office'. Indeed, his administrative burdens were so heavy as to make the asylum almost a self-contained world, wherein

the medical officer is especially prompted – if he wish to stand well with the Committee – to develop the moral management and domestic economy to the utmost; to exhibit well-kept wards, well-clothed and well-

[1] ibid., p. 34.

[2] For protests against the dismissal of the medical officer of the Norfolk County Asylum, see *Asylum Journal*, 7, 15 August 1854, pp. 99–102. For the discharging of Dr Millson, the first superintendent of the Northampton County Asylum, see Chapter 6 below.

[3] E. Freidson, *Profession of Medicine*, p. 10, emphasis in the original.

fed patients, well-filled workrooms, and a well-stocked and worked farm; and, above all, a good balance from the patients' earnings, as a set-off to the cost of their maintenance.[1]

The relevant group with which to compare the status of psychiatrists remained the medical profession as a whole, though judging by their responses, the latter seem to have found the mad-doctors a somewhat embarrassing excrescence. Almost twenty years after the establishment of their professional association, and despite numerous efforts to rectify the situation, psychiatrists had to concede that

the study of mental disorders is studiously excluded from the medical curriculum, alienist physicians, as they are therefore well called, work in a department of science the first principles of which are not recognized by their medical brethren, and seem often to speak a language not understood by those around them . . . so few of even our most accomplished professors [of medicine] have any knowledge of the various types of mental derangement . . .[2]

And according to Hunter and MacAlpine, the 'segregation of psychiatry from medicine if anything became more pronounced as time went on'.

By and large, asylum superintendents seem to have accepted this somewhat ambiguous professional status, and to have worked uncomplainingly within the limits of the authority granted them by their employers. It was otherwise with some of the leading figures in the field, those who, by their eminence, had attained positions outside the county asylum system,[3] or who had managed to pursue careers outside that system entirely.[4] These men were clearly not satisfied with psychiatry's marginal status in medicine, and realized that their professional autonomy was compromised by the obvious lack of application of the medical model in the huge custodial

[1] J. T. Arlidge, 'An examination of the practice of bloodletting in mental disorders, by Pliny Earle', *Asylum Journal of Mental Science*, 2, 1856.

[2] T. Harrington Tuke, cited in R. A. Hunter and I. MacAlpine, op. cit., p. 1053.

[3] E.g. John Charles Bucknill and Lockhart Robertson, former superintendents of the Devon and Sussex County Asylums respectively.

[4] E.g. Arlidge, Maudsley, Granville.

institutions of the period. It was from their ranks that the most vigorous critics of the asylums' complacent custodialism were recruited. And it was they who sought, almost desperately, to assert that all aspects of the treatment of insanity were a medical province, and that asylum doctors should therefore be immune from interference by unqualified laymen. The profession was warned that 'the notion that medicine is inoperative in mental disorder has produced much mischief' and was urged to guard against 'the exclusion or . . . the undue disparagement of physical means of cure and alleviation', lest there be a return to the 'past when the skill and experience of the physician was thought to be less important than the watchful care of the matron or steward'. It was the asylum superintendent's task to emphasize that 'the just medium has been passed, and the insane are suffering by the present extreme views' which depreciated the value of medicine. On the contrary, the importance of conventional medical treatment must be repeatedly stressed.[1]

The difficulty here lay in the fact that it did little good to advocate a greater emphasis on medical techniques as a means of raising psychiatry's prestige, or to attribute the low status of asylum doctors to 'the laudation by physicians of the so-called moral means of treatment, and the oblivion into which medical aid has been allowed to fall', when the medical remedies which could prove their worth in practice simply did not exist. An alternative tack therefore became popular with those intent on raising the profession's prestige and resisting outside, 'lay' interference. If the proportion of patients cured failed to rise in the years following the rapid expansion of the asylum system, so that claims that the medical

---

[1] J. T. Arlidge, 'An examination of the practice of bloodletting in mental disorders, by Pliny Earle'; W. A. F. Browne, *The Moral Treatment of the Insane: A Lecture*, London, Adlard, 1864, p. 5; W. Charles Hood, *Statistics of Insanity*, London, Batten, 1862, p. 104. Since there were plainly no effective medical therapies for the treatment of the insane, it is not at all clear how the authorities' scepticism about the value of medical treatment could have been harming the insane, though it is obvious why their *doctors* should find it detrimental. As Arlidge pointed out, 'It has induced magistrates to hold medical men in little estimation as *physicians* of asylums, and to view them merely as useful and superior stewards in directing the general management and moral treatment, and as safeguards of casualties and of accidental disease.'

(i.e. pharmaceutical) treatment of insanity had greatly improved were likely to be received with scepticism, there remained one aspect of the condition of lunatics where no one doubted that there had been progress. As Daniel Hack Tuke put it, 'so far as this includes moral treatment and management, it has advanced in all civilized countries in a manner calculated, all will admit, to cause the liveliest feelings of satisfaction'. In consequence, those who were convinced that 'There is no more dangerous delusion in the range of lunacy than this notion that the care and treatment of the insane is not wholly medical',[1] now sought to claim that moral treatment itself (or as some preferred to call it, 'medico-moral treatment') was something only physicians were qualified to dispense.

Beginning with the simple *assumption* that 'the moral system of treatment can only be properly carried out under the constant superintendence and by the continuous assistance of a physician',[2] the profession eventually developed a more elaborate set of arguments for the position that moral treatment by itself provided sufficient justification for ensuring that it is 'the medical authority that controls everything in an asylum for mental disease', entirely free of all outside interference. As Granville put it,

It would be just as reasonable, or unreasonable, for the lay officials of an ordinary hospital to prescribe the drugs or instruments with which physicians and surgeons treat physical disease, as for lay authority to be combined with the medical in an asylum for the insane . . . for the simple and obvious reasons, that disease of the mind is amenable only to the influence of moral remedies, and the discipline, the control, the daily routine and management of the insane are the 'drugs' with which the physician of the mind must work the cure of his cases.[3]

As this implies, all aspects of asylum administration were now alleged to form part of the system of moral treatment, a system whose components were so closely linked one to another that unschooled intervention at any point threatened the whole edifice.

---

[1] J. T. Arlidge, *On the State of Lunacy*, p. 104; D. H. Tuke, *History of the Insane*, p. 484; J. M. Granville, *Care and Cure of the Insane*, II, 1877, p. 149.

[2] *Asylum Journal*, 'Editorial' 1, 3, 1854, p. 33.

[3] J. M. Granville, op. cit., I, pp. 77, 150.

From the very outset, the design of the physical structure of any asylum required continuous consultation with, and deference to, the accumulated expertise of this branch of the medical profession. After all, 'An asylum is a special apparatus for the cure of lunacy, and ought to be constructed under the direction of the physician by whom it is to be employed, or by an expert in the uses to which it will be subsequently applied.' And once the asylum was in operation, magistrates' committees must somehow be taught to resist the temptation to meddle in questions which were beyond their competence to decide. As to where that boundary might lie, if the more uninhibited protagonists of medical control were to be believed, almost everything was beyond any layman's competence. Granville, for instance, reported that the Middlesex magistrates had ordered their superintendents to make changes in the asylum's diet, so as to lessen its monotony. But while their actions were clearly well-intentioned, and the consequences in this particular instance were harmless (or even beneficial), 'It is impossible to admit that a lay committee has any ground or qualification for the task of forming a judgement on a point of this nature.' Apparently only a physician was qualified to recognize and 'treat' monotony. The trouble was, that 'This, unfortunately, is what visiting committees do not perceive',[1] and persisted in not perceiving. Questions of diet, decoration, and amusement were ones in which many laymen continued to feel they were as qualified as any professional (as, of course, the originators of moral treatment had contended they were); and consequently, for all the well-wrought arguments of men like Granville, asylum committees continued to interfere in the administration of their asylums whenever it suited them to do so.

3. Medical Authority in the Asylum

So far, I have been largely concerned with the external aspects of the psychiatric profession's efforts to consolidate its position – that is, with the threats to the asylum doctors' status and dominance originating outside the institution. Although decisions in these areas clearly had implications, often serious ones, for the superintendents' conduct of the asylums themselves, there also existed a set of

[1] ibid., pp. 15, 127.

problems which bore more directly on the issue of the physician's authority within the institution.

John Arlidge, who for a time had served as resident medical officer at St Luke's, complained that asylums had grown so large that 'asylum superintendents . . . are driven to a system of routine and general discipline, as the only one whereby the huge machine in their charge can work, and look upon recoveries as casual or undesigned coincidences'.[1] What he overlooked was the potent protective function such a situation provided for the psychiatric profession. For one of the crucial problems for any occupation whose results blatantly fail to measure up to its claims is to insulate its members from the consequences of this failure – partly, of course, those which may flow from the discontent of its clients; but also, and perhaps of equal importance, the loss of morale and belief in themselves among its own members.

The asylum doctors' inability to do anything for the over-whelming majority of their patients meant that interaction with inmates threatened daily denial of their effectiveness. In this situation, being asked to undertake impossibly heavy caseloads in a patently over-large institution provided the profession with a convenient scapegoat on which to blame many of its troubles. As one would expect in the circumstances, there were complaints that because the physician had 'his mile or so of wards and offices to perambulate daily', and four or five hundred inmates to consider, he could not possibly be expected to employ the full resources of his healing art; and stories were told before official inquiries to illustrate just how unreasonable it was, in consequence, to expect cures, given the trying conditions doctors were forced to work under. But there was no sustained effort on the part of the asylum doctors to reduce their task to manageable proportions, or to secure adequate staffing of asylums.

On the contrary, they resisted suggestions which would have relieved them of the burden of caring for chronic patients;[2] and instead of welcoming efforts by outsiders to rid them of their administrative functions, so as to allow them to devote their full energies to the cure of patients, they fiercely resisted all such

[1] J. T. Arlidge, *On the State of Lunacy*, p. 103.
[2] See Chapter 6 below.

proposals, and insisted on burying themselves ever deeper in administrative concerns. Asylums were so large, and so crowded with physically decrepit specimens, that the superintendent's assistant physicians, who were forced to have some daily contact with the patients, could safely spend all that time in providing routine medical care for ordinary physical ailments; thereby, of course, affording confirmation that they were engaged in supplying a medical service to the inmates.

Even the assistants, however, found ways to minimize the amount of time they were forced to spend in the unpleasant and disturbing company of (live) patients. Particularly popular, if the figures given in the annual reports of the Commissioners in Lunacy are to be believed, was research on dead bodies, which even though it might be repetitive and lead nowhere, at least bore a passing resemblance to more conventional medical practices! In the meantime, the dirty work of dealing with the patients on a day-to-day, hour-by-hour basis was left to a staff of attendants, themselves recruited from the dregs of society, men and women who, in return for long hours spent in close, defiling contact with the insane, received suitably low status and financial rewards. Thus insulated from the reality of asylum existence, the superintendent was able to remain a remote, if benevolent despot, his position above the crowd and freedom from too close and frequent contact with the patients protecting him from the contamination, not just of his social position, but, indirectly, of his authority as well.[1]

Perhaps a more serious threat to the asylum doctor's authority than his potential loss of confidence in his own skills, or of the deference shown him by his patients, was one which is generic to all types of professional authority, but which was here experienced

---

[1] The pernicious effects of too familiar and intimate association with one's inferiors upon the deference accorded those of higher status (which was so deeply rooted a feature of Victorian society) were duly noted by Granville (op. cit., I, p. 99), who warned, 'The circumstance of a superintendent's wife acting as matron involves a sacrifice of social position injurious, if not fatal, to success. It is above all things indispensable that medical superintendents of asylums should be educated gentlemen; and if that is to be the case, their wives cannot be matrons. Indeed, it is inconceivable that a man of position and culture would allow his family to have any connection with an asylum.' So much for his emphasis that the insane were 'sick people'!

in a peculiarly acute form. As Freidson has pointed out, 'the authority of expertise is in fact problematic, requiring in its pure functional form the time-consuming and not always successful effort of persuading others that its "orders" are appropriate',[1] rather than relying, as does bureaucratic authority, on the application of rewards and penalties to obtain compliance. Obviously, the task of persuasion is made easier to the extent that a given group of experts can provide plausible evidence that its approach brings substantially superior results to those which would have ensued in the absence of the application of their special skills, and/or the more nearly the experts and those for whom their service is intended share a common universe of discourse. Both of these factors, however, served only to exacerbate the problems psychiatry faced in maintaining its professional authority. In the first place, the asylum doctors' basic claim to possess expertise in the treatment of insanity was a fragile one, and not one in support of which they could readily produce convincing evidence in the form of large numbers of cures. Secondly, it is probable that there existed here an even more profound disjunction than usual between professional and lay world views. Neither the uneducated classes recruited as attendants in asylums, nor the social derelicts who formed the bulk of the asylums' population, were likely to share to any significant degree the profession's perspective on insanity. That perspective, after all, was a relatively novel one; and it was one to which the asylum doctors had been concerned to convert the élite, not the masses.

Even in those instances where the special skill possessed is demonstrably powerful and effective, 'professions have attempted to solve the problem of persuasion by obtaining institutional powers and prerogatives that at the very least set limits on the freedom of their prospective clients and that on occasion even coerce their clients into compliance. The expertise of the professional is institutionalized into something similar to bureaucratic office.'[2] Consequently, where claims to the authority of expertise are themselves weak and tenuous, one can certainly expect that the quest to supplement this with the authority of office will acquire extraordinary urgency and importance.

[1] E. Freidson, *Professional Dominance*, New York, Atherton, 1970, p. 131.
[2] ibid.

In the context of the asylum, securing the authority of office meant restricting the position of asylum superintendent to medical men, and investing that position with power over *all* aspects of asylum administration, including personnel questions as well as matters more strictly related to the treatment of patients. In the earliest asylums, the medical profession accumulated such powers almost fortuitously. The asylums were small, and the local magistrates were but little inclined to pay two salaries where one would do. Accordingly, once the justices had been convinced that lunatics required almost constant medical assistance, the doctor employed for this purpose was generally expected in addition to take charge of the day-to-day administration of the asylum.

However, the rapid expansion of the number of lunatics and the associated rise in the average size of public asylums posed something of a threat to this cosy arrangement. For in asylums containing several hundred inmates, 'when to the medical and moral treatment of the patients are added the multifarious duties comprised under the terms "general management and superintendence" . . . it will be readily conceded that . . . those labours are far too onerous to be adequately performed by a single individual'.[1] A logical solution to the problem, which could be expected to occur to some asylum committees at least, was to hire a full-time lay administrator to assume the routine duties of running the institution, thus allowing the asylum doctor to devote his full time and energy to the task for which his professional training had presumably prepared him, the cure of patients.

The superintendents, though, evinced no desire whatsoever to adopt this policy or to rid themselves of their mounting burden of administrative duties. On the contrary, they insisted on assuming them. Where, as at Hanwell, asylum committees attempted to institute such a separation of powers, the physicians in residence, backed by the profession as a whole, did their best to render such schemes unworkable.[2] More generally, recognizing that the

[1] *Commissioners in Lunacy, Report on Bethlem Hospital*, 1852, p. 15.

[2] On the two occasions (1838–9 and 1843–4) on which the Hanwell Committee sought to install a lay administrator, the superintendent then in office promptly resigned. In both instances, his successors as resident medical officers fought fiercely with their lay competitor. Within weeks, the degree of administrative chaos and internal disorder was such as to force the magistrates to dispense with the layman and reinstitute uniform medical control.

question of lay versus medical administrators 'is one in which the profession as a body has a direct concern, and in which every practitioner of "psychological medicine" must feel his *status* immediately involved', psychiatry's publicists sought by all means at their disposal to convince the public that 'the interests of science and the obligations of true economy alike require that public asylums should be "hospitals" under medical management . . .'[1] These efforts were crowned with success. Asylum committees everywhere, even those which had flirted with the idea of lay administrators, conceded what the doctors wanted. Rather than dividing his authority with a lay administrator, the medical superintendent was to be given the assistance of one or more assistant physicians to perform the necessary medical chores, while he concentrated almost his entire energies on administration. Henceforth, the further an asylum doctor's career progressed, and the more experience he gained, the less his contact with the insane. But at least psychiatry had buttressed its weak claims to the authority of expertise with the authority of a near-autocratic office.

[1] J. M. Granville, op. cit., I, p. 150, emphasis in the original.

Chapter Six

'Museums for the Collection of Insanity'*

Some Persons of a desponding Spirit are in great Concern about that vast Number of poor People, who are Aged, Diseased, or Maimed; and I have been desired to employ my Thoughts what Course may be taken, to ease the Nation of so grievous an Incumbrance. But I am not in the least Pain upon that Matter; because it is very well known, that they are every Day *dying*, and *rotting*, by *Cold* and *Famine*, and *Filth* and *Vermine*, as fast as can reasonably be expected.

(Jonathan Swift, *A Modest Proposal for Preventing the Children of poor People in Ireland, from being a Burden to their Parents or Country*)

1. The Growth of the County Asylum System

According to the 1845 Lunatic Asylums Act, every county and borough in England and Wales had a statutory obligation to provide, within three years, adequate asylum accommodation at public expense for its pauper lunatic population. Most made efforts to comply with the law: by the end of 1847, thirty-six of the fifty-two counties had built asylums of their own. Nevertheless, the reluctance in many quarters to incur the large capital expenditures necessarily required by such a programme did not simply disappear once the reformers had won the battle on the Parliamentary level, and they were forced to concede that 'considerable opposition has arisen in several counties to any proposals for erecting a county asylum'.

Unwilling to provoke a full-scale conflict with local authorities by invoking the powers the Act gave them to compel compliance,

* Francis Scott in the *Fortnightly Review*, 1879.

lest by doing so they stirred up the widespread if temporarily dormant fear of central direction, the Commissioners in Lunacy and their allies sought instead to use their powers of persuasion to bring errant magistrates into line. John Conolly, whose successful introduction of the non-restraint system into the huge establishment at Hanwell had done much to give substance to the claim that asylum treatment of the insane represented a humanitarian advance over the rigours of the gaol and the workhouse, now became one of the most able publicists on behalf of the creation of county asylums. In a series of essays first appearing in the *Lancet* in 1846, re-published as the monograph *On the Construction and Government of Lunatic Asylums* in the following year, he restated the reformers' standard objections to providing for the insane in private mad-houses or in wards attached to workhouses, contending that only a purpose-built, publicly supported asylum would suffice. In similar fashion, the Commissioners in Lunacy used their annual reports as a handy medium for propaganda on behalf of the merits of county asylums. The prospect of cure provided an attractive basis on which to advocate the creation of costly new institutions, and both in their regular reports, and in the supplemental report they issued in 1847 on the proper moral and medical treatment of insanity, they urged the certainty of a high proportion of cures, provided only that the counties shouldered their responsibilities and furnished sufficient asylums wherein recent cases of insanity could receive prompt treatment. Asylum superintendents sought to employ their own reports to further this same spirit of optimism and to insist on the potential benefits of early intervention.

To avoid the danger that all this work might remain just an exercise in preaching to the converted, the Commissioners engaged in lengthy correspondence with the magistrates of areas reluctant to implement the Act's provisions. While these further efforts to convince the recalcitrant of the error of their ways were not always immediately successful, they did provide a continous discreet pressure which eventually wore down the opposition of all but the most determined adversaries. Counties like Cambridge and Sussex, and boroughs like London and Norwich, fought a prolonged rear-guard action, but eventually most capitulated without the Commissioners being forced to resort to compulsion. As more and more counties made provision for their pauper lunatics at public expense, so licensed houses catering to paupers began to close, increasing the pressure on the remaining local authorities to follow suit. By 1854, the number of counties which had made public provision for their insane had risen to 41, and by the end of the decade, the task of obtaining at least an initial commitment to the care of the pauper insane on the part of each county and borough was substantially complete. The legal commitment to the asylum had now been strengthened by a considerable financial investment in this solution.

2. The Accumulation of Chronic Cases

In one highly significant respect, the extensive programme of asylum construction had departed from the provisions of the 1845 Act. The Metropolitan Commissioners' tour of inspection had convinced them that

the disease of Lunacy . . . is essentially different in its character from other maladies. In a certain proportion of cases, the patient neither recovers nor dies, but remains an incurable lunatic, requiring little medical skill in respect to his mental disease and frequently living many years. A patient in this state requires a place of refuge, but his disease being beyond the reach of medical skill it is quite evident that he should be removed from Asylums instituted for the cure of insanity in order to make room for others whose cases have not yet become hopeless. If some plan of this sort be not adopted the Asylums admitting paupers will necessarily continue full of incurable patients . . . and the skill and labour of the physician will thus be wasted upon improper objects.[1]

Accordingly, their Report recommended, and the Act embodied, a provision permitting the erection of separate receptacles for the chronic at the discretion of any county authority. Once the legislation was enacted, however, no constituency pressed for its implementation, and no county chose to do so.

The asylum doctors conceded, even insisted, that 'the pauper lunatic is not merely to be secured; he is, if possible, to be restored

[1] *Report of the Metropolitan Commissioners in Lunacy*, 1844, p. 92.

to reason'.[1] But for a number of reasons, they resisted the notion that this goal could best be realized by providing separately for the acute and the chronic. The publicly stated grounds for this opposition were that any such system, while superficially attractive, would necessarily be productive of a repetition of the very abuses the reform of the lunacy laws had been designed to avoid. In particular, it would be difficult, if not impossible, to recruit suitable staff, and to maintain the requisite morale and dedication in institutions which were avowedly custodial. Furthermore, in all save cases of confirmed idiocy, there always remained a possibility, however remote, of cure, so that it would be both cruel and unwise to consign even apparently hopeless cases to places where efforts directed towards their restoration would cease. The Lunacy Commissioners simply adopted the opinion of the profession as their own, and therefore did not press local authorities to provide for such a segregation. And the magistrates themselves, who were reluctant to incur the expense of erecting and providing for the management of two separate institutions, opted instead for the immediate capital savings of a single asylum for curable and incurable alike.

Underlying the asylum superintendents' no doubt genuine concern lest institutions for the incurable should degenerate into the snakepits from which asylums were meant to rescue the insane, one suspects that they were also seeking to inhibit the construction of a set of organizations which might potentially compete with their own for the limited funds available. Almshouses for the chronic were particularly dangerous, since they would not only be a cheaper alternative, but according to existing plans, would also achieve part of their savings by dispensing with the expense of a full-time medical staff. In view of their subsequent inability to cure most of those labelled insane, it was fortunate for the asylum doctors' own future that they resisted any such proposals – for had they been left to cope with only those they themselves considered curable, control over almost all lunatics would quickly have passed out of their hands. Instead, the continued retention of chronic cases in ordinary asylums in time allowed them to make a graceful retreat from the

[1] John Conolly, *The Construction and Government of Lunatic Asylums*, London, Churchill, 1847, p. 58.

difficult and risky task of curing significant numbers of lunatics. Having chosen to deal with cases that were acknowledged to be, by and large, beyond hope, the asylum doctors gradually manoeuvred to redefine success in terms of comfort, cleanliness, and freedom from the more obvious forms of physical maltreatment, rather than the elusive and often unattainable goal of cure.

Table 3 Asylum Superintendents' Estimates of the Number and Percentage of Curable Patients in Asylums in England and Wales in 1844

	Private			Pauper		
Type of Asylum	Total Patients	Number Curable	Per cent Curable	Total Patients	Number Curable	Per cent Curable
Provincial Licensed Houses	1,426	412	28·9	1,920	637	33·2
Metropolitan Licensed Houses	973	153	15·7	854	111	13·0
County Asylums	245	61	24·9	4,244	651	15·4
Charity Hospitals	536	127	23·7	343	59	17·2
Military/Naval	168	18	10·7	—	—	—
Bethlem	265	181	68·5	90	no estimate	
St Luke's	177	93	52·5	31	16	51·6

Source: Metropolitan Commissioners in Lunacy, 1844 Report, pp. 185, 187.

As Table 3 shows, even in 1844, before the influx of the mass of pauper inmates generated by the expansion of the county asylum system, the esimated number of curable cases in most types of asylum was really quite low. With the exception of Bethlem and St Luke's, both institutions which rigorously selected their inmate population to exclude those who lacked a high potential for recovery, no class of asylums estimated that as many as a third of its patients would ultimately recover; in most cases, fewer than a fifth were expected to do so. The discrepancy between these rather low figures and the optimistic projections some of those running the institutions were simultaneously employing in an effort to secure the erection of more institutions at public expense was attributed to the public's reluctance or inability to secure prompt asylum treatment for their insane relatives. Cure rates for recent cases were asserted to be much higher; and the combination of a wider availability of asylum treatment, greater public confidence in the treatment accorded the insane, and the educational campaign of the medical superintendents themselves, stressing the advantages of early treatment, was expected to effect a substantial improvement in the asylum's overall performance as a curative institution.

The predicted rise in the proportion of cures quite simply failed to occur. At the Littlemore Asylum, for instance (the joint asylum for the counties of Oxfordshire and Berkshire), 17·1 per cent of the total number resident were discharged as recovered in 1847, the first full year of its operation. In his next annual report, however, William Ley, the superintendent, was obliged to caution his readers that such a favourable outcome was due to a combination of fortuitous circumstances, and hence was unlikely to be repeated: 'The Recoveries in 1847 were unusually numerous, arising from the class of Patients admitted, and from the greater quiet maintained in the Asylum – The average rate of Discharge by recovery in 1848 has been ten per cent upon the whole number of patients.' The chaplain's report suggests how quickly optimism about curability had evaporated, in this asylum at least:

It is a melancholy reflection to think, that out of the number of those who attended the Services, how few, in all probability, will ever again have their reasoning faculties restored; but I still trust that their constant attendance at the Sunday Services and daily Prayers, will be productive of an eternal benefit to them, so that my ministry among these my afflicted fellow-creatures may not be altogether in vain.[1]

The Littlemore Asylum was, if anything, more successful as a curative institution than the majority of the county asylums. At all events, Ley discharged more of his patients as recovered than did most of his counterparts, something he did not neglect to draw to the attention of the local magistrates. From the outset, super-

[1] *Littlemore Asylum Annual Report*, 1848, pp. 4, 8.

intendents of county asylums complained that they were being swamped by hopeless cases. In the first year of the Derby County Asylum's operation, Hitchman, the director, commented: 'The majority of the Patients admitted here have not only been in a chronic state of insanity, but also in a feeble state of bodily health.' The tendency of the asylum to become the resting place for the broken-down and physically decrepit grew still more marked in subsequent years. The diary of John Millar, the first superintendent of the Bucks Asylum at Stone, indicates that a similar pattern held there too. On 24 March 1857, for instance, less than three years after the asylum first opened its doors, Millar estimated that while nine males and eleven females might possibly be restored to reason, the condition of the remainder – sixty-six males and 100 females – was quite hopeless. His dismissal later that year brought no essential change in this respect. Humphry, his successor, conceded in his first report that 'there is reasonable hope of recovery in only 13 of the 213 persons then resident in the asylum'.[1] Since only a fraction of the inmates were sent back to the community recovered (or even 'improved') each year, and since the elimination of others by death had slowed as the eradication of the grosser instances of physical neglect reduced mortality rates, over time the asylums became clogged with masses of incurables, and the proportion cured tended to fall even further.

The superintendents continued to blame the asylum's apparently poor performance in what they had initially claimed to be their most vital task on their inability to secure enough cases of incipient insanity before time had confirmed the disease and while their largely unspecified, but undoubtedly powerful, techniques were maximally effective. The large numbers of existing chronic cases were also at least partially to blame for the problem: 'It is greatly to be regretted that owing to the want of room, the difficulty of obtaining Admission to Asylums, and the mistaken kindness and reluctance on the part of relatives and friends in many Cases, the early removal of Patients to Asylums should be so long delayed . . . thereby diminishing their chances of recovery.'[2] Yet no matter how

---

[1] *Derby County Asylum Annual Report*, 1852, p. 29; *Bucks County Asylum Annual Report*, 1858, p. 9.

[2] *Hanwell County Asylum Annual Report*, 1871, p. 33.

many new asylums the magistrates were persuaded to build, and no matter how hard the asylum doctors promoted the idea that early treatment was in the long run the most economical response to insanity, curable cases apparently never materialized.

Table 4 Estimated Number Curable in Asylums in England and Wales in 1860 and 1870

| | 1860 | | | 1870 | | |
	Patients	Number Curable	Per cent	Patients	Number Curable	Per cent
Provincial Licensed Houses	2,356	361	15·4	2,204	285	12·9
Metropolitan Licensed Houses	1,944	253	13·0	2,700	283	10·5
County and Borough Asylums	17,432	1,952	11·2	27,890	2,149	7·7
Registered Hospitals	1,985	320	16·1	2,369	436	18·4

Sources: 14th Annual Report of the Commissioners in Lunacy, 1860, p. 117; 24th Annual Report, 1870, p. 97.

Table 5 Cure and Mortality Rates in County and Borough Asylums 1870–90

	Number cured on total number resident – per cent	Number died on total number resident – per cent
1870	8·54	8·48
1880	8·31	7·40
1890	7·68	8·20

Sources: 25th Annual Report of the Commissioners in Lunacy, 1871, pp. 112–115; 35th Annual Report, 1881, pp. 148–51; 45th Annual Report, 1891, pp. 96–9.

7

When the Lunacy Commissioners published tables estimating the likely proportion of inmates who would recover at some time in the future, comparable to that published in 1844, every single type of institution exhibited a decline from earlier levels. The county asylum superintendents' prophecies – self-fulfilling or otherwise – that less than one in ten of their patients would recover were apparently accurate. Between 1870 and 1890, the proportion they claimed to cure continued to fall steadily, until ultimately more of their charges left the asylum in coffins each year than were restored to society in the possession of their senses.

3. Mammoth Asylums

The collapse of the asylum's pretensions to provide cure was matched by the decay and disappearance of all the crucial features of moral treatment – those elements which were supposed to distinguish the asylum from the prison. The departure from early ideals was perhaps most visible in the architecture of these institutions. The buildings themselves offered mute testimony to the fact that the asylum was now 'a mere refuge or house of detention for a mass of hopeless and incurable cases'. Whereas it had been an article of faith with the reformers that 'the main object to be borne in mind, in the construction of lunatic asylums, is to combine cheerfulness with security, and to avoid everything which might give the impression that he is in prison', within little more than a decade there were complaints that county asylums were 'built externally on the model of a palace, and internally on that of a workhouse'.[1]

The Lunacy Commissioners viewed this development more complacently than most outside observers, though a note of criticism crept into many of their reports. Of Colney Hatch, the second asylum for the County of Middlesex, they commented: 'Several of the wards of both divisions in the old block, are very dark and gloomy towards the centre . . . the wards generally, still have a very comfortless look . . . Everywhere there is a deficiency of

[1] J. M. Granville, *The Care and Cure of the Insane*, I, London, Hardwicke & Bogue, 1877, p. 8; 'Lunatic Asylums', *Westminster Review*, 43, 1845, p. 168; 'Lunatic Asylums', *Quarterly Review*, 101, 1857, p. 383.

comfortable and ordinary domestic furniture.'[1] Generally, however, they were satisfied with small improvements, such as flowered
wallpaper, a few cheap framed prints on the walls, and an enlargement of tiny and heavily barred windows.

Other critics were less charitably disposed. Mortimer Granville,
who investigated conditions in the metropolitan asylums on behalf
of the *Lancet* during the mid-1870s, commented that

the Middlesex County asylum at Colney Hatch is a colossal mistake . . .
It combines and illustrates more faults in construction and errors of
arrangement than it might have been supposed possible in a single
effort of bewildered or misdirected ingenuity . . . the wards are long,
narrow, gloomy, and comfortless, the staircases cramped and cold, the
corridors oppressive, the atmosphere of the place dingy, the halls huge
and cheerless. The airing courts, although in some instances carefully
planted, are uninviting and prison-like.

At the City of London asylum at Dartford, the staircases were
'cramped and draughty', the lavatories 'very defective', and the
structure as a whole, while given to 'outward show', was pervaded
by a 'spirit of parsimony' with respect to the internal arrangements.
Hanwell, too, was a classic example of the asylum architecture of the
period, typified by 'long, cold corridors, huge wards, and a general
aspect of cheerlessness'. From without,

it is a vast and straggling building, in which the characteristics of a
prison, a self-advertising charitable institution, and some ambitious piece
of Poor Law architecture struggle for prominence. The gates are kept by
an official who is attired in a garb as nearly as possible like that of a
gaoler. All the male attendants are made to display the same forbidding
uniform.

Small wonder then, that for all the protests that such ideas were
unfounded, 'many among the higher, and nearly all among the
lower classes, still look upon the County Asylum as the Bluebeard's
cupboard of the neighbourhood'.[2]

[1] *Commissioners in Lunacy, 16th Annual Report*, 1862, p. 139.
[2] Granville, op. cit., I, pp. 75, 145, 154; 'Lunatic Asylums', *Quarterly
Review*, 101, p. 353.

Gigantic asylums such as these were already common within a decade of the passage of the 1845 Act. Colney Hatch, which opened in 1851, was from the outset designed for more than 1,000 patients. Its wards and passages amounted in the aggregate to more than six miles. The exterior was 'almost palatial' in character:

> Its facade, of nearly a third of a mile, is broken at intervals by Italian campaniles and cupolas, and the whole aspect of the exterior leads the visitor to expect an interior of commensurate pretensions. He no sooner crosses the threshold, however, than the scene changes. As he passes along the corridor, which runs from end to end of the building, he is oppressed with the gloom; the little light admitted by the loop-holed windows is absorbed by the inky asphalte paving, and coupled with the low vaulting of the ceiling, gives a stifling feeling and a sense of detention as in a prison. The staircases scarcely equal those of a workhouse; plaster there is none, and a coat of paint, or whitewash, does not even conceal the rugged surface of the brickwork. In the wards, a similar state of affairs exists: airy and spacious, they are without a doubt, but of human interest they possess nothing.[1]

With the exception of the external harmony of its architectural style, in which respect it was somewhat atypical, Colney Hatch might have served as the archetype of the county asylums of the latter decades of the nineteenth century. Propelled by the overriding desire to economize, local magistrates almost universally adopted the practice of tacking on wing after wing, story upon story, building next to building, in a haphazard and fortuitous fashion, as they strove to keep pace with the demand for accommodation for more and more lunatics. For all the Lunacy Commissioners' attempts to impose order on the chaos, as asylums grew steadily larger in the course of the century, and yet remained stubbornly over-crowded and overrun by hopeless and decrepit cases, it became impossible to aspire to providing more than minimal custodial care. Asylums began to seem 'more like towns than houses'; they became institutions which 'partake rather of the nature of industrial than of medical establishments'.

Increasing size was the one aspect of the drift towards custodialism that the Lunacy Commissioners strove hardest to resist.

[1] 'Lunatic Asylums', *Quarterly Review*, 101, p. 364.

Throughout the 1850s, for example, they conducted an acrimonious correspondence with the Middlesex magistrates over plans to expand Hanwell and Colney Hatch, both of which already contained well in excess of 1,000 inmates. Here, as elsewhere, their inability to compel compliance with their directives proved decisive. All new asylums, or plans to extend existing institutions, needed their prior approval, but this failed to provide them with adequate leverage to force the justices to adopt their views. Local authorities balked at the proposal that they should respond to the growing demand for asylum accommodation by providing for a proliferation of small, costly institutions. Whenever the Commissioners rejected their plans to extend already large institutions, asylum committees simply made minor modifications to the existing designs and re-submitted them. The Commissioners' complaints that 'the more extended the asylums are, the more abridged become their means of cure', that 'it is manifest that anything like individual treatment must be limited to a very small proportion of cases, and we fear that with the mass of the Patients the Superintendents must necessarily depend upon the good conduct and trustworthiness of the attendants', were met by a stony indifference.

Given their conviction that any asylum, no matter how far it strayed from the initial conception of what an asylum should be, was better than no asylum at all, the Lunacy Commissioners then faced three not very palatable alternatives. They could continue to reject the proposals, in which case the lunatics for whom there was no room in existing asylums would be deprived of the benefits of asylum treatment, and would likely languish under not very salubrious conditions in the local workhouses. They could appeal to the Home Secretary, who possessed ultimate authority in these matters, except that he usually sided with the magistrates. (The central government was no more inclined than its local representatives to sanction 'excessive' expenditures on a segment of the disreputable poor.) Or they could bow to the inevitable, concede that further opposition was 'impracticable', and approve the plans themselves. Perceiving the futility of resistance, their objections grew less and less frequent, though periodically they plaintively noted that 'each succeeding year . . . confirms us in the opinions we have so often expressed as to the many evils resulting from the congregation of very large numbers of the insane under one roof and one management'. Each succeeding year also brought a further increase in the average size of the patient population of county and borough asylums.

Table 6 Average Size of County and Borough Asylums in England and Wales in the Nineteenth Century

Date	Number of Asylums	Average Size
1 Jan. 1827	9	116·0
1 Jan. 1850	24	297·5
1 Jan. 1860	41	386·7
1 Jan. 1870	51	548·6
1 Jan. 1880	61	657·2
1 Jan. 1890	66	802·1

Source: Annual Reports of the Commissioners in Lunacy, except 1827 figures, which are from K. Jones, *Lunacy, Law, and Conscience*, London, Routledge & Kegan Paul, 1955, p. 116.

4. The Custodial Institution

Within these mammoth institutions, the reality of the patient's existence departed further and further from the conditions in the outside world, for his return to which the asylum was still ostensibly preparing him. As Browne put it:

> In the vast asylums now extant . . . all transactions, moral as well as economic, must be done wholesale.[1]

They have grown into lunatic colonies of eight or nine hundred, or even a thousand or more inhabitants, comfortably lodged and clothed, fed by a not illiberal commissariat, watched and waited on by well-paid attendants, disciplined and drilled to a well-ordered routine.[2]

[1] W. A. F. Browne, *The Moral Treatment of the Insane: A Lecture*, London, Adlard, 1864, p. 18.

[2] J. T. Arlidge, *On the State of Lunacy and the Legal Provision For the Insane*, London, Churchill, 1859, p. 102.

And the key to comprehending asylum existence was obviously routine.

Critics insisted that such organized monotony was

very well suited to a workhouse, but totally unfitted to an asylum for mental cure. Individuality is entirely overlooked; indeed the whole asylum life is the opposite of the ordinary mode of living of the working classes. When the visitor strolls along the galleries filled with listless patients, the utter absence of any object to afford amusement or occupation strikes him most painfully. It is remarked with infinite approval now and then by the Commissioners that the walls have been enlivened with some cheap paper, that a few prints have been hung in the galleries, that a fernery has been established – matters all very well in their way, but utterly inadequate to take the place of the moving sights of the outside world.[1]

Superintendents of the larger asylums conceded that 'it is totally impossible there to do more than know [the inmates] by name'.

'Individual interest in patients is all but dead.' How could it be otherwise? For 'their number renders the inmates mere automatons, acted on in this or that fashion according to the rules governing the great machine'.[2] Even the patients' diversions and recreations were organized and bureaucratized, shaped to fit the asylum's timetable and routine. In the words of the superintendent at the Northampton General Asylum: 'Amusement has now become so much an established and recognized part of the treatment of the insane, that it is requisite that it should be conducted in a regular and systematic manner.' What this meant in practice is suggested by a description of one of the patients' balls now becoming a feature of asylum life:

On the occasion of our visit there were about 200 patients present . . . In a raised orchestra, five musicians, three of whom were lunatics, soon struck up a merry polka, and immediately the room was alive with dancers . . . Had the men been differently dressed, it would have been impossible to have guessed that we were in the midst of a company of lunatics, the mere sweepings of the parish workhouses; but the prison uniform of sad coloured grey appeared like a jarring note amidst the

[1] 'Non-Restraint in the Treatment of the Insane', *Edinburgh Review*, 131, 1870, p. 223.

[2] J. T. Arlidge, op. cit., p. 107.

general harmony of the scene . . . At nine precisely, although in the midst of a dance, a shrill note is blown, and the entire assembly, like so many Cinderellas, breaks up at once and the company hurry off to their dormitories.[1]

The mechanical metaphor recurs again and again in contemporary descriptions of the asylum. Granville insisted that 'you want rather to encourage self-control than to convert a patient into a machine or a part of a machine'. But his own investigations of asylums showed that

the classification generally made is for the purpose of shelving cases; that is to say, practically it has that effect . . . in consequence of the treatment not being personal, but simply a treatment in classes, there is a tendency to make whole classes sink down into a sort of chronic state . . . I think they come under a sort of routine discipline which ends in their passing into a state of dementia.

The asylum was 'a mere house of perpetual detention', in which, characteristically, there was an 'utter absence of any means for engaging the attention of the Patients, interesting them in any occupations or amusements or affording them a sufficient variety of exercise outdoors'. In consequence, inspections of the patients found that 'besides a large number crouching on the floors, many were in or upon their beds, some for very trivial causes, and some, as if they had merely sought relief there from the noise and monotony of the galleries'.[2]

From the outset, the advocates of moral treatment had laid much stress on the therapeutic benefits of providing employment for asylum inmates, a suggestion which met with a ready response from

[1] *Northampton General Lunatic Asylum Annual Report*, 1861, p. 10; 'Lunatic Asylums', *Quarterly Review*, 101, pp. 375–6. Such dances were an exception to the general insistence upon a strict separation of the sexes. Apparently such separation was meant to extend even to the corpses: one of the principal defects noted by the Lunacy Commissioners at the Cambridge Asylum was 'the present dead-house, which serves for both sexes (an arrangement, we think, objectionable)' (*Commissioners in Lunacy, 25th Annual Report*, 1871, p. 131).

[2] *House of Commons Select Committee on the Operation of the Lunacy Law*, 1877, pp. 396–7, 388; *Commissioners in Lunacy, 16th Annual Report*, 1862, p. 138.

those charged with providing receptacles for the pauper insane. An inquiry into the number of patients employed and the type of tasks they performed was accordingly diligently made by the Lunacy Commissioners on each of their visits to an asylum, and the answers carefully written up in their subsequent reports. Two things clearly emerge from this mass of material. In the first place, the employment provided was hardly that envisaged by the early reformers. Instead of having as its primary goal the benefits which would accrue to the patients, the jobs provided were those that enabled the institution to run more smoothly and more cheaply – doing the laundry, repairing clothes and uniforms, acting as farm labourers on the asylum farm, or performing various menial tasks around the institution. Secondly, even given a generous definition of what constituted employment, a sizeable proportion of the inmates were not given any task, however trivial. Many patients were simply left to rot.

5. The Maintenance of Order

For those who had to run these enormous receptacles for the insane, the question of most obvious concern was how such collections of crazy people – who had been placed in an institution because of their failure to conform to the ordinary rules and conventions of society – could be brought to sustain some semblance of order. The abandonment of the traditional weapons for achieving this, chains and the whip, was constantly invoked as the symbol of the humanity with which the patients were now treated when compared with past enormities, and as a shield against the perception that asylums had, on the reformers' own terms, proved a disastrous failure. On the face of things, this made the asylum administrators' task much more difficult, but in practice it was scarcely a major handicap. As is so often the case in the area of social control, the behaviour which restraint had been designed to regulate turned out to be exacerbated, if not produced, by the very measures taken to control it. Its abolition showed that restraint

was in fact creative of many of the outrages and disorders to repress which its application was commonly deemed indispensible . . . the wards of lunatic asylums no longer exhibit the harrowing description of their former state. Mania, not exasperated by severity, and melancholia, not deepened by the want of all ordinary consolations, lose the exaggerated character in which they were formerly beheld.[1]

With the employment of a larger number of attendants and the continuing availability of solitary confinement or 'seclusion' for the most stubbornly uncooperative inmates, the more extravagant prophecies of doom uttered by those attached to the old methods of management proved largely unfounded.

A subtle irony lay behind the whole subject of the control of asylum inmates' behaviour. For the creation of such a network of expensive specialized institutions in the first place had drawn its legitimacy from the constantly reiterated contention that lunatics were sick and/or not responsible for their own actions. Yet, if these vast asylums were to operate at all, patients had to be made to conform to the rules of the institutions, and this could only be done by utilizing the ordinary system of rewards and punishments to elicit the desired behaviour. But the resort to positive and negative sanctions was a tacit concession that it made some sort of sense to hold the lunatic responsible for his actions, and that by doing so his behaviour could be manipulated. In practice, then, the definition of actions as symptoms could not be maintained if the institution was to continue to function, and could scarcely be discarded if asylum doctors were to continue to maintain the fiction that their work was essentially medical in character.[2]

The need to disguise this awkward reality largely explains the linguistic contortions to which asylum superintendents resorted when speaking of the techniques they used to control their patients, and, in particular, their disingenuous insistence that disciplinary measures were, in fact, 'medical treatment'. In the same breath, John Millar could concede that 'the shower bath is used as a corrective discipline. The matron uses the shower bath for swearing,

[1] Conolly, cited in Granville, op. cit., I, p. 111.
[2] As Erving Goffman puts it in *Asylums* (Garden City, New York, Doubleday, 1961, pp. 350–66; London, Penguin, 1970), 'the interesting point here is that psychiatric staff are in a position neither to forgo the fiction of neutrality nor to sustain it'. I have obviously drawn heavily here on his analysis.

bad language and filthy habits'; and then assert: 'The whole question [of its use] I consider to be entirely within the province of the Superintendent, as much as any other medical treatment he may think necessary to employ.'[1] The use of drugs to tranquillize patients undoubtedly increased in the course of the nineteenth century:

Since the abolition of mechanical restraint in asylums there is no doubt that the use of medicines intended to produce sleep has very largely increased; not perhaps those that would send patients off into a state of positive somnolency, but to quiet them down; such, for example, as chloral, bromide of potassium, and remedies of that class.

Again, the rationale was explicitly therapeutic, and Granville was angry at what he saw as a perversion of medical techniques:

The use of narcotics in the fashion I am condemning is only a modi-fication of the old practice of giving patients antimony under the pretence of reducing the fever heat and fury of mania, or of employing a strong shower-bath, the douche, or the cold pack with the same ostensible purpose. The pretence of curative treatment was a sophistry. The real object was to secure quiet wards, and the modern version of the same policy is a free use of sedatives.[2]

The tranquillity the Lunacy Commissioners valued so highly had other sources as well. One of the less obvious ways of ensuring that obstreperous patients did not remain that way for long was the practice of keeping all inmates on a diet barely above starvation level:

The dietary in the asylums, certainly around London, is much below the normal standard, according to the received quantities. I have calcu-lated the dietaries at different asylums, or got them calculated, and I find that they are below the average determined by Dr Lyon Playfair's inductive experiments for even moderate exercise; they are barely above

[1] Bucks County Asylum, Superintendent's Diary, 18 August 1856.
[2] *House of Commons Select Committee*, 1877, p. 397; Granville, op. cit., I, p. 59.

the requirements for quiet. An excited person in an asylum would be wasting more tissue than would be replaced by such a diet.[1]

Order was also maintained by depriving recalcitrant inmates of 'privileges' which helped make the intolerable bearable. Browne, for instance, conceded that 'there is a penal code in every pauper asylum in this country, but it is of a very mild description. The punishment consists generally in the deprivation of a man's tobacco, or in his enforced absence from the amusements provided; the balls, concerts, and entertainments.'[2] Less mentionable in official circles was the use of physical violence by attendants to compel the inmates' obedience. Yet the fact that almost every year, despite the difficulty of obtaining evidence sufficient for a conviction, the Commissioners' reports contain details of prosecutions brought against attendants for breaking patients' ribs, or even bringing about their deaths, indicates that such practices continued, albeit less frequently and openly than before.

6. Asylums for the Upper Classes

While county asylums contained the overwhelming majority of those incarcerated for insanity, their admissions were restricted by law to pauper lunatics, i.e. those maintained in whole or in part at public expense by parishes or poor law unions. Fee-paying upper- and upper-middle-class patients patronized an entirely separate network of institutions, consisting of a mixture of the old charity or 'registered' hospitals and the profit-making private licensed houses. And, as one might expect, there were some sharp differences

[1] *House of Commons Select Committee*, 1877, p. 307. Such a policy had an additional advantage: it saved on the cost of maintenance.

[2] *House of Commons Select Committee*, 1877, p. 72. The following revealing exchange occurred a little later in J. C. Browne's testimony: Q. 'They have so much sense of responsibility, in fact, that they are influenced by the knowledge that they will be deprived of those luxuries if they violate the rules of the asylum?' A. 'Most certainly; and it is the practice in almost every county asylum in England to act on that principle, and to assume a knowledge of right and wrong in the majority of inmates.' As Goffman has so skilfully shown, those who live outside a total institution ordinarily do not appreciate the terrible significance having to do without trivial things possesses for those confined in such a bleak environment.

between these establishments and those catering to paupers, differences which were naturally most marked in the asylums servicing the aristocracy.[1]

From the outset, private patients were accommodated in small asylums. For example, the Lunacy Commissioners' first report showed that the average size of the ninety-six provincial licensed houses taking private patients, eliminating one atypically large institution, was almost exactly thirty-six patients; most took fewer than a hundred, and several as few as two. Moreover, unlike county asylums, the size of the institutions taking private patients scarcely grew in the course of the nineteenth century. In 1879, only thirteen of the thirty-three metropolitan licensed houses and twelve of sixty provincial licensed houses contained thirty patients or more. On 1 January 1890, the average patient population of a metropolitan licensed house was seventy-six patients, and of a provincial licensed house only thirty-two. Consequently, private patients were spared the more grossly institutional features characteristic of the public asylums.

Medical attention was much more assiduous, and given the much lower doctor/patient ratio, the average patient was likely to have at least some contact with a physician in the course of the week. The proportion of attendants was usually much greater than the ratio of 1:10 or 1:12 which was the standard in the better county asylums. 'In some of the Private Establishments receiving Patients of a high class (such as Dr Fox's Asylum at Brislington, Dr Willis's at Shillingthorpe, and Mr Newington's at Ticehurst) the number of Attendants and Servants averages about one for every two patients.'[2]

---

[1] One thing that should constantly be borne in mind is that the differences between the various kinds of institutions catering to private patients were almost as great as those between private and pauper asylums. One crude index of this is the range of fees charged to inmates. In 1879, these broke down as follows: 'In 32 of the houses, receiving about 1,300 patients, the average payment is under £100 per annum. In 22, receiving about 750, the average payment is from £100 to £150 per annum . . . In 18 the average payments range from £150 to £200. In 13, from £200 to £280. In four from £280 to £330, and in one house, Ticehurst, they reached £470, including the cost of carriages and other expensive luxuries' (*Commissioners in Lunacy, 33rd Annual Report*, 1879, p. 113).

[2] *Commissioners in Lunacy, 2nd Annual Report*, 1847, p. 56.

With the establishment of a regular system of inspection and the removal of pauper patients, the grosser forms of abuse and mal-treatment of patients seem by and large to have disappeared from these asylums. In return for their much larger payments, most private patients were kept in much greater comfort than their pauper counterparts. Of no county asylum could it be said, as it was of the metropolitan licensed houses, that 'the accommodation provided for the patients of the private class in no way differs from what is usually found in an ordinary [sc. upper-class] dwelling house'. While chronic pauper cases were herded about in a dull, witless mass, their upper-class equivalents usually received relatively unregimented domestic care. At Ashbrooke Hall, for example, a Mrs Hitch received 'six quiet and harmless female patients . . . Each patient has an attendant and is visited by a medical man at least once a month – these ladies go to church, and their amusement is provided for, by outdoor occupation, and music and other means of amusement is provided indoors . . . The patients live in Mrs Hitch's family.' At Kenton House, a similar institution near Exeter, 'two ladies receive excellent accommodation of a quiet domestic kind, and much personal care and attention from the lady having charge of them.'[1]

A number of these receptacles for the upper classes more closely resembled an asylum, though. Among the best, and certainly the most expensive of these was Ticehurst, a favourite with the aristocracy. Founded in the eighteenth century, it remained in the hands of the Newington family throughout the nineteenth century. In the early 1800s, it already possessed grounds of approximately fifty acres, afterwards increased to 300 acres; and by 1830, it was equipped with an aviary, bowling green, pagoda and summer house, music room, reading room, and so forth. Throughout the century, its patient population fluctuated between sixty and eighty, evenly divided between the sexes. An extraordinarily large staff attended to the wants of the inmates: 'The Medical Superintendents, three in number, are assisted by seven lady superintendents and com-panions, four gentlemen acting as companions.' The latter, 'living as they do, constantly with the patients, must materially influence

[1] *Ashbrooke Hall Licensed House Visitors' and Patients' Book*, 31 August 1886 and 1 March 1877; *Commissioners in Lunacy, 26th Annual Report*, 1872, p. 32.

for the good the demeanour and general conduct of the attendants, and the comfort to the patient to have one of his own position as his companion in his room and during his walks must be very great'. In 1879, there were in all over 150 attendants of one sort or another – 'twenty-seven male attendants, thirty nurses, forty-three indoor domestics, thirty-eight outdoor, including coachmen and gardeners', as well as fifteen carriages and twenty-six horses. Almost every visit by the Commissioners produced a comment on the 'great comfort [which] as usual prevailed in every part of the Establishment . . . the fact that this is a private asylum is, as far as possible, veiled by the comfort and elegancies of the House and furniture'. Not surprisingly, 'the general feeling is undoubtedly content with the domestic arrangements . . . indeed it would be difficult to add to the comforts which the Patients have in this Establishment, absolute liberty excepted'. Lest the asylum's 300 acres of grounds provided insufficient diversions, two houses were acquired by the sea, at West Cliff and St Leonard's, to which patients could repair for a change of air and scenery.

At the asylum itself, every effort was made to occupy and amuse the patients. Lectures were given on popular subjects. There were fortnightly concerts in the summer, 'as many as thirty-six patients taking part in them'. Many patients dined regularly with their physicians. 'An excellent theatre with scenery' was constructed for the use of the patients. Some patients were 'taken to festivities in the neighbourhood, cricket matches, archery, fetes, flower shows, and others have been taken out for picnics'. Horses, donkeys, and carriages were available for riding, and a pack of hounds for hunting. (Aristocrats could not be deprived of their favourite diversion simply because they were crazy.) In short, while moral treatment may have disappeared without trace in the public asylums, it was applied with a vengeance at some of the private ones. In the words of the Commissioners, 'the recreation grounds are large and well-adapted to restore health to diseased minds . . . and we can speak in high terms of . . . the efforts made to promote the recovery and welfare of those placed here for treatment'.[1]

---

[1] *Ticehurst Asylum Visitors' Book*, 30 May 1877; 23 March 1874; 10 June 1880; 9 October 1871; 5 December 1870; 8 December 1877; 27 July 1878; 16 October 1890; 7 December 1877.

The results, to say the least, were disappointing. In report after report, the Commissioners were compelled to acknowledge that 'we spoke to all, but did not obtain many relevant replies'; 'all are apparently in good health but no one shows any sign of mental improvement'; and so on. As a rule, Ticehurst performed less well with respect to cures than many county asylums: to take just the years 1870, 1880, and 1890, in each twelve-month period, the numbers discharged cured as a percentage of the total numbers resident were respectively 3·75 per cent, 5·68 per cent, and 4·13 per cent. It was not alone in this respect, as Table 7 shows. In general, the proportion of cures achieved by all this effort was abysmally low. Apparently, the rich could buy greater attention and more eminent psychiatrists for their crazy relatives, but not more cures; so that for all the lavish expenditure of funds, private asylums remained, in Bucknill's words, 'institutions for private imprisonment'.

Table 7 Percentage of Cures of Private Patients in Asylums in England and Wales, Calculated on the Whole Number Resident, 1 January–31 December

Type of Institution	1870	1880	1890
Metropolitan Licensed Houses	7·57%	6·25%	5·75%
Provincial Licensed Houses	11·15%	7·43%	6·41%
Registered Hospitals	12·11%	9·05%	11·25%

Sources: Commissioners in Lunacy, 25th, 35th, and 45th Annual Reports, 1871, 1881, 1891.

7. Warehousing the Patients

Though several of the Lunacy Commissioners had been in the forefront of the effort to secure reform, and had then been at pains to emphasize the asylum's virtues as a curative institution, they adjusted their levels of expectation without visible discomfort to reflect the custodial reality which from the outset characterized almost all types of asylums. Indeed, the pressures emanating from the Commissioners' office generally served rather to reinforce than to mitigate the custodialism of the system. The optimism surrounding the achievement of reform persisted, at least in attenuated form, through the remainder of the 1840s and perhaps even into the early 1850s, and the Commissioners' reports in those years did pay some attention to the issue of cure. In 1847, they went so far as to issue a supplementary report largely devoted to a survey of existing techniques and methods of curing mental disorder as practised in English asylums of the period, hoping thereby to raise the general proportion of cures and to stimulate further advances in the field. But as the actual results achieved in the new asylums began to belie the easy optimism about curability which characterized these early years, they began to concentrate their attention on more mundane administrative matters. To judge by the space and emphasis allotted each topic, by the mid-1850s the question of curing asylum inmates ranked considerably below the urgent issue of the composition of the inmates' soup. Henceforth, the asylum's role in providing treatment and cures was emphasized only when defending asylums against proposals to retain lunatics in workhouses, or when magistrates failed to build enough asylum accommodation to keep up with the demand.

Over the many years it took to achieve their goals, lunacy reformers had developed a faith in the virtues of the institution which was not easily destroyed. But it was not just a human reluctance to admit their own mistake which led the Commissioners to collaborate in and encourage the adoption of an efficient custodialism as the primary goal of the asylum system. In the first place, the bourgeois emphasis on the virtues of self-discipline and regularity which was so prominent a feature of the ideology of moral treatment was not always carefully distinguished, even in the minds of its principal advocates, from a celebration of order and obedience for their own sakes – and such a perversion of the original intent was particularly likely to occur and to be overlooked once asylums began to deal with an essentially lower-class population. In a sense, the potential for its transformation into an instrument of repression was always latent in moral treatment. Equally important, the campaign for lunacy reform had derived much of its energy and had attracted much of its support from those who sought to protect helpless paupers from the abominable conditions and cruelties to which they had been subjected in private madhouses. From such a perspective, it is at least understandable that the abolition of chains and the elimination of the grosser excesses of the earlier institutions could be viewed as the fulfilment of the promise of reform, impeding the perception of their replacement's perhaps equally unattractive features.

The Commissioners' standard of comparison was explicitly not the goals the reformers had set for themselves, but rather the previous conditions in the worst private madhouses. They pointed to examples like Warburton's houses at Bethnal Green, where prior to an efficient system of inspection,

mechanical restraint was carried out to such an extent that there were *seventy* out of about four hundred patients almost invariably in irons . . . there was no bath, no library, not even a book or a newspaper; little or no employment; no means of amusement; a small and inefficient staff of attendants (there being only one to about fifty patients) . . . the rooms were defective in cleanliness, warmth and general comfort . . . parts of the asylum were damp and offensive from want of drainage . . .

and so on.[1] Given such a starting point, it was difficult *not* to find evidence of improvement, even in institutions which remained clearly custodial.

As the rising cure-rate which the Commissioners had originally hoped for failed to materialize, they adopted still more conservative criteria on which to base their judgement as to an asylum's effectiveness. The reader of the four- and five-hundred-page reports the Commission produced year after year soon encounters certain words and phrases which then recur with monotonous regularity, indicating the Commissioners' pleasure or displeasure with what they found, while revealing at the same time the implicit values which lay behind their actions. Good asylums were those where the bedding was 'clean and sufficient'; the treatment 'humane and judicious'; the patients 'orderly, quiet, free from excitement and satisfactorily clothed'; the institution 'clean and tidy'; mortality rates low and attendance at chapel high; and where there was a general air of efficiency. On the other hand, institutions which

[1] *Commissioners in Lunacy, 2nd Annual Report,* 1847, p. 85.

deviated in any of these respects, those whose physical structure was defective or whose water supply was insufficient, could expect to be censured.

The performance of medical superintendents was not assessed in terms of how successful they were in treating or curing patients, or how diligently they were pursuing research into the causes or treatment of mental disorder. Such matters were scarcely mentioned. Instead, asylum doctors were praised for the efficient performance of mundane administrative tasks, for their 'kindliness' and their efforts to provide for the comfort of their charges; and reprimanded if they failed to keep up to date with the mountain of legal paperwork – case books, admission records, discharge records, books recording instances of restraint and seclusion, and so on – required by the lunacy statutes. Any deviations from routine, even those which had a therapeutic intent, were likely to draw a stern reproof from the Commissioners, since they almost inevitably involved some increased risk, however slight, that the patients would abscond or succeed in doing away with themselves. The intent was the humane one of preventing a repetition of the abuses to which lunatics had been exposed prior to 1845. But the consequence was to stifle initiative and innovation on the part of the asylum doctors, and to foster a dull, protective environment where merely keeping the patient alive became an end in itself.

Not surprisingly in the circumstances, asylum superintendents were content to turn necessity into a virtue. When the county asylums built in accordance with the 1845 Act first opened, the superintendents had emphasized that 'the recovery or improvement of the inmates is to be the primary consideration, and . . . [is] the purpose [for which] the Asylum was specially intended'. The custodial care of long-term patients was to be only a secondary, residual function. As the prospect of curing significant numbers came to seem more and more remote, however, the Commissioners' attitudes and preferences enabled the doctors to make a relatively smooth transition to a situation where these priorities were almost precisely reversed. The asylum's ability to keep crazy people out of harm's way, and to provide them with more humane care than they would otherwise receive, increasingly became the justification for its continued existence. 'In fact', the public were informed, a County Asylum which receives pauper patients, chronic cases of ordinary Insanity from other Counties, as well as Idiot children from its own and other districts can never hope to show a very high percentage of recoveries. But the asylum is carrying out the objects of its creation – namely the cure of curable cases and the care of all cases of the Insane who are incurable,[1]

even if the ratio of incurable to curable cases had turned out to be much larger than had been originally anticipated.

Aware of the overwhelmingly lower-class composition of the awkward, inconvenient, and troublesome people the asylums had now collected within their walls, and conscious of the lack of alternative structures and mechanisms for coping with such a potentially disruptive lot, most of those who counted in Victorian England found it easy to reconcile themselves to the collapse of earlier pretensions to cure. With scarcely a murmur of protest, both national and local élites were converted to the merits of a holding operation which kept these undesirables, the very refuse of society, out of sight, and preferably out of mind. On the national level, the Select Committees of 1859–60 and 1877, both of which inquired into the treatment of the insane, exhibited little or no concern with the issue of the cure of (or rather the asylums' failure to cure) lower-class patients. The 1859–60 Committee displayed some anxiety about the condition of those pauper lunatics still confined in workhouses, but otherwise merely sought to establish that serious instances of physical abuse of the insane, such as those uncovered by parliamentary inquiries earlier in the century, had indeed disappeared. Both this Committee and the one appointed in 1877 obviously retained an unshakable faith in the fundamental applicability of the asylum solution, and their major shared concern was simply to prevent the accidental or conspired-at incarceration of sane (upper- and upper-middle-class) individuals. Likewise, the central government's decision in 1874 to grant each parish a subsidy of four shillings a head for every pauper lunatic confined in an asylum (an action which was announced long after it was apparent that asylums were little more than convenient dumping grounds for

[1] *Bucks County Asylum Annual Report*, 1854, p. 22; *Northampton County Asylum Annual Report*, 1888, p. 12.

the decrepit), represented a tacit – if very practical – endorsement of the value of custodialism.

The comments of Poor Law officials, who were shown over asylums when they came to inspect their local lunatics, indicate that they too were ready to compliment the asylum administrators on the excellence of their custodial care, and were seldom inclined to question the value of the enterprise just because cure proved out of reach. Following one such visit, the officials from the Devizes Union noted complacently that 'most of the Lunatics belonging to this union seem to be very hopeless cases (many of them never having possessed any mind cannot of course become sane) and the Medical Superintendent who very courteously went through the Establishment with me stated that he thought that there were only about two cases which would be likely to recover'. Subsequent visits gave little hope of change: 'There does not appear to be much probability of the ultimate recovery of the patients . . . The Medical Superintendent could only give hope of being discharged to three patients.' The inspectors from Highworth and Swindon Union were taken over the asylum, 'which we found in excellent order, the whole of the wards and corridors and day rooms being made as bright and cheerful and particularly clean and attractive for the unfortunate inmates as possible'. The forty-six inmates from their Union unfortunately showed no sign of mental improvement: 'What is still more sad is the report of the Medical Superintendent that out of this large number, not more than two men and three women can reasonably be expected to be ultimately discharged from restraint.'[1] Such therapeutic nihilism being accepted as a fact of life, local officials typically concentrated, as here, on emphasizing the amenities and physical comfort of the institution.

8. Pressures to Economize

The emerging consensus among almost all the interested parties on the value of a custodial operation was bolstered by the Lunacy Commissioners' staunch adherence to the notion that institutionalization remained the only acceptable solution to the problems of insanity. While this alliance could not entirely stifle complaints

[1] *Wiltshire County Asylum Visitors' Book*, 1876–87, pp. 42, 103, 185–6.

about the asylum doctors' performance and suggestions that the asylum system had failed and ought to be disbanded,[1] it could and did operate to blunt the force and effectiveness of these attacks. But this relative immunity was bought at a price: the availability of funds for a custodial operation aimed at warehousing a predominantly lower-class population was never likely to be great. Consequently, asylums were perpetually starved of money – not to the extent that they had to close, for that would release their inmates back into the community, and the community tolerance for the presence of the defective and decrepit in its midst was by now quite low – but always sufficiently effective to preclude the provision of more than a minimum of care.

Local authorities were always reluctant to spend 'extravagant' sums of money on paupers. Consequently, although this became a more intense and pervasive concern in later years, magistrates on many asylum committees sought from the outset to keep costs to a bare minimum. As they became more experienced at running such large institutions, and perhaps less concerned to provide expensive accommodation once cures failed to materialize, they often realized considerable savings. To take just one example, in 1848, two years after the Littlemore Asylum opened its doors, the weekly charge to each parish for each patient was 11s. a week. By 1851, the magistrates had succeeded in reducing it to 8s. a week; and despite rising prices for provisions and being compelled to pay higher wages to the asylum staff, two years later they had effected a further reduction to only 7s. 6d.

A few asylum committees, convinced of the doctors' ability to make good their claims to cure, were prepared to permit larger expenditures in the expectation that the recoveries which would result would justify the apparently greater costs incurred. Such a policy was not popular with the local Poor Law officials, as the experience of the Buckinghamshire Asylum indicates. From its opening, the magistrates exhibited a marked defensiveness about costs. In their very first report, which was distributed to all the parish Poor Law officers, they sought to persuade their audience

[1] For a discussion of this critique of the asylum, see Andrew T. Scull, *Decarceration: Community Treatment and the Deviant: A Radical View*, Englewood Cliffs, N.J., Prentice-Hall, 1977, Chapters 6 and 7.

that 'in this as in many other instances a liberal policy is identical with a true economy, as a means of saving the local rates, and the duty of humanity to arrest the incipient disease before it has time to assume a chronic and hopeless character, coincides with the pecuniary interests of the ratepayers'. They felt compelled to treat the subject at some length, because 'an erroneous impression seems to have prevailed in some quarters that the accommodation to be afforded in a Lunatic Asylum was no more than that required in a Union Workhouse, and that the Building might be erected for much the same cost, the essential difference between the two Institutions and the capacity, habits, and necessities of the inmates being greatly overlooked.'

Evidently the committee's efforts failed to carry conviction. Two years later, the asylum superintendent took up the same task. Millar's defence of the asylum was typically spirited:

Odium is cast upon those having [the insane's] immediate care because an expenditure is incurred greater than is to be found to be sufficient in the Unions for Sane persons, the disease, habits, and propensities of the Insane being quite overlooked. Why those suffering from a disorder the most terrible to which the human race is liable, which the world regards with fear and horror, which affixes a stigma on the sufferer for life, and against whose recovery a premium is even offered, should be branded with the vagrant and the mendicant, thus exposed to a degradation and economy which even the convicted criminals – those pests and outcasts of society – are spared, appears to me to be an evil which requires amendment. Parochial authorities never complain that convicts cost about ten shillings a week.[1]

This was stirring stuff, though scarcely calculated to make Millar many friends. From the outset, he had been firmly committed to a curative régime, and had sought to minimize the barriers between the asylum and the community by allowing patients frequent opportunities to visit the nearby town of Aylesbury. In essence, he had staked his future on being able to produce a sufficient proportion of cures, and initially, at least, had won the support of the magistrates. But he simply could not stem the influx of chronic and hopeless cases. The following year, after more than three years

[1] *Bucks County Asylum Annual Report*, 1854, pp. 5, 10; *Annual Report*, 1856, p. 14.

of uniformly favourable, even enthusiastic, reports on his conduct of the asylum by both the magistrates and the Lunacy Commissioners, he was abruptly dismissed, ostensibly for permitting administrative irregularities on the part of the asylum staff. Unable to produce the results to justify their liberal approach, the magistrates appear to have capitulated to local pressures for economy. Under Millar's successor, Humphry, the asylum became just another custodial institution, and later in the century the Buckinghamshire magistrates were to prove as adept as their counterparts elsewhere at cheeseparing.[1]

The link between an asylum's popularity in the local community and its cost to local taxpayers was further demonstrated by events at Northampton in the 1870s and 1880s. The Northamptonshire magistrates had for many years avoided incurring the heavy expenses the erection of a county asylum necessarily entailed. The legal requirements of the 1845 Act had been circumvented by a unique arrangement whereby the local charity hospital (the Northampton General Lunatic Asylum, which had opened in 1839) took all the county pauper patients on a contractual basis. During the 1860s, however, the pressures on the physical capacity of this asylum became acute, and it became apparent that further buildings would be required to house the rising numbers of pauper lunatics. The county's contract with the asylum trustees was now about to expire anyway, and the Commissioners in Lunacy took the opportunity to press for the erection of a conventional county asylum at a separate site, refusing to countenance the renewal of the existing contract. Local resistance to the idea was fierce, but for once the Commissioners obtained the backing of the Secretary of State, and the local authorities were reluctantly forced to concede defeat. Grudgingly, they embarked on an asylum building programme. Here too, the statutory requirement that the Commissioners approve all the plans and specifications checked any inclination they might have had to economize on construction costs; and they were compelled to build, not just an asylum, but a costly asylum.

---

[1] The complacent acceptance of a custodial role is evident even in the tone of the annual reports, which lose the interest and optimism of the earlier years and become just another dull bureaucratic routine – a development, incidentally, which is common to all asylum reports in the course of the century.

When the asylum finally opened its doors, its unpopularity with the local people was made patently clear in letters and editorials in the local newspaper, the *Northampton Herald*. The general sentiment was that 'the long suffering ratepayers have not much to be proud of except it is a most hideous building'. The Lunacy Commissioners visited and pronounced themselves highly satisfied with the condition of the asylum, which only served to inflame local ire further:

Of course the Commissioners in Lunacy were much gratified by their visit. They have not to pay . . . But now comes almost the worst part of the story. You Sir and I and other victims, would expect to obtain something for their money, a building that the county would be proud of . . . And what have we obtained? – a monstrously ugly structure whose chief architectural feature is a 'tall chimney'.

The opposition continued, and extended even to allegations that behind the high walls and the trees which shielded the asylum from the public gaze, patients were being brutally maltreated. But the prime target was always the alleged extravagance with which the asylum was administered. The superintendent, Dr Millson, had rashly insisted that since the asylum was supposed to be a hospital, patients were entitled to more than the spartan existence of a workhouse environment. The *Herald* began to suggest that the magistrates' committee running the asylum 'were dissatisfied with the lavish expenditure of public money evident in everything, even to the cups and saucers, which were far better in quality than necessary'.[1] In April 1878, under fire from all directions, Millson submitted his resignation.

In less than a year, his successor effected a remarkable reversal of public attitudes. On 4 January 1879, the *Herald* informed its readers that 'the county Lunatic Asylum now, as far as its management is concerned, seems to have entered upon a satisfactory course'. In subsequent issues, obvious delight was expressed at the condition of the hospital. A passage in the asylum report for the year indicates how such a spectacular transformation had been achieved. The surplus accommodation in the new buildings had

[1] *Northampton Herald*, 10 March 1878; 25 May 1878; 16 February 1878.

been filled with lunatics from other counties and boroughs whose asylums were already full:

there are now in the Asylum 128 out-county and private patients, irrespective of those chargeable to the boroughs of Northampton and Peterborough. The trouble which these cases entail on the staff is very considerable; but the profits accruing from them are also considerable, and should the Asylum need any further additions or alterations, the Northampton ratepayer will not again be called upon for the money.

It was this fact, that the asylum was now running at a profit, which was emphasized over and over again in press comments, and in the institution's own annual reports. In 1880, 'the cost of patients' maintenance was reduced from three years ago . . . although this was effected despite an increase in the dietary and the clothing supplies'. The following year, 'another reduction in maintenance was reported . . . bring the charge at this hospital to an amount lower than the general average of similar institutions'. The overcrowding, which was by now quite severe, undoubtedly helped in this respect. By 1886, the average cost per patient per week had fallen from the original founding rate of 10s. 6d. to 8s. And while the continual influx of patients eventually forced some minor alterations to the original structure, to raise the capacity from less than 500 initially to 700 in September 1883 and 850 by 1889, the profits from out-county patients were sufficient to pay for the needed 'improvements'. 'Thus the necessity for having recourse to the County Rates has been avoided',[1] and the asylum was able to maintain its new-found popularity.

The patients' overcrowded living conditions were clearly not a feature confined to the Northampton County Asylum. Almost every year, the Lunacy Commissioners reported that such conditions were widespread. Other institutions, too, saw it as a way of avoiding increased capital expenditure. And since it allowed fixed

[1] *Northampton County Asylum Annual Report*, 1878, p. 16; *Annual Report*, 1880, p. 14; *Annual Report*, 1881, p. 8; *Annual Report*, 1877, p. 8. In 1881, the Lunacy Commissioners commented that in some of the male wards, 'patients vary from 60 to 70 while there are beds for but 27'. A similar state of affairs in 1880 had led to the conversion of a lavatory on the male side and a sewing room on the female side into dormitories.

costs, such as the superintendent's salary and repairs to buildings, to be spread more thinly over a larger number of cases, it helped to reduce or stabilize maintenance costs for each patient. Caterham and Leavesden were explicitly custodial institutions opened for the metropolitan area's chronic lunatics. Patients were gathered together there in huge, barn-like dormitories, and were such hopeless cases that almost none were expected to (or did) leave them, except in coffins. (In an average year, fewer than one per cent were discharged cured.) In 1885, the weekly cost of each inmate dumped at these asylums was, respectively, 7s. 11d., and 7s. 3½d. It is indicative of the success of the policy of saving money through excessive overcrowding of facilities and the practice of a cheese-paring economy, that at county asylums claiming to provide therapeutic treatment, costs were not very different – for example, at both the Worcester County Asylum and the Wiltshire County Asylum, the charge was 7s. 10¾d.

9. The Outcome of Reform

The worst predictions of men like Hill, Reid, and Conolly had thus been borne out, and asylums were now so large as to make even the pretence of treatment a mockery. Indeed, 'even the fresh cases which come in, being associated with such large numbers, drift into a state of dementia'. The distressing truth which confronted those who looked back on the work of the reformers in the early part of the century was 'how closely the complaints and aims of the reformers, in the days when there were few county or borough asylums, resemble our own. It is in respect to the very evils these . . . institutions were designed to remedy that they are themselves conspicuously defective'.[1]

The asylum's early association with social reform gave a humanitarian gloss to these huge, cheap, more or less overtly custodial dumps where the refuse of humanity was now collected together. At the same time, the medical control of asylums, and the propaganda about treatment rather than punishment, served to legitimate further the custodial warehousing of these, the most difficult and problematic elements of the disreputable poor. Such a policy

[1] *House of Commons Select Committee*, 1877, pp. 386, 391–2.

functioned to 'herd lunatics together in special institutions where they can be more easily visited and accounted for by the authorities',[1] and its practical advantages sufficed to ensure the continued expansion of existing asylums and the construction of many new ones.

Working-class opposition to the elimination of parish relief, and their hatred of the new workhouse 'Bastilles', had brought only a limited modification of the rigours of the new Poor Law, and not its abandonment. The poor thus had little alternative but to make use of the asylum as a way of ridding themselves of what, in the circumstances of nineteenth-century working-class existence, was undoubtedly an intolerable burden, the caring for their sick, aged, or otherwise incapacitated relatives. From the bourgeoisie's perspective, the existence of asylums to 'treat' the mentally ill at public expense could be invoked as a practical demonstration of their own philanthropic concern with the less fortunate. But far from asylums having been 'altruistic institutions . . . detached from the social structures that perpetuate poverty',[2] one must realize that they were important elements in sustaining those structures: important because of their symbolic value, and as a reminder of the awful consequences of non-conformity. Arlidge's bitter comment on the outcome of reform succinctly summed up the consequences of its central achievement, the creation of vast receptacles for the confinement of those without hope:

In a colossal refuge for the insane, a patient may be said to lose his individuality and to become a member of a machine so put together, as to move with precise regularity and invariable routine; a triumph of skill adapted to show how such unpromising materials as crazy men and women may be drilled into order and guided by rule, but not an apparatus calculated to restore their pristine condition and their independent self-governing existence. In all cases admitting of recovery, or of material amelioration, a gigantic asylum is a gigantic evil, and figuratively speaking, a manufactory of chronic insanity.[3]

[1] J. C. Bucknill, *The Care of the Insane and their Legal Control*, London, Macmillan, 1880, p. 122.

[2] Herbert Gans, preface to Colin Greer, *The Great School Legend*, New York, Basic Books, 1971.

[3] J. T. Arlidge, op. cit., p. 102.

Chapter Seven

The Social Production of Insanity

'But I don't want to go among mad people,' Alice remarked.
'Oh, you can't help that,' said the Cat: 'we're all mad here. I'm mad.
  You're mad.'
'How do you know I'm mad?' said Alice.
'You must be,' said the Cat, 'or you wouldn't have come here.'

(Lewis Carroll, *Alice's Adventures in Wonderland*)

HAMLET: 'Ay marry, why was he sent into England?'
CLOWN: 'Why because he was mad. He shall recover his wits there; or
if he do not, it is no great matter there.'
HAMLET: 'Why?'
CLOWN: ' 'Twill not be seen in him; there the men are as mad as he.'

(William Shakespeare, *Hamlet*)

The reformers had launched their proposals backed by the claim
and sustained by the conviction that proper asylum treatment
would cure a significant proportion of the insane, and so reduce the
incidence of insanity. The public had been assured that providing
county asylums 'will, no doubt, require a considerable sum in the
first instance, but hereafter the parishes will be relieved from a very
heavy and increasing burden'.[1] It would be something of an under-
statement to suggest that these expectations proved delusory.
Indeed, it remains perhaps the most paradoxical feature of the
entire reform process that the adoption of a policy avowedly aimed
at rehabilitation and the rise of a profession claiming expertise in
this regard should have been accompanied by a startling and

[1] Sir A. Halliday, *The Present State of Lunatics and Lunatic Asylums*, 1828,
p. 24.

continuing rise in the proportion of the population officially recognized as insane.

1. Rising Numbers of Madmen

Figures presented in the Report of the 1807 Select Committee, the first of the numerous nineteenth-century Parliamentary investigations into the lunacy question, gave 2,248 as the official tally of all persons identified as insane in England and Wales at the beginning of that year, on which basis the incidence of insanity was roughly 2·26 cases in every 10,000 of the general population – scarcely a rate calculated to produce anxiety that this was a common condition.[1] As efforts at 'reform' focused further attention on the plight of the insane, however, so their estimated proportion in the total population began to rise.[2] 'In 1810', before the first county asylum built under the 1808 Act opened its doors, 'the existing number of the insane in this kingdom was estimated by Dr Powell at one in 7,300; in 1820 by Dr Burrows, at one in 2,000; and in 1829 by Sir Andrew Halliday, at 16,500 or one in 769'.[3] The Metropolitan Commissioners' 1844 Report provided official confirmation that such a rapid rise, at least in the number of cases known to the authorities, had indeed taken place. The number of insane now amounted to over 20,000 and the incidence had risen to 12·66 cases per 10,000, almost six times that reported in 1807. This increase now became another of the reformers' arguments for new legislation to deal with the insane. For insanity was now a serious social problem, and 'pauper Lunatics have unfortunately become so numerous throughout the whole kingdom, that the proper construction and cost of asylums for their use has ceased to be a subject which affects a few counties only, and has become a matter of national interest and importance'.[4]

[1] *House of Commons Select Committee*, 1807, p. 5.

[2] I want to defer for the moment any discussion of the adequacy or accuracy of these and subsequent data on the numbers of lunatics. For the present, I am solely concerned to demonstrate the extent of the increase in the number of people *officially identified* as insane, and to illustrate its effect on the prevailing conceptions of just how serious a problem insanity was.

[3] John Thurnam, *Observations and Essays on the Statistics of Insanity*, London, Simpkin Marshall, 1845, p. 170, footnote.

[4] *Metropolitan Commissioners in Lunacy, 1844 Report*, p. 30.

The achievement of reform – the construction of asylums and the employment of doctors to effect the cure of the insane – did not bring about a halt or even a diminution in the rapid upward spiral of cases of lunacy. Between 1844 and 1860, while the population as a whole grew by just over 20 per cent, the number of lunatics all but doubled; and the growth in the number of the insane continued to far outstrip the rate of increase of the general population for the rest of the century. By 1890, there were 86,067 officially certified cases of mental illness in England and Wales, which meant that in the forty-five years immediately following the establishment of a compulsory system of public asylums for the early treatment and cure of lunatics, while the total population had risen by a mere 78 per cent, the number of lunatics had more than quadrupled. To put it another way, in 1844 the rate of certified cases of mental illness in the population as a whole was 12·66 per 10,000; by 1890, the figure was 29·6 per 10,000.

In the years immediately following the opening of the county asylum system, those who ran the asylums tended to dismiss the apparent rise in numbers as a temporary phenomenon. Their claim was that before asylum treatment had been made widely available, there had been a submerged reservoir of crazy people, hidden from public view, and hence not recorded in official statistics. Asylum committees were convinced that they had adequate 'reasons to believe that, since the asylum had been opened, and the advantages it affords to lunatics have become known and recognized throughout the county, many poor insane persons, long previously neglected at home', were brought into the institution. Families now realized that the inhumanity of the madhouse was a thing of the past, and had become aware of the benefits which scientific treatment in an asylum could confer, so that those with a lunatic in the closet or attic brought forth cases 'never before known to the parish officers'.[1]

Obviously, such a state of affairs could not be expected to continue for ever. The community ought sooner or later to run out of this accumulated surplus. But unfortunately for the asylum

---

[1] Report of the Visiting Justices of the Wandsworth County Asylum, Surrey, 1850, cited in J. M. Granville, *The Care and Cure of the Insane*, I, London, Hardwicke & Bogue, 1877, p. 224.

Table 8 Total Population, Total Number Officially Identified as Insane, and Rate of Insanity per 10,000 People in England and Wales

1 Jan.	Population	Number officially identified as insane*	Rate per 10,000	Source of data on number insane
1807	9,960,000	2,248	2·26	House of Commons 1807
1819	11,106,000	6,000	5·40	Burrows 1820
1828	13,106,000	8,000	6·10	Halliday 1828
1829	13,370,000	16,500	12·34	Halliday 1829
1836	14,900,000	13,667	9·18	Parliamentary Return 1836
1844	16,480,000	20,893	12·66	Metropolitan Commissioners in Lunacy
1850		NOT AVAILABLE		
1855	18,786,914	30,993†	16·49	Commissioners in Lunacy Annual
1860	19,902,713	38,058	19·12	Reports
1865	21,145,151	45,950	21·73	
1870	22,501,316	54,713	24·31	
1875	23,944,459	63,793	26·64	
1880	25,480,161	71,191	27·94	
1885	27,499,041	79,704	28·98	
1890	29,407,649	86,067	29·26	

* Includes lunatics confined in asylums, but also those in workhouses, at large in the community, etc.

† The Commissioners found 20,493 lunatics in asylums of all types in 1855; lacking a complete enumeration of all lunatics not so confined, they estimated that these amounted to some 10,500 persons. (Commissioners in Lunacy Annual Report 1855, Vol. 9, p. 39.)

authorities, it began to appear as though the rise in the number of lunatics *would* go on for ever. Consequently, this explanation, at least when standing alone, quickly came to seem inadequate. The Lunacy Commissioners might argue that a by-product of their inspection of workhouses, and their other activities, was the uncovering of previously unnoticed cases of insanity, but even they conceded that this was no longer sufficient to account for the persistent sharp increase in the total number of the insane.

Naturally enough, such a rapid accumulation did not occur without arousing public unease and concern at the course of events. Most people drew the obvious conclusion that the changes in official statistics reflected a real increase in the incidence of the disorder, and the Lunacy Commissioners commented that 'the opinion generally entertained was that the community are more subject than formerly to attacks of insanity'. Public fear of the legions of crazy men and women that society was apparently spawning at time verged on panic. Bucknill, for rhetorical effect, complained of 'the customs and laws which the sane majority has sanctioned for what is called the care and treatment, but to speak more truly for the custody and control, of that which is still fortunately the insane minority of the people'; but such hyperbole was lost on a general public which was convinced that such statements were almost literally true. Not three years previously, an editorial in *The Times* had commented that 'if lunacy continues to increase as at present, the insane will be in the majority, and, freeing themselves, will put the sane in asylums'.[1]

It was partly to allay these anxieties that the Commissioners had sought to explain (or rather to explain away) the reasons for the multiplication of cases of lunacy. On other grounds, though, they could scarcely have avoided examining the question. The progressive increase in insanity was obvious to those with even the most casual acquaintance with the subject. It can hardly be a source of wonder that those officially charged with overseeing the asylum system on a full-time basis should have chosen to investigate the reasons for such a development.

[1] *Commissioners in Lunacy Annual Report*, 1861, p. 84; J. C. Bucknill, *The Care of the Insane and their Legal Control*, London, Macmillan, 1880, pp. 1–2; *The Times*, 5 April 1877.

We must remember that those engaged in this enterprise were trying to account for a paradoxical state of affairs. The 'scientific' discovery of mental illness, and the adoption of a more 'rational' approach based upon this discovery which aimed at treating and curing the lunatic rather than neglecting him or incarcerating him in a gaol or workhouse, were advances which might have been expected to coincide with a decline in the prevalence of insanity. Instead they were associated with an explosive growth in the number of the insane. When the Lunacy Commissioners sought to reconcile this seemingly contradictory state of affairs, they did so as men who had been among the prime movers in the reform process, and who were convinced of the superiority and value of the medical approach to insanity. Naturally, therefore, they were disposed to look for answers which laid the blame on something other than reform, and which accounted for the apparent failure of the asylum in practice.

2. Official Explanations of the Increase

In 1844, more than 80 per cent of those diagnosed as insane were classified as paupers. Subsequently, the increase in the number of lunatics came overwhelmingly from their ranks. Between 1844 and 1860 the number of pauper lunatics rose by 96·4 per cent, while that of private lunatics grew only 24·4 per cent. Understandably, the Commissioners concentrated their attention on explaining the reasons for the increase among the former. Seeking 'to take into account every circumstance bearing directly or indirectly on the condition of the insane poor, which might have the apparent effect of increasing their number . . .', the Commissioners first checked the most obvious point. Perhaps there had been a rise in the number of paupers, accounting for all or part of the increase in insanity among this class? On the contrary, 'we have positive information that pauperism has decreased . . .' The Poor Law Board had recently produced figures which showed that 'the decrease in the average number of paupers of all classes in receipt of relief at one time in 1859, as compared with 1849, is 20·5 per cent, and as regards able-bodied paupers, the decrease in 1859, as compared with 1849, is 40·7 per cent'. The other suggestion which most readily presented itself was, at least as far as the Commissioners were concerned, equally easily disposed of. The rise could not reflect an increased incidence of insanity among the lower classes, since 'we have been unable to discover any material changes in the social conditions of the labouring population rendering them more prone to mental disease'.[1] If there were no increase in the proportion of paupers in the general population which could account for the increasing number of pauper lunatics, and if those paupers who remained were no more susceptible to insanity than their predecessors had been, one conclusion seemed inescapable: the figures which showed that such an upward trend existed must somehow be faulty. Accordingly, the Commissioners sought to reassure the public that the rise was more apparent than real.

In the first place, they contended, the methods of gathering statistics on insanity had previously been slipshod and inadequate. Local authorities had often failed to keep accurate accounts in the first place, and had compounded the error by submitting careless reports to the central government. The more thorough and uniform system of reporting they themselves had introduced had had the effect of adding large numbers to the official national statistics, even though such cases had existed all along. Much of the apparent rise could thus be attributed to 'the large number of cases previously unreported, and only recently brought under observation'.[2] Other factors were also at work. The alleged failure of the Poor Law authorities to send their cases of lunacy to asylums at a sufficiently early stage in the disease meant that asylums were filled to overflowing with the most inveterate and hopeless cases. The Commissioners conceded that it was impossible to determine with precision the effect of institutionalization on the life span of the insane, as the necessary figures on mortality rates prior to the rise of the asylum system were lacking;

But we are warranted in assuming that when destitute and diseased persons are placed under care in Establishments well-conducted, well-regulated, and specially adapted for their protection and treatment, and

---

[1] *Commissioners in Lunacy Annual Report*, 1861, p. 77.

[2] ibid., p. 78; see also *House of Commons Select Committee on the Operation of the Lunacy Law*, 1877, p. 6, evidence of Lord Shaftesbury.

in which they receive succour, abundant food, and careful medical supervision, the result will be the prolongation of lives which would otherwise have been of short duration.[1]

Partial confirmation of this hypothesis was provided by figures on mortality rates in asylums, which showed a sharp diminution since the early 1840s, when they ran as high as 18 per cent and more per annum in some Metropolitan Licensed Houses; a decrease which coincided with the introduction of the new system of inspection and the general improvement of asylum conditions. The greater life expectancy associated with asylum care accentuated the existing tendencies towards the long-term accumulation of chronic cases; and their increased longevity had the apparent effect of augmenting the incidence of insanity in the community.

More cases of insanity had existed in the community in the past than anyone had realized because they had often been mistaken for something else. Recent 'scientific' advances now enabled such cases to be recognized for what they 'really' were, and, for the first time, to be looked after and treated properly. 'There can be very little doubt', the Commissioners in Lunacy informed Parliament, 'that the system of observation and inquiry adopted of late years, however imperfect it still may be, had led to the detection and classification as Insane, of many persons formerly looked upon as ordinary Paupers'.[2]

These, then, were the most common official explanations of why the statistics of insanity showed a persistent rising trend. By and large, they all suggested that the apparent increase was primarily a statistical artifact and did not reflect the true state of affairs. In addition, however, there was one other theory which enjoyed periodical bursts of popularity among some of the asylum doctors, and the public also. Advocates of this position conceded that there had indeed been some real increase in the prevalence of insanity, an increase they attributed to the stresses attendant upon life in a higher 'mechanical civilization'. This view was first articulated by

[1] *Commissioners in Lunacy Annual Report*, 1861, p. 79.

[2] ibid., p. 78. As I shall argue at more length below, this remark, and similar ones about recognizing previously 'misclassified' cases of insanity, unconsciously suggest what was actually going on, an expansion of the boundaries of the mad.

Powell, and subsequently received support from Halliday, both of whom adduced the rise over time in the number of people identified as insane as the principal evidence for such a position. Browne, too, was convinced that 'the occupations, amusements, follies, and above all the vices of the present race are infinitely more favourable for the development of the disease than any previous period'.[1]

Later in the century, Bucknill and Tuke exhibited a greater scepticism about the quality of the statistical data in favour of this generalization. Nevertheless, they then succeeded in reaching an identical conclusion, though by a somewhat more circuitous route. Direct measures of the comparative prevalence of insanity at different periods being somewhat unreliable, the issue could only be resolved by observing 'whether the most frequent causes of insanity are to be found in greater force in civilized societies'. Evidently realizing that an audience of orthodox adherents of a Victorian evolutionism which as a matter of course equated a 'higher' civilization with progress in almost all spheres would find the conclusion that a more civilized existence was also more productive of mental defectives an unpalatable one, they sought to soften the blow. They too, 'regarding the question in an abstract and theoretical point of view . . . should certainly be disposed to expect that the development of civilization . . . would conduce to the mental health of any people subjected to its influence'. But from a different perspective, one was forced to recognize the possible drawbacks of the pace and fluidity of modern life, at least when taken to extremes. So that 'practically, we submit, that, in consequence of the abuse of the very blessings attendant on the progress of civilization, and of the temptation which civilization offers to overtask the faculties; and, lastly, in consequence of the greatly increased degree in which the emotions are developed, the result is, that an advanced civilization tends to increase the number of the insane'.[2]

[1] Richard Powell, *Observations on the Comparative Prevalence of Insanity at Different Periods*, London, Woodfall, 1813; Sir Andrew Halliday, *A Letter to Lord Robert Seymour: with a Report on the Number of Lunatics and Idiots in England and Wales*, London, Underwood, 1829, p. v; W. A. F. Browne, *What Asylums Were, Are, and Ought to Be*, Edinburgh, 1837, pp. 51–5.

[2] J. C. Bucknill and D. H. Tuke, *A Manual of Psychological Medicine*, Philadelphia, Blanchard & Lee, 1858, pp. 48, 58.

Actually, neither Bucknill and Tuke, nor their predecessors who had argued for the same conclusion, had proved in any scientifically acceptable sense that a connection existed between civilization and insanity. Their case seems plausible only because of what they claimed were the causes of insanity; but no scientific evidence was (has yet been) produced to demonstrate that 'artificiality', 'excitement', 'stress', and the like are instrumental in bringing about insanity. Moreover, since 'civilization' consisted of precisely those things which were supposed to cause insanity, the alleged proof turns out to have been a mere tautology. While this is not to say, of course, that the original hypothesis is necessarily false, only that it remains unproven, it does leave open the possibility that the statistical rise in insanity has quite different sources.

For a somewhat different set of reasons, the suggestion that an improved system of reporting cases of insanity was a major factor lying behind the rise in the apparent incidence of the 'disease' is similarly unsatisfactory. It does possess a certain surface plausibility, deriving from the fact that from 1844 onwards, the statistics of insanity were indeed more carefully collected than they had hitherto been. When the 1807 Select Committee presented the figures it had obtained, it felt bound to caution the Report's readers that 'these are so evidently deficient in several instances that a very large addition must be made in any computation of the whole number'. And while subsequent numbers given by Burrows and Halliday were based on official returns, both considered it necessary to 'correct' those figures by adding an estimate of cases omitted from the returns for one reason or another; so that prior to the 1844 Report of the Metropolitan Commissioners in Lunacy, no entirely satisfactory accounting existed. On the other hand, it strains credulity to believe that the early nineteenth-century observers underestimated the incidence of what they called insanity as badly as the figures make it seem. While the 1807 Select Committee thought in terms of a 'large' addition to existing figures, the tone of their report nowhere suggests that they considered the real rate to be five or six times the existing estimate (as it would have needed to be to account for the size of the discrepancy between these and later statistics).

The Committee's recommendation that sixteen District Asylums, 'calculated to contain as large a number as possible, not exceeding three hundred', should be erected to provide for all the country's insane population indicates that they thought the likely under-estimate was of the order of one or two thousand, or roughly fifty to a hundred per cent; for the total capacity of such a system would have been only 4,800. Two pieces of evidence suggest that such a conclusion was not wildly unreasonable. In 1807, Dr Andrew Halliday conducted a parish by parish survey of the counties of Norfolk and Suffolk to provide a check on the official returns, and found a total of 112 and 114 lunatics respectively, as compared with the reported figures of 42 and 103 – an increase of approximately 56 per cent.[1] Using Halliday's data, the rate of insanity per 10,000 people in each county (based on populations in 1811 of 291,982 and 239,153 respectively) was 3·83 and 4·77, compared with a national rate, calculated from the Committee's figures, of 2·26.

Evidence from Bedfordshire provides further confirmation of the fact that, even when careful inquiries were instituted in the early nineteenth century to discover the number of insane persons in a county, the rate of incidence of insanity, while greater than that given in the 1807 Report, was not spectacularly so. When the local county asylum opened in 1812, there was found to be a shortage of lunatics with which to fill it, only twelve candidates for admission being received. Threatening letters to parish overseers, warning that heavy fines would be levied were they found to be concealing cases to avoid incurring the expense of asylum treatment, and a sub-sequent tour of the county by Samuel Whitbread, explicitly under-taken to drum up more inmates to fill the new institution, failed to produce more than twelve additional cases. The census of the previous year had estimated a population of 70,203 for the county. This would suggest a rate of insanity of approximately 3·59 per 10,000 people, once more only slightly greater than the 2·26 which the 1807 figures gave for the country as a whole.[2]

By the time Burrows and Halliday made their estimates of the prevalence of insanity, the number of asylums and madhouses had

[1] *House of Commons Select Committee*, 1807, pp. 7, 27, and Appendices 2 and 3, letters from Andrew Halliday.

[2] *Bedfordshire County Asylum Minutes*, 15 July, 3 October 1812 (in Bedfordshire County Record Office).

already increased considerably, as, if they were to be believed, had the number of lunatics. Once again it seems unlikely that their estimates were as bad as the Lunacy Commissioners later implied. Both were men with a long and extensive acquaintance with questions related to insanity. Both prepared their estimates with considerable care, and were aware of and corrected for the most serious discrepancies in the official returns. And given their mutual concern with rousing public attention to the seriousness of the problem of insanity, one would expect them, if anything, to have erred on the side of generosity when estimating the numbers requiring treatment.

There is yet a further objection to the hypothesis that a more accurate enumeration was a major factor. The system of collecting data on all aspects of insanity which was established on a permanent

Table 9 Total Population, Total Admissions into all Asylums in the Year, and Admissions Expressed as a Rate per 10,000 of the Total Population of England and Wales, 1855-1890

	Population estimated for middle of year	Total admissions excluding transfers	Rate of admissions per 10,000
1855	18,786,914	7,366*	3·92*
1860	19,902,713	9,512*	4·77*
1865	20,990,946	10,424*	4·96*
1870	22,501,316	10,219	4·54
1875	23,944,459	12,442	5·19
1880	25,480,161	13,240	5·19
1885	27,499,041	13,354	4·85
1890	29,407,649	16,197	5·51

Source: Annual Reports of the Commissioners in Lunacy.

* For these years, the Commissioners' figures on admissions include patients transferred from one asylum to another. Accordingly, the ratio of admissions to population is overstated by an unknown, but sizeable amount. In 1870, for example, transfers amounted to 10·7 per cent of total admissions, and in 1880, to 11·7 per cent. Assuming (conservatively) that transfers in the period 1855-65 were approximately 10 per cent of admissions, the rate of admissions per 10,000 people would reduce to 3·53 in 1855, 4·30 in 1860, and 4·47 in 1865.

basis in 1846 remained substantially unchanged during the rest of the century. Yet the increase in the recorded cases of lunacy slowed little, if at all, in the latter part of the nineteenth century. It might take a few years, perhaps even a decade, for the full effects of the new arrangements to show themselves, but in the absence of further major changes in the way that data were gathered, assertions that increases in the rate of insanity reflected a more exact count come to seem progressively more implausible.

The Commissioners' contention that much of the rise in the lunatic population merely reflected the accumulation of chronic cases in asylums has a somewhat more solid foundation in fact. Since not much more than a third of each year's admissions recovered the use of their wits, and the annual mortality rate likewise amounted to about a third of annual admissions, a fairly substantial proportion of each year's intake remained behind to swell the total number of insane people in the population. Even so, taken alone, this factor obviously did not account for the increase. For one thing, as the Commissioners themselves realized, the growth in numbers was simply too rapid for that. Secondly, as the admission rates per 10,000 of the general population indicate, although there were some fluctuations from year to year, the secular trend which underlay these was clearly in an upward direction. Finally, if the accumulation of chronic cases was the sole, or even the single, major factor in the rise in the rate of insanity, we would expect the increase to have been approximately the same in the case of both private and pauper patients; for the cure rates in most private asylums were even lower than in their public counterparts, and mortality rates were roughly comparable. Yet in practice, the number of private patients rose 101·4 per cent between 1844 and 1890, while the number of pauper patients increased more than three and a half times as fast, by some 363·7 per cent.[1]

3. An Alternative Explanation

All of the 'explanations' given at the time for the growth in numbers

---

[1] The other 'explanations' we have considered so far are subject to analogous objections, since they too fail to indicate why patient numbers should rise so much more rapidly among the paupers than among the private patients.

8*

of the insane share two fundamental assumptions: (1) that there is some finite universe of 'crazy people' out there in the world; and (2) that identifying who is and who is not to be defined as mad is an activity governed by some objective, uniform, and unchanging standard. Neither assumption will withstand critical examination.

Definitions of insanity and discussion of how the condition is to be recognized abound in early nineteenth-century 'psychiatric' literature. The problem is, that while the definitions are full of medical terms and phrases, and are frequently long and cumbersome, they make no progress at all towards the actual identification of cases. Indeed, their uselessness for all practical purposes (save as support for the contention that identifying such a complex entity is an expert's task), is so great that many of these very same writers cheerfully concede, elsewhere in their treatises, that their formal distinctions are of no help whatsoever when it comes to the question of deciding someone's sanity.

The arbitrariness of the whole business is suggested by the need most writers felt to coin a definition of their own. The verbal gymnastics are entertaining, even if the results are somewhat meagre. A man is sane only 'when . . . the manifestations of his mind, his sentiments, passions, and general conduct, continue either to improve or to keep in accordance with the exhibitions of his previous powers and habits';[1] so that 'strictly speaking, every individual who exhibits an involuntary alteration in his mental manifestation denoting the most trifling disorder is not at that moment in a state of perfect sanity or health, that is, he is insane'.[2] Alternatively, the insane person is 'one whose intellect has been perverted'.[3] His insanity is 'a consequence of loss of nervous tone . . . all insane phenomena may be ascribed to the two well-known consequences of loss of nervous tone (acting coincidently), – namely excess of nervous energy or irritable accumulation, and paralysis or loss of nervous tone'.[4] At the same time, medical science shows us

[1] W. C. Ellis, *A Treatise on the Nature, Symptoms, Causes, and Treatment of Insanity*, London, Holdsworth, 1838, p. 16.

[2] ibid., pp. 30–31.

[3] Thomas Mayo, *Medical Testimony and Evidence in Cases of Lunacy*, London, Parker, 1854, p. 4.

[4] Henry Monro, *Remarks on Insanity: Its Nature and Treatment*, London, Churchill, 1850, p. vi.

that 'Insanity . . . is inordinate or irregular, or impaired action of the mind, of the instincts, sentiments, intellectual or perceptive powers, depending upon and produced by an organic change in the brain.'[1] We should understand that 'a precise definition of madness cannot be attempted as its degrees and intensity depend upon the extent to which the mental faculties have been perverted from their normal condition'; but the impossible may yet be attempted, and it turns out that 'every morbid state that influences our reflective, observant and imaginative faculties, disables an individual from conducting the processes of reasoning, or the sound and healthy exercise of his mental attributes, constitutes insanity'.[2] Finally, although one cannot obtain 'much help from definitions given by different medical authorities, for not only were some of them, as Dr Good has truly observed, "so narrow as to set at liberty half the patients at Bethlem or the Bicêtre and others so loose and capacious as to give a strait waistcoat to half the world", but . . . when medical men were required to explain what meaning they attached to the word Insanity, they generally satisfied themselves by giving such as had been repeated by one author after another, apparently without examination'; one should not be dissuaded from offering another: 'Insanity . . . is *the impairment of any one or more of the faculties of the mind, accompanied with, or inducing, a defect in the comparing faculty*'.[3]

On top of the basic pathology were then piled a myriad of sub-types and varieties: idiocy, fatuity, monomania, mania, and melancholia all assumed a veritable plethora of disguises. With definitions such as these, it can scarcely be a source of wonder that lesser luminaries who tried to rely on the pontifications of the most eminent men in the field were soon obliged to abandon the attempt in despair. Monro's complaints were typical:

All who have charge of asylums must well know how very different the clear and distinct classification of books is from that medley of symptoms which is presented by real cases . . . to be nice in dividing instinctive

[1] W. A. F. Browne, op. cit., p. 6.

[2] J. G. Millingen, *Aphorisms on the Treatment and Management of the Insane*, London, Churchill, 1840, pp. 3, 1.

[3] J. Conolly, *An Inquiry Concerning the Indications of Insanity*, London, 1830, pp. 292–3, 300, emphasis in the original.

insanity from moral insanity, is a subtlety more easily accomplished in books than in practice, and more useful in a legal than a medical point of view. Again, to divide one sort of dementia from another – to go to the length Mr Esquirol has, and distinguish imbecility by four stages . . . is curious rather than useful.

As for himself, he preferred the simpler, but more useful distinction between acute, chronic, and imbecilic insanity. 'I have tried in vain to classify cases to any practical purpose on any more rigid plan than I have mentioned above. It is useless to paint pictures with more vivid colours than nature presents, and worse than useless if practical men (or rather, I would say, men obliged to practice) receive these pictures as true representations.'[1]

Events seem to have borne out Haslam's gloomy conclusion that to discover 'an infallible definition of madness . . . will I believe be found impossible'. After three decades of fruitless efforts to prove him wrong by an array of medical experts on the subject, the judgement remained the same. Unfortunately, 'the attempts of medical writers to define insanity, have not been more successful than those of legal authorities to define what constitutes unsoundness of mind. It is, perhaps, not possible to propose a definition which shall be both positively and negatively correct; that is, which shall include all who are insane and exclude all who are not.' The consequences of trying were evident: 'Medical men have been subjected to much ridicule in our courts of law for the great variety, and sometimes total dissimilarity, of opinions entertained by them with reference to a correct definition of insanity. The great fault consists in attempting to define with precision what does not admit of being defined.'[2]

This might perhaps have amounted to no more than a mere verbal dispute over definitions, of no practical importance, had there existed fundamental agreement on the criteria for distinguishing the mad from the sane. But this was far from the case. Indeed, the best authorities were convinced that no such rules could be drawn up.

[1] H. Monro, op. cit., pp. 1–2, 3.

[2] John Haslam, *Observations on Madness and Melancholy*, 2nd edn, London, Callow, 1809, p. 5; J. M. Pagan, *The Medical Jurisprudence of Insanity*, London, Ball & Arnold, 1840, p. 25; William B. Neville, *On Insanity: Its Nature, Causes and Cure*, London, Longman *et al.*, 1836, p. 7.

'[Medical men] have sought for and imagined a strong and definable boundary between sanity and insanity, which has . . . been imaginary and arbitrarily placed.'[1] These efforts notwithstanding, 'no palpable distinction exists, no line of demarcation can be traced between the sane and the insane. It must be confessed, that the line is either ideal or purely geometrical.' General agreement was easily secured in extreme cases of violent mania or complete dementia, but with these exceptions, 'the task of declaring this to be reason and that insanity is exceedingly embarrassing, and, to a great degree, arbitrary. People have puzzled themselves to discover this line, a terra incognita, in fact, which does not exist.'[2] Yet if the decision as to what was or was not to count as madness was essentially 'arbitrary', the assumption that the universe of crazy people was in any sense strictly delimited was clearly not substantiated.

Lacking any other basis, the defenders of medicine's claim to possess a special skill in diagnosing cases of insanity were forced to appeal to clinical experience to legitimize and certify the authenticity of the individual practitioner's decisions. At first sight, it might be somewhat disconcerting to learn that 'the practitioner's own mind must be the criterion, by which he infers the insanity of any other person'. In practice, though (they claimed), this was not as risky a procedure as it might seem. In the first place, 'it may be assumed that sound mind and insanity stand in the same predicament, and are opposed to each other in the same manner, as right to wrong, and as truth to lie. In a general view no mistake can arise, and where particular instances create embarrassment, those most conversant with such persons will be best able to determine [their sanity].'[3] Secondly, 'it must be borne in mind, that a great unanimity may exist among experienced observers as to the presence of certain mental states, characterized by certain generally accepted names, which states, at the same time, it would be very difficult to describe in any form of words, insomuch that the undefined name, in the use of which all experienced men are agreed respecting these states, will convey to all a more clear and distinct impression than any attempt

[1] J. Conolly, op. cit.
[2] W. A. F. Browne, op. cit., p. 8.
[3] J. Haslam, op. cit., pp. 37, 38.

at definition or even description'.[1] Finally, the public were assured, 'although . . . contrariety of sentiment has prevailed concerning the precise meaning of the word madness, mental practitioners have been sufficiently reconciled as to the thing itself: so that when they have seen an insane person, they have readily coincided that the patient was mad'.[2] But apart from these vague assurances, no evidence was produced to demonstrate the reliability or the validity (whatever that might mean in this context) of the decisions taken by individual medical men. The stress was entirely upon first hand experience or 'judgement'. Yet, 'such emphasis', as Freidson has noted, 'is directly contrary to the emphasis of science on shared knowledge, collected and tested on the basis of methods meant to overcome the deficiencies of individual experience. And its efficacy and reliability are suspect.'[3]

The implications of this situation were profound. Beyond the initial hard core of easily recognizable behavioural and/or mental disturbance, the boundary between the normal and the pathological was left extraordinarily vague and indeterminate. In consequence, insanity was such an amorphous, all-embracing concept, that the range of behaviour it could be stretched to encompass was almost infinite. The asylum doctors themselves were but little inclined to resolve this ambiguity in favour of a narrow construction of their own sphere of competence. On humanitarian grounds, since they had convinced themselves that asylums were benevolent and therapeutic institutions, and believed that laymen were incompetent to cope with, and liable to maltreat the mad, they were impelled to seek out still more cases, rather than to reject any who were proffered. There were other incentives providing support for the adoption of such an orientation. Most notably, there was an obvious link between how serious a problem insanity was perceived to be, and the importance and prestige bestowed upon those thought to be experts in its treatment. Naturally, by increasing the population which fell within their purview, the profession also became entitled to obtain increased resources to support their activities.

[1] T. Mayo, op. cit., p. 14.
[2] J. Haslam, op. cit., p. 2.
[3] E. Freidson, *Profession of Medicine*, New York, Dodd, Mead, 1970, p. 347.

Taken together, these considerations impelled the profession to 'solve' these boundary problems by incorporation rather than by exclusion. In practice, they did not all go as far as Haslam, who succeeded in establishing a finite universe of crazy people by the simple expedient of defining everyone as mad.[1] Such an approach was liable to provoke ridicule, and so prove counterproductive. In any event, apparently more sober and restrictive definitions possessed more than sufficient latitude. Perhaps without even being conscious in many cases that this was what they were engaged in doing, the profession began to create whole new realms of madness, all the while leaving their original verbal definitions intact.

It is this shift in the way the term was applied, rather than improvements in record-keeping or the alleged influence of civilization on the incidence of insanity, that I believe was the second major factor behind the rapid rise during the nineteenth century in the number of people identified as insane. Yet although it should be clear by now that the asylum doctors were quite content, indeed positively eager, to take on the duties of coping with an ever larger population of mad people, one must beware of the tendency to conclude that the mere existence of even a considerable degree of professional imperialism provides a sufficient explanation of the ever wider practical application of the term insanity. If the profession was eager, the public had also to be willing. For it is doubtful whether many groups of experts possess a secure enough position to impose an outlook too widely divergent from that of the general public; and certainly a group whose claims to special expertise and competence were as fragile as those of the asylum doctors could not have succeeded in doing so.

One important consequence, however, did flow from the asylum doctors' outlook. Since the profession had, in effect, evinced a willingness to deal with almost any and all people whose behaviour the community found intolerable, it was this *lay* conception of what was and was not behaviour which could be borne which fixed the boundary between the sane and the insane. So that it is to this

---

[1] Compare his 'expert' testimony at the trial of a Miss Bagster in 1832: He avowed, 'I never saw any human being who was of sound mind.' On being pressed as to whether he meant this literally, he responded acidly, 'I presume the Deity is of sound mind, and he alone.' Cited in W. A. F. Browne, op. cit., p. 7.

extra-professional world that one must look for the sources of a more expansive view of madness.

Very early on in the history of the asylum, it became apparent that its primary value to the community was as a handy place to which to consign the awkward and unwanted, the useless and potentially troublesome. Quite obviously, there is no absolute standard by means of which people are placed or not placed in one of these categories. On the contrary, the whole notion of intolerable behaviour, of which these are merely particular examples, is clearly a culturally and situationally variable one. The importance of the asylum lies in the fact that it makes available a culturally legitimate alternative, for both the community as a whole and the separate families which make it up, to keeping the intolerable individual in the family. The very existence of the institution not only provides a dump for all sorts of inconvenient people; it also, by offering another means of coping, affects the degree to which people are prepared to put up with inconvenience. Thus I would argue that the asylum inevitably operated to reduce family and community tolerance (or, to put it the other way round, to expand the notion of the intolerable), to a degree which varied with how grandiose and well accepted the helping claims of those who ran it were. In so doing, it simultaneously induced a wider conception of the nature of insanity.

The historical evidence does not allow a direct test of this hypothesis, but there are a number of indirect ways of deciding whether or not it is correct. Among the most important of these are the following: (1) If who is defined as mad is primarily dependent upon community and family tolerance of such things as dependency, inconvenience, and inability or refusal to abide by ordinary social conventions, then the poor, who have fewer resources for coping with deviant, dependent and awkward relatives, and who are less able to resist pressures from others to incarcerate such intractable individuals, should contribute the bulk of this increase. (2) If the availability of institutions is in fact productive of decreased tolerance, then expansion of the asylum system should always produce increased numbers of crazy people. As a correlative of this, one would expect estimates of the prevalence of insanity to reflect the degree of institutional provision for the insane; so that at the beginning of the nineteenth century, when such provision was slight or non-existent in most areas, these estimates should seem almost ludicrously low by comparison with later ones, arrived at once the asylum system is firmly established. Whenever asylums are built, there should be a persistent tendency to underestimate the demand for accommodation; no matter how careful a survey is made of the local requirements, it should always turn out to be wrong. More strikingly, additional facilities built to meet the apparent excess demand ought swiftly themselves to be filled to capacity, and the original cycle should then be repeated all over again for so long as more money is available for more buildings. (3) If the asylum's main function is to serve as a dumping ground for the awkward and inconvenient, though often harmless, then it should in fact be filled with such. Moreover, since these are the sort of people whom nobody is very keen to see return to the community, there ought, particularly as the passage of time accentuates these characteristics of the patient population, to be comparatively little pressure placed on psychiatrists to fulfil their early claims to cure, even though they prove, if anything, less successful than in the past in this respect.[1]

At first sight, the official statistics on insanity kept by the Lunacy Commissioners fail to provide any straightforward way of deciding whether the yearly increase in the number of the insane came disproportionately from the poorer segments of the community. The records of admissions of new cases are aggregated into a single undifferentiated total. But the annual figures of the total number of lunatics *were* broken down into two component parts – private and pauper lunatics. And since the performance of private and pauper asylums with respect to cures and mortality rates was so essentially similar, these complicating factors can be set on one side. Any differences in the speed with which patients accumulate in the two sectors can thus be expected to reflect accurately an underlying difference between them as regards the appearance of fresh cases of insanity.

How accurately, though, did the distinction between pauper and private patients correspond to a lunatic's social class? And how reliably was the distinction made in practice? A lunatic was termed

---

[1] The evidence for the latter proposition has already been presented in Chapter 4, so I shall not repeat it here.

a pauper lunatic if the money for his maintenance came in whole or in part from public funds. This was a simple distinction to make, and since the Lunacy Commissioners insisted that records be accurate on this point, misclassification must certainly have been exceedingly rare. The label 'pauper', of course, carried with it an additional stigma which almost every family which could possibly do so sought to avoid. Had they been inclined to place their pockets ahead of their pride, they would doubtless have found the equally parsimonious local authorities a formidable barrier to overcome. So that, as the term itself would suggest, pauper lunatics were quite definitely recruited from only the poorer segments of the community. It would be wrong, however, to conclude that they were drawn simply from the ranks of the official pauper class. On the contrary, many must have come from the 'respectable' working classes, for, 'except among the opulent classes, any protracted attack of insanity, from the heavy expenses which its treatment entails, and the fatal interruption it causes to everything like active industry, seldom fails to reduce its immediate victims, and generally also their families with them, to poverty, and ultimately to pauperism'.[1] But quite plainly, the division between the pauper and the private lunatic reflected accurately the basic class division of Victorian society.

If we begin by looking at the data on lunatics in asylums for the decade 1849–59, the first in which the county asylum system became fully operational, a simple pattern emerges; one which, with minor variations, remains essentially unaltered until at least the end of the century, and quite possibly beyond. On 1 January 1849, the total number of patients in all types of asylums was 14,560; by 1 January 1859, it had risen to 22,853. Almost all the increase had taken place in the county and borough asylums, which now accommodated 15,845 inmates compared with only 6,494 ten years earlier. By comparison, the numbers in private licensed houses had actually declined by 1,915. These figures reflected the fact that although there had been a spectacular rise in the number of pauper lunatics confined in asylums, the number of private patients institutionalized had remained virtually static. While the number of pauper patients had grown from 10,801 to 18,022, an increase of 7,221, the figures

[1] *Commissioners in Lunacy Annual Report*, 1855, p. 35.

for private patients showed an increase of only 1,072, from 3,759 to 4,831. Moreover, even this slight rise was largely a statistical artifact, since the 1859 total included a number of elements – the patients at Bethlem, military and criminal lunatics – which had not been counted in arriving at the 1849 total; so that the Commissioners were doubtful whether there had been 'any increase in the number of Registered Private Patients during the period of ten years ending 1st January 1859'.[1]

To some extent, the availability of the institution decreased the tolerance of all sections of society. In the words of Joseph John Henley, General Inspector of the Local Government Board,

I . . . think there is a disposition among all classes now not to bear with the troubles that may arise in their own houses. If a person is troublesome from senile dementia, dirty in his habits, they will not bear with it now. Persons are more easily removed to an asylum than they were a few years ago.

But it was among the poor that this change was most marked:

. . . persons in humble life soon become wearied of the presence of their insane relatives and regardless of their age desire relief. Persons above this class more readily tolerate infirmity and can command the time and attention. The occasion may never occur in the one case, which is urgent in the other. Hence an Asylum to the poor and needy is the only refuge. To the man of many friends it is the last resort.

Huxley, another asylum superintendent, reached essentially the same conclusion.

Poverty, truly, is the great evil; it has no friends able to help. Persons in middle society do not put away their aged relatives because of their infirmities, and I think it was not always the custom for worn-out paupers to be sent to the asylum . . . It is one more of the ways in which, at this day, the apparent increase of insanity is sustained. It is not a real increase, since the aged have ever been subject to this sort of unsoundness.[2]

---

[1] *Commissioners in Lunacy Annual Report*, 1861, pp. 75–6.
[2] *House of Commons Select Committee*, 1877, p. 166; *Northampton General Lunatic Asylum Annual Report*, 1858, p. 11; J. T. Arlidge, *On the State of Lunacy and the Legal Provision for the Insane*, London, Churchill, 1859, p. 95.

Table 10 Number of Private and Pauper Lunatics, that Number Expressed as a Rate per 10,000 of the General Population, and Pauper Lunatics as a Percentage of the Total Number of Lunatics

	Private		Pauper		Total number of lunatics	Pauper lunatics as a % of the total number of lunatics
	Number	Rate/10,000	Number	Rate/10,000		
1844	4,072	2·47	16,821	10·21	20,893	80·5
1860	5,065	2·54	32,993	16·58	38,058	86·8
1865	5,790	2·74	40,160	18·99	45,950	87·4
1870	6,280	2·79	48,433	22·94	54,713	88·0
1875	7,340	3·09	56,403	23·55	63,743	88·1
1880	7,620	2·99	63,571	24·94	71,191	89·6
1885	7,751	2·82	71,215	25·89	78,966	90·1
1890	8,095	2·75	77,257	26·27	85,352	91·0

Sources: 1844 Report of the Metropolitan Commissioners in Lunacy, and Annual Reports of the Commissioners in Lunacy.

Workhouse authorities, too, sought to use the asylums to 'relieve their wards of many old people who are suffering from nothing else than the natural failing of old age', as well as to rid themselves of troublesome people in general.[1] 'A very large amount of additional accommodation having been thrown open . . . the Parochial Authorities have availed themselves of it, and removed to Asylums numbers of paupers who would otherwise have remained in Workhouses or cottages.'[2] The asylum doctors played their part by employing a double standard of insanity: 'Orders for the admission of Paupers into the County Asylum are given more freely than would be thought right as regards the imputation of Lunacy, towards persons equally debilitated in body and mind who have the means of providing for their own care.'[3] Table 10 provides a graphic illustration of the effects of these class-linked differentials in community tolerance and in the availability of resources for coping with difficult people. The number of private patients rises only gradually and modestly; the number of pauper lunatics all but quadruples.

The general relationship between the construction of asylums and the increase in insanity again suggests that on the whole it was the existence and expansion of the asylum system which created the increased demand for its own services, rather than the other way round. In the first place, it is simply remarkable how small the insane population was estimated to be when the first significant growth of the asylum system began in the late eighteenth century. When the York Asylum was first proposed, for example, in 1772, those planning the new institution prudently decided that they needed some estimate of the potential demand for its services. Accordingly, they conducted a careful inquiry 'as to the number of lunatics in the Three Ridings [of Yorkshire]'. When the survey was complete, the number of cases uncovered 'was found *so alarming* that it was determined to erect a building capable of receiving fifty-four patients . . .'[4] One doubts whether a finding that, in a popula-

[1] *House of Commons Select Committee*, 1877, p. 152, evidence of Dr Balfour, medical inspector of the London workhouses.

[2] *Commissioners in Lunacy Annual Report*, 1861, p. 15.

[3] *Littlemore County Asylum Superintendent's Report*, 1855.

[4] [J. Blackwell], 'Report on the Treatment of Lunatics', *Quarterly Review*, 74, 1844, p. 420.

tion probably well in excess of half a million, asylum provision was needed for fifty-four patients would have been viewed with 'alarm' a century later. Rather the response would likely have been to inquire into the reasons why this community had had the good fortune to escape the plague of insanity.

Twenty years later, William Tuke secured the establishment of the Retreat in the same city to provide for the care of all insane English Quakers. When the Retreat was proposed, insanity was thought to be a very rare condition among so sober and level-headed a group as the Quakers. Haslam, in his *Observations on Madness*, had claimed that their judicious religious beliefs and personal habits made them 'nearly exempt' from its ravages. Consequently, 'the projectors of the Retreat were thought, by some of their own friends, to be making too large a provision for its wants, in proposing a building for thirty patients'.[1] Indeed, many Quakers originally opposed the whole project, on the grounds that there were insufficient numbers of Quaker lunatics to justify it, and that to fill any institution, inmates would have to be admitted who were not members of the Society of Friends. In practice, however, the supply of patients proved more than adequate. The average number of Quaker inmates each year between 1796 and 1820 was 49; between 1820 and 1840 it rose to 71. Apparently the Quakers were as liable to insanity as everybody else.

If the opening of the York Retreat had produced more Quaker lunatics than anyone had hitherto realized existed, an analogous pattern was observed when many of the county asylums built under the 1808 Act began to receive patients. At Nottingham, for instance, where the first county asylum in the country was opened in 1811, the parish authorities had reported a total of thirty-five cases of insanity in the 1806 return to Parliament. To err on the side of caution, the magistrates built the asylum to accommodate 76–80

---

[1] Cited in Samuel Tuke, 'Introductory Observations' to *On the Construction and Management of Hospitals for the Insane* by M. Jacobi, London, Churchill, 1841, p. liv. In Jonathan Swift's Ireland insanity was also perceived to be a rare condition. When Swift died, he left a legacy in his will to establish a lunatic asylum in Dublin, on the model of Bethlem, for 140 patients. Fearing that so many lunatics might not be found, he added a provision that surplus beds could be used for other purposes.

patients, and were mortified when this was almost immediately found to be totally inadequate. Initially, not every community found the alternative offered by the new institutions equally seductive. Perhaps because their economic 'backwardness' brought with it a certain insulation from the corrosive effects of capitalism on the strength of family ties, the inhabitants of some regions proved less eager to consign their troublesome relatives to the asylum. In many Welsh counties, where subsistence farming remained the dominant form of economic activity, such attitudes persisted well into the second half of the nineteenth century.[1] Away from the Celtic fringe, counties like Bedford succumbed much more quickly. Long before the 1845 Asylums Act, the initial shortage of inmates for the local asylum had been replaced by such a superfluity of applicants that the local magistrates had been forced to enlarge the original structure considerably. When the Metropolitan Commissioners conducted the first nationwide survey of the adequacy of existing provisions for lunatics, they drew attention to how general a phenomenon this was:

it must be observed as a remarkable circumstance with respect to counties having pauper Lunatic Asylums, that it has been found necessary to enlarge almost every asylum of that sort that has hitherto been erected. The Asylums for the counties of Bedford, Cornwall, Gloucester, Kent, Lancaster, Leicester, Middlesex and Nottingham, and for the West Riding of York have all been enlarged, and some of them several times.[2]

When the 1845 Act made county asylums compulsory everywhere, this pattern simply spread through the rest of the country. County asylums had been expected to reduce the lunatic population by providing early treatment and hence cure; but everywhere,

---

[1] As late as 1872, for example, approximately 60 per cent of the known lunatics in Cardiganshire, Carmarthenshire, and Pembrokeshire still resided at home with relatives and others. In Anglesey the proportion was as high as 72 per cent. By contrast, in the more economically advanced and increasingly industrial county of Glamorgan, it had declined to less than 27 per cent. A case-by-case survey of the treatment of the non-institutionalized lunatics in the first three counties found that they were treated for the most part kindly by their families, and that their relatives were vehemently opposed to institutionalization. See *Commissioners in Lunacy Annual Report*, 1876, pp. 75–6, 346–9.

[2] *Metropolitan Commissioners in Lunacy 1844 Report*, p. 84.

notwithstanding very considerable pains have been taken, on the proposition to build a new asylum, to ascertain the probable number of claimants, and a wide margin over and above that estimate has been allowed in fixing on the extent of accommodation provided, yet no sooner has the institution got into operation, than its doors have been besieged by unheard of applicants for admission, and within one third or one half of the estimated time, its wards have been filled and an extension rendered imperative.[1]

By the mid-1850s, most county institutions had been open for only five or six years. Yet in their 1856 Report, the Lunacy Commissioners were lamenting 'the crowded state of nearly all the County Asylums, and the urgent necessity of making further immediate provision for the care and treatment of the Insane Poor . . . in nearly every County the accommodation provided in Asylums is, at present, or shortly will be, inadequate'. Building more asylums and expanding the existing ones failed to resolve the underlying problem. By 1867, there were forty-nine county and borough asylums, taking a total of 24,748 patients, compared with the sixteen receiving 4,336 in 1844. 'Notwithstanding this large increase of provision for Pauper Lunatics, the pressure for further accommodation in many districts is most urgent, particularly in Middlesex, Lancashire, and Yorkshire, the most urban counties, with the largest asylums and the greatest provision for their insane.'[2] At the Littlemore Asylum, which after 1850 took patients from both Oxfordshire and Berkshire, 'it was believed, from a Parliamentary return, that the number of Pauper Lunatics (inclusive of idiots) maintained by the parishes of the whole Union, did not exceed 480 . . .', and increased accommodation was provided for the Berkshire patients on this basis. When this swiftly proved inadequate, the asylum authorities adopted the standard conclusion 'that this Return was but imperfect'.[3] To cite one more example, the Surrey Asylum at Wandsworth was opened in 1841 with provision for 350 patients. By 1843 it was overcrowded and had to be enlarged; three years later, further enlargement was necessary, and provision was now made for 875 patients. This brought only a

[1] J. T. Arlidge, op. cit., p. 7.
[2] *Commissioners in Lunacy Annual Report*, 1867, pp. 67–8.
[3] *Littlemore County Asylum Annual Report*, 1863, pp. 13–14.

brief respite, for by 1853 accommodation was again insufficient. The magistrates now balked at further capital expenditures, and by cramming additional patients into the existing structure, it was made to suffice. Finally, in 1862, with Wandsworth taking 1,083 patients (more than three times the original estimate of what was required), construction of a second asylum at Brookwood was begun. That, too, was designed to take more than 1,000 patients.

The general pattern of an initial estimate of demand, which then proves wildly wide of the mark, leading to the construction of additional facilities designed to more than meet the apparent deficit, which themselves prove grossly inadequate, leading to a repetition of the whole cycle, is perhaps exhibited most clearly in the case of the Middlesex asylums, which provided for most of London's lunatics. Provision for pauper lunatics in public asylums in Middlesex began with the erection of Hanwell Asylum, completed in 1831. The original intention had been to build an asylum for 300 inmates, but following the figures revealed by the Parliamentary Return of 28 April 1830, it was decided to make provision for 500. At the time, this seemed not unreasonable, for although the return had shown a total of 824 lunatics and idiots, 480 of these were reported to be harmless, and 228 of these were not in any kind of confinement. In 1834, however, Ellis, the superintendent, reported that 'no fresh patients can be received, except on vacancies occurring from the cures or deaths of some of the present inmates; and the applications for admission are so numerous, that, with the utmost success that can be hoped for in cures, many months must now elapse after an application has been made before a patient can be received'. A year later, 'it was reported to contain a hundred patients more than it had been built for; after another two years, it had to be enlarged for 300 more . . .'[1] At the end of the decade, it had space for 1,000 patients, and applications were still piling up.

Following an 1844 return to the Quarter Sessions which showed that there were 722 more lunatics in the county than there was space for in Hanwell, the magistrates decided that more accommodation would have to be provided. Their initial plan simply to add on to the existing structure meeting with objections from the Lunacy Commissioners, they proceeded to build a second separate asylum

[1] *Commissioners in Lunacy Annual Report*, 1857, p. 12.

for over 1,200 patients, a generous margin over those known to exist. 'Colney Hatch was opened in 1851; within a period of less than five years, it became necessary to appeal to the ratepayers for further accommodation . . .' The Hanwell Annual Report for 1855 concluded gloomily that 'it is probable . . . notwithstanding the additional accommodation lately made . . . that there must be at this moment 500 unprovided for'. The magistrates resisted pressures from the Lunacy Commissioners to provide yet another asylum, commenting that 'a third Asylum is a vast and expensive evil', especially since the patients were almost entirely 'the most hopeless and the most objectionable'.[1] Instead, they simply adapted Hanwell and Colney Hatch to take in the neighbourhood of 2,000 patients each.

Inevitably, history repeated itself once again. By the late 1860s, the shortage of beds was so acute that surplus patients were sent outside the county, wherever room could be found for them, some as far away as Yorkshire. The opening, over the next few years, of the two huge custodial warehouses at Caterham and Leavesden for the most chronic cases from the metropolitan area provided considerable relief, for each took over 2,000 cases. Again, however, this proved merely temporary. In 1877, a third regular asylum had to be opened at Banstead, only for the increase to swell beyond even its capacity. By 1880, the asylum for insane children at Darenth had to be converted to take adults as well, the overflow from Caterham and Leavesden. And even after this addition, the superintendent at Hanwell once more reported that 'the demand for beds continues largely in excess of the Asylum accommodation . . .'[2]

I have suggested that asylums were largely dumps for the awkward and inconvenient of all descriptions. The comments of the

---

[1] *Commissioners in Lunacy Annual Report*, 1857, p. 12; *Hanwell County Asylum Annual Report*, 1855, p. 9.

[2] *Hanwell County Asylum Annual Report*, 1882, p. 5. One other interesting piece of information supporting the idea that the availability of the asylum creates its own supply of lunatics is provided in the *Commissioners in Lunacy Annual Report*, 1861, pp. 79–80. Maidstone and Canterbury, two boroughs in Kent, then possessed equal populations. While Maidstone had made provision for its lunatics to be admitted to the Kent County Asylum, however, Canterbury had not: 'the returns now show double the number of Insane Paupers in the provided over the unprovided borough'.

asylum superintendents and the Lunacy Commissioners on the character of asylum inmates provide abundant support for this view. From the moment most asylums opened, they functioned as museums for the collection of the unwanted. John Millar, the superintendent at the Buckinghamshire Asylum, commented on the nature of his earliest admissions in his diary. Of eleven males brought in on 1 February 1853, for instance, 'Four . . . are incurable, two of them being advanced in years and two are paralytic. There is also a hopeless epileptic.' Suffolk Asylum in 1852 included ten people 'nearly seventy years of age, nine over seventy, three over eighty; sixteen in a state of bodily exhaustion; nine either idiots from birth, or imbeciles for a very long period; one child with well-known disease of the heart, and a woman, a cripple, scrofulous, blind and deaf'. The Worcester Asylum received many patients between sixty and eighty years old, 'while others were the subjects of organic disease of the brain, lungs and heart, or suffered from long-continued mental disease, or from the superannuation of old age'. At Kent, 'the age of eleven persons admitted in 1853 averaged 64, and twelve were from 72 to 75. In many of these the malady was simply decay of the mind, or was due to apoplectic seizures, and attended by palsy.' John Bucknill of the Devon County Asylum found that

Patients have been admitted suffering from heart disease, aneurism, and cancer, with scarcely a greater amount of melancholy than might be expected to take place in many sane persons at the near and certain prospect of death. Some have been received in the last stages of consumption, with that amount only of cerebral excitement so common in this disorder; others have been received in the delirium or stupor of typhus; while in several cases the mental condition was totally unknown after admission, and must have been unknown before, since an advanced condition of bodily disease prevented speech, and the expression of intelligence or emotion, either normal or morbid.[1]

Frequent reference to the large proportion of cases of senile decay among asylum admissions continued to be made in later years, and by the fourth quarter of the nineteenth century, some asylum superintendents had begun to object to the burden that this

[1] All taken from county asylum annual reports, cited in J. Arlidge, op. cit., pp. 92–6.

group was to care for, and to suggest that asylum treatment was inappropriate for this class[1] – not that this dissuaded either the Poor Law officers or the families of such people from continuing to send them. Quite apart from the inconvenient and decrepit old people, there was no shortage of other individuals whom the community was glad to get rid of. Asylums became a dumping ground for a heterogeneous mass of physical and mental wrecks – epileptics, tertiary syphilitics, consumptives in the throes of terminal delirium, cases of organic brain damage, diabetics, victims of lead poisoning, the malnourished, the simple-minded, and those who had simply given up the struggle for existence.

This, for Bucknill, was the great difference 'between the inmates of the old madhouses and the modern asylum – The former containing only obvious and dangerous cases of lunacy, the latter containing great numbers of quiet and harmless patients whose insanity is often difficult to determine'.[2] More specifically, among the

[1] E.g. 'In several instances the patients have been so old and feeble that they have had to be carried direct from the vehicle that brought them to bed, and there they remain until they die . . . All the treatment the majority of them require is simply kind nursing and sustaining diet; and this ought to be secured as well in the Workhouse as in the Asylum, and thus avoid the risk of removal.' (*Hanwell County Asylum Annual Report*, 1875, p. 23.) 'Very old and palsied people continue to be sent and very few, almost none, are in even moderate bodily health . . . I fail to see any reason for not retaining many . . . in work-houses. Doubtless their minds are somewhat enfeebled by the causes above-named, but they cannot be considered as truly imbecile or insane. *If they are so, every person who lives beyond his sixtieth or seventieth year, or who may have an attack of paralysis* is liable to be so classed.' (*Caterham Lunatic Asylum Annual Report*, 1873, pp. 4–5, emphasis in the original.)

[2] J. C. Bucknill, op. cit., p. xxvii. Compare also Granville's comment that 'It is impossible not to recognize the presence of a considerable number of "patients" in these asylums who are not lunatic. They may be weak, dirty, troublesome, but they are certainly no[t] . . . affected with mental disease.' Indirectly, his contention that 'Speaking generally the causation of insanity everywhere, special organic disease apart, is an affair of three W's – worry, want and wickedness. Its cure is a matter of three M's – method, meat and morality' (J. M. Granville, op. cit., I, pp. 264, 48), reveals more about the sort of people being sent to asylums than about the causes of 'mental illness'; more about the persistence of the middle-class prejudice in favour of order and discipline than the existence of any scientifically grounded therapy for its cure.

inmates who filled the new madhouses which existed before the alleviating action of the lunacy laws . . . outrageous madness was the rule, and the detention of patients after they had become tranquil and harmless was against the rule. Nowadays, our numerous asylums swarm with a motley crowd of persons of weak minds or low spirits; with tranquil and reasonable persons said to have suicidal tendencies if they are not always under supervision; with paralytics and epileptics, and with persons in various stages of mental decay; no doubt all of them, with very rare exceptions, persons of unsound mind, but not madmen or lunatics, or even insane persons, as our fathers understood these terms.[1]

It is surely not the least of the many ironies with which lunacy reform abounds that its very success in making available the 'humanitarian' and 'scientific' alternative of asylum treatment tended to encourage families to abandon the struggle to cope with the troublesome – a temptation many fell prey to:

The very imposing appearance of these establishments acts as an advertisement to draw patients towards them. If we make a convenient lumber room, we all know how speedily it becomes filled up with lumber. The county asylum is the mental lumber room of the surrounding district; friends are only too willing, in their poverty, to place away the human encumbrance of the family in a palatial building at county expense.[2]

In consequence,

the law providing that madmen, dangerous to themselves and others, shall be secluded in madhouses for absolutely needful care and protection, has been extended in its application to large classes of persons who would never have been considered lunatics when this legislation was entered upon. Since 1845, medical science has discovered whole realms of lunacy, and the nicer touch of a finikin civilization has shrunk away from the contact of imperfect fellow-creatures, and thus the manifold receptacles of lunacy are filled to overflow with a population more nearly resembling that which is still at large.[3]

---

[1] J. Bucknill, op. cit., p. 3.
[2] [Andrew Wynter], 'Non-Restraint', *Edinburgh Review*, 131, 1870, p. 221.
[3] J. Bucknill, op. cit., p. 4.

Chapter Eight

The Legacy of Reform

In any society the dominant groups are the ones with the most to hide about the way society works. Very often therefore truthful analyses are bound to have a critical ring, to seem like exposures rather than objective statements, as the term is conventionally used [to denote mild-mannered statements in favour of the status quo] . . . For all students of human society, sympathy with the victims of historical processes and scepticism about the victors' claims provide essential safeguards against being taken in by the dominant mythology. A scholar who tries to be objective needs these feelings as part of his ordinary working equipment.

(Barrington Moore, *The Social Origins of Dictatorship and Democracy*)

1. Competing Accounts of Lunacy Reform

Whatever lunacy reform ultimately achieved for its ostensible clients, it certainly has had its uses for the retrospective (and contemporary) vindication of the humanity of the English bourgeoisie. Perhaps few present-day observers can quite summon up the note of positive enthusiasm and complacent self-congratulation with which the Victorian middle classes regarded their museums of the mad. Even the least informed of us feels a certain scepticism and discomfort when confronted with the claim that 'the county asylum is the most blessed manifestation of true civilization the world can present'.[1] Yet still the reformers' claims for the purity and humanitarianism of their own motives (supplemented by the labours of generations of historians who saw in the evolving treatment of the mentally distracted a source of support for their own

[1] Cited in Andrew Wynter, *The Borderlands of Insanity*, 2nd edn, London, 1879, p. 112.

Whiggish predilections) have served to inculcate in most people the notion that the rise of the mental hospital represents progress towards enlightenment and a practical expression of concern and assistance for one's suffering fellow-man.

Perceptions of this sort are not easily overturned or modified. After all, not only do they correspond to what the most powerful protagonists in these events wished to believe about themselves and embody what they wanted us to accept about their actions; such beliefs also perpetuate a set of myths with enduring contemporary value. Moreover, their optimistic assumptions are embedded in the very language we use – words like 'reform', 'psychiatrist', 'mental hospital', and so on – and it is a sociological truism, but true nonetheless, that the concepts which we use to delimit and discuss any particular segment of reality inevitably colour our perceptions of that reality. In the circumstances, there has been an understandable tendency to discount facts which fail to fit a 'progressive' interpretation as atypical and exceptional, and to attribute them to the inevitable imperfection of all human institutions.

However, the attractions of the facile equation of history with progress had long since lost their lustre in most historical circles, and during the 1960s this disenchantment somewhat belatedly began to spread to discussions of lunacy reform. There can be little question but that the historians now adopting this more critical stance were influenced by the growing disillusion in intellectual and policy-making circles with the value of the nineteenth-century asylum's present-day successors. Their work both reflected and gave further sustenance to the currently fashionable anti-institutional ideology (of which more in a moment).

Equally salient in the formulation of a more sceptical perspective were ideas drawn from the sociology of deviance, and, more particularly, those known as 'societal reaction theorists', who had made agencies of social control one of the focal points of their research. For central to this work was an ironical claim: that control structures, far from being a basically benign and defensive response to individual pathology, themselves acted to shape, create, and sustain deviance; that 'the very effort to prevent, intervene, arrest and "cure" persons of their alleged pathologies may . . . precipitate or seriously aggravate the tendency society wishes to guard against'.[1] Revisionists who re-examined nineteenth-century responses to the insane in the light of these notions drew a portrait which amounted to a virtual mirror image of the old Whiggish picture. Where one saw flaws and imperfections in a fundamentally sound approach, the other saw institutions with but few redeeming features – not a scientific or therapeutic response to illness, but a penal, custodial repression of threats to the social order.

Such polemical assaults (while they have for the most part been limited to discussions of conditions in the United States) have had their uses in dissipating some of the fog of righteousness which has enveloped and nearly smothered past efforts to come to terms with the treatment of the insane in the nineteenth century; but they have scarcely provided a satisfactory alternative analysis of the phenomenon. Like the sociological tradition upon which they draw, the work of men like Szasz and Rothman portrays those consigned to asylums as caught up in some largely arbitrary scapegoating process, and views the lunatic as the 'put-upon victim, with the social control agencies the villain of the piece'.[2] But this is grossly to oversimplify and distort what happened. It romanticizes those incarcerated as crazy, and plays down the degree to which their behaviour was (and is) genuinely problematic. Even worse, by way of response to the central question of why an institutional approach to madness emerged in the first place, these writers can offer little more than either crude conspiracy theory; or an account pitched in terms of a nebulous cultural *angst* – arising one knows not whence – about the stability of the social order.[3]

The very weaknesses and excesses of these revisionist explanations have prompted the revival, albeit in a more sophisticated and

[1] David Matza, *Becoming Deviant*, Englewood Cliffs, N.J., Prentice-Hall, 1969, p. 80.

[2] J. Lorber, 'Deviance as Performance: The Case of Illness', *Social Problems*, 14, 1967, p. 309. See Thomas Szasz, *The Manufacture of Madness*; New York, Dell, 1970 (London, Routledge & Kegan Paul, 1971); Robert Perrucci, *Circle of Madness*, Englewood Cliffs, N.J., Prentice-Hall, 1974; David Rothman, *The Discovery of the Asylum*, Boston, Little Brown, 1971.

[3] Szasz's work inclines towards the conspiratorial view; Rothman's to cultural idealism. For more extensive criticism of the latter's approach, see Andrew T. Scull, 'Madness and Segregative Control: The Rise of the Insane Asylum', *Social Problems*, 24, 1977, pp. 337–51.

seductive modern guise, of the traditional meliorist interpretation. One must concede that, looked at without rose-tinted spectacles, Victorian lunatic asylums present in many ways a dismal and depressing picture. But if the *results* can scarcely be applauded, or must be damned with faint praise, the benevolent *intentions* remain. Apparently, the history of lunacy reform records the efforts of a largely well-intentioned group of men (and the occasional woman), whose endeavours mysteriously always produced accidental and unintended unpleasant consequences. However unattractive, the institutions they founded were not 'inherently evil'. On the contrary, 'mental hospitals were not fundamentally dissimilar from most human institutions, the achievements of which usually fall far short of the hopes and aspirations of the individuals who founded and led them'.[1]

But this simply will not do either. For the view of reform as the product of the 'accidental', malevolent distortions of a Manichean world represents a denial of or a failure to come to terms with the multiple ways in which structural factors constrain, prompt, and channel human activities in particular directions. On a deeper level, consequences which appear unintended and 'accidental' considered from the viewpoint of the individual actor, remain susceptible to investigation and explanation. As I have tried to demonstrate here, the genesis and subsequent development of specialized segregative techniques for the handling of the mad was neither fortuitous, nor the product of the mere piling up of a series of incremental, *ad hoc* decisions which were bereft of any underlying dynamic or logic. Instead, the trajectory taken by lunacy reform in nineteenth-century England must be seen as the product of historically specific and closely interrelated changes in that society's political, economic, and social structure; and of the associated shifts in the intellectual and cultural horizons of the English bourgeoisie.[2]

[1] Gerald Grob, *Mental Institutions in America: Social Policy to 1875*, New York, Free Press, 1973, p. 342.

[2] For an analysis of how these changes prompted equally major transformations in the English crime control apparatus in this period, see Steven Spitzer and Andrew T. Scull, 'Social Control in Historical Perspective: From Private to Public Reponses to Crime', in D. F. Greenberg (ed.), *Corrections and Punishment: Structure, Function, and Process*, Beverly Hills, Sage Publications, 1977, pp. 281–302.

9

2. 'Experts' and the Control of Deviance

The cumulative impact of the entire process has proved extraordinarily long-lasting. We have examined the social processes by which 'madness' became 'mental illness'. Quite clearly, people's responses to bizarre and otherwise inexplicable behaviour continue to be mediated by and through that socially constructed meaning, just as the medical monopoly over the treatment of the mad, first established in the mid-nineteenth century, remains substantially secure. Indeed, in many respects, medicine is even more firmly entrenched in this field than at the close of the nineteenth century – though, notwithstanding extravagant claims for the effectiveness of anti-psychotic medication,[1] not because of any dramatic improvements in its therapeutic performance.

At the close of the nineteenth century, the professional status of asylum doctors remained distinctly questionable. Conspicuously mired in the status of salaried employees, and forced to confront and cope with a clientele consisting almost exclusively of the least attractive members of the lower orders of society, they shared with similarly situated groups like workhouse doctors and public health officers at best a tenuous hold on social respectability and but a paltry measure of the autonomy usually granted to those engaged in professional work. Since then, however, practitioners of psychological medicine have, with somewhat more success, laid claim to these standard accoutrements of professional status.

Paradoxically, I suggest that psychiatry's retention of its institutional base in the asylum was of extreme importance in accounting for the long-term improvement in its fortunes – for the asylum assured its cognitive monopoly and guaranteed a (captive) market for its services. Given these advantages, psychiatry needed only to develop a plausible esoteric theory, and a course of professional training to transmit it, in order to persuade the public of its expertise and thus to secure its independence from outside scrutiny and interference in its line of work. Here I suspect a key role was played by Freudian ideas, notwithstanding the obvious impracticality of applying them in an asylum context. For the

---

[1] Cf. Andrew T. Scull, *Decarceration: Community Treatment and the Deviant – A Radical View*, Englewood Cliffs, N.J., Prentice-Hall, 1977, Chapter 5.

Freudian system possessed a combination of almost unsurpassable virtues as a professional ideology. It had the great merit of being non-testable, and hence non-refutable; and, like Marxism, it lent itself to simplification for the simple and sophistication for the sophisticated. Requiring prolonged and costly training, it developed in its devotees a presumptive expertise which readily justified the rejection of outside, non-professional interference; a dogma which even provided an 'explanation' of why such 'irrational' resistance to its method should arise in the first place – thus discrediting its critics while protecting itself from the dangerous task of actually having to supply substantive answers to the objections they might raise. Moreover, by encouraging the development of the whole new realm of office practice, coping with upper-class neurotics, psychiatry was at once able to dilute the ill-effects of overly-close association with the poor, the stigmatized, and the unwanted; and to establish among the élite its credentials as a doubly worthy enterprise. Thereafter, having secured psychiatry's position *vis-à-vis* the insane, it provided the basis for the profession's subsequent efforts to engulf other forms of deviance, and reduce these too to a medical paradigm.

On their own terms, with respect to their ability to 'cure' their subjects, the experts on the control of deviance in modern societies have been spectacularly unsuccessful – which raises the question of why they are still accorded the status of experts. Looking at the case of psychiatry, with which I have here been concerned, it is clear that in practice psychiatrists in the nineteenth century did little more than act as caretakers of custodial dumping institutions. Nor did it require much sophistication or inquiry to uncover the fact. It was too blatantly obvious to be overlooked – or so it might seem. Yet despite this, the medical superintendents of asylums continued to claim and to be recognized as experts in the treatment of 'mental illness'. Only a few cranks, and some of the asylum inmates,[1] seem to have voiced the opinion that the emperor had no clothes.

Such a persistent, almost wilful blindness must derive from

[1] A constant complaint made by inmates of English lunatic asylums to the Lunacy Commissioners, throughout the nineteenth century, was that they did not belong in asylums, and that nothing was being done to cure them anyway.

9*

something more than the sacred and hence unquestioned quality with which modern societies have endowed science and certified expertise. It is true, of course, that such unexamined deference is habitually exhibited in its most acute form in the realm of medicine. Indeed, the doctor-patient relationship is so structured as to demand routinely that the client abdicate his own reasoning capacity.[1] In its place is fostered a naïve child-like faith that the physician is operating in the patient's best interests; and that when he does so, he is guided by an esoteric training and knowledge giving him insights which are beyond the powers of ordinary mortals to grasp or understand. But when all is said and done, modern medicine, much of the time at least, has results, if not God, on its side. British psychiatry at the end of the nineteenth century (and most of the 'experts' currently engaged in the control of deviance) clearly did (do) not.

And yet, if asylums, and the activities of those running them, did not transform their inmates into upright citizens, they did at least get rid of troublesome people for the rest of us. By not inquiring too deeply into what went on behind asylum walls, by not pressing too hard to find out what superintendents actually did with their patients, and by not being too sceptical of the officially constructed reality, people were (are) rewarded with a comforting reassurance about the essentially benign character of their society and the way it dealt (deals) with its deviants and misfits. Granting a few individuals the status and perquisites ordinarily thought to be reserved for those with genuine expertise and esoteric knowledge was a small price to pay for the satisfaction of knowing that crazy people were getting the best treatment science could provide, and for the comfortable feelings which could be aroused by contemplating the contrast between the present 'humane' and 'civilized' approach to the 'mentally ill' with the barbarism of the past.

3. Community Treatment

The state-supported network of mental hospitals, the second major

[1] Cf. E. Freidson, *Professional Dominance*, New York, Atherton, 1970, pp. 119–21.

legacy of the nineteenth-century reform movement, has met with a more mixed fate. Until the middle of the present century, the institutional response remained the dominant approach to the problems posed by the mentally ill. The pattern of consistent year-by-year increases in the number of inmates confined in mental hospitals, so noticeable a feature of the nineteenth-century asylum system, persisted almost unchanged until 1954. And for most of the two subsequent decades, mental hospital admissions have continued to rise quite sharply, keeping the now decrepit nineteenth-century structures in constant use. Nevertheless, this latter period has witnessed a major departure from historical precedent, a reversal of the remorseless secular increase in the size of the mental hospital population. In the face of a century-and-a-half-old trend in precisely the opposite direction, the number of patients resident in English mental hospitals has fallen sharply, from 148,000 in 1954 to fewer than 96,000 two decades later. Still more abrupt has been the mental hospitals' decline from official favour, to the point where they are now written off as 'doomed institutions', to be run down and closed within the foreseeable future. Under mounting attack because of their negative effects on those they treat, segregative techniques in their traditional form are now steadily losing ground to newer 'community-based' alternatives.

Madness seems to attract more than its share of myths. In the nineteenth century, the myth of the Noble Savage – free from the stress, the artificiality, the vices of modern life (and thus free from the insanity which was part of the price of civilization) – was given a widespread currency. The propagation of such a notion had obvious value for those bent on reforming the treatment of lunatics and bringing them the benefits of modern science; for only the adoption of their programme of a network of specially designed, medically run asylums could hope to stem the rising tide of madness with which the advance of civilization threatened Victorian England. The contemporary equivalent of the Noble Savage (in some intellectual circles at least) seems to be a mythical pre-institutional Golden Age, when the population at large enjoyed the blessings of living in 'communities' – an innocent rustic society, uncorrupted by the evils of bureaucracy, where neighbour helped neighbour and families gladly ministered to the needs of their own troublesome members, while a benevolent squirearchy looked on, always ready to lend a helping hand. Once again, a myth has had its uses for those bent on changing social policy, this time providing a counterpoint to a mass of social scientific research on the mental hospital which amounts to a full-blown assault on its therapeutic failings.[1] For such people, lunacy reform is seen as simply one colossal mistake.

Certainly, there is much in what I have said about the nineteenth-century asylum which can but serve as grist for their mill. But realism about the awfulness of asylum existence ought not to prompt us to opt for a blind faith in the virtues of its presumed antithesis. One can – indeed, I think must – be deeply sceptical about claims made on the mental hospital's behalf: yet one must not fall prey to equally groundless fantasies and illusions about the available alternatives. If one were to believe the devotees of the contemporary cult of the community, if we would only bring the mentally disturbed back into our midst, not only would we avoid the isolating and labelling effects of commitment to an institution, but 'by enlisting the good will and the desire to serve, the ability to understand which is found in every neighbourhood, we shall meet the challenge which such groups of persons present . . .' Apparently, what is needed is a return to

a simpler time not so very long ago . . . when the problems of the mentally retarded and disturbed, the aged and the troubled young, were dealt with in the communities where each of these people lived. A greater continuity or integration of the entire age spectrum seems to have prevailed in those days: . . . and those who were deficient in intelligence or emotional balance were not only tolerated but accommodated.[2]

We may reasonably doubt whether such idylls existed in seventeenth- or eighteenth-century England, the Paradise presumably Lost when the insane were consigned to the asylum. The available

---

[1] E.g. Erving Goffman, *Asylums*, Garden City, New York, Doubleday, 1961 (London, Penguin, 1970); W. Caudill, *The Psychiatric Hospital as a Small Society*, Cambridge, Mass., Harvard University Press, 1958; I. Belknap, *Human Problems of a State Mental Hospital*, New York, McGraw Hill, 1956; R. Perrucci, op. cit.

[2] B. Alper, foreword to Y. Bakal (ed.), *Closing Correctional Institutions*, Lexington, Mass., Lexington Books, 1973, pp. vii–viii.

evidence on the treatment accorded the insane in the community in this period is sketchy and inadequate, a situation complicated by the then prevalent failure to distinguish at all carefully between the mad and other deviant and dependent groups. Nevertheless, what we *do* know of the treatment either of the clearly frenzied or of problematic people in general lends little support to such romantic speculations. Nor should this come as a surprise, given what we know of the general tenor of eighteenth-century English social life, particularly, though not exclusively, among the lower orders. Even among their 'betters' the widespread credence given to the idea of the continuity of all forms of creation, including man, in the imperceptible gradations of a single great chain of being brought with it a ready acceptance of the notion that some men were indistinguishable from brutes – an easy equation between apes and savages, and between apes and men lacking in 'reason'.[1] And what we know of the treatment of brutes in this period scarcely inspires confidence about the treatment of human beings equated with them.

Nor have recent experiences with 'community treatment' proved much of an advertisement for its virtues. Cutting through the clouds of rhetoric and wishful thinking with which the subject abounds, it is apparent that the whole policy was undertaken with little prior investigation of its likely effects, and that even now we lack 'substantiation that community care is advantageous for clients'.[2] While the acutely disturbed continue to receive some attention, frequently being dealt with through short-term hospitalization, this contrasts 'with a second class service, or no service at all, for the chronic patient'.[3] Many of those expelled from mental hospitals become lost in the interstices of social life, and turn into drifting

[1] See the discussion in W. F. Bynum, *Time's Noblest Offspring: The Problem of Man in the British Natural Historical Sciences*, unpublished Ph.D. dissertation, Cambridge University, 1974. The seminal work on this belief system is A. O. Lovejoy's *The Great Chain of Being*, New York, Harper, 1960.

[2] J. and E. Wolpert, 'The Relocation of Released Mental Hospital Patients into Residential Communities', mimeo, Princeton University, 1974, pp. 14–19. The following paragraphs draw upon my *Decarceration: Community Treatment and the Deviant – A Radical View*.

[3] J. K. Wing, 'How Many Psychiatric Beds?', *Psychological Medicine*, 1, 1971, p. 190.

inhabitants of those traditional resorts of the down and out, Salvation Army hostels, settlement houses, and so on. In those cases where families have attempted to deal with members discharged from mental hospitals, they have frequently experienced severe difficulties in coping – indeed, they have only been induced to do so by the authorities' persistent refusal to accede to their requests for rehospitalization.[1]

In the United States, where the non-institutional approach has been pursued still more vigorously than in England, such outcomes would seem relatively benign. There, for thousands of the old already suffering from mental confusion and deterioration, the new policy has meant premature death.[2] For others, it has meant that they have been left to rot and decay, physically and otherwise, in broken-down welfare hostels or in what are termed, with Orwellian euphemism, 'personal-care' nursing homes. For thousands of younger psychotics discharged into the streets, it has meant a nightmare existence in blighted city centres, amidst neighbourhoods crowded with prostitutes, ex-felons, addicts, alcoholics, and the other human rejects now repressively tolerated by their society. Here they eke out a precarious existence, supported by welfare cheques they may not even know how to cash. They spend their days locked into or out of dilapidated 'community-based' boarding houses. And they find themselves alternatively the prey of street criminals, and a source of nuisance and alarm to those 'normal' residents of the neighbourhood too poverty-stricken to leave. All in all, it is difficult to avoid the conclusion that 'in the absence of after-care and rehabilitation services, the term "community care" [remains] . . . merely an inflated catch phrase, which conceal[s] morbidity in the patients and distress in the relatives'.[3]

4. The Therapeutic State

Psychiatrists, and other social control experts for that matter,

[1] G. Brown, M. Bone, B. Dalison, and J. K. Wing, *Schizophrenia and Social Care*, London, Oxford University Press, 1966, Chapters 3 and 5, esp. pp. 51ff.

[2] See R. Marlowe, 'When they closed the doors at Modesto', in *Where is my Home?* mimeo, Scottdale, Arizona, 1974, pp. 110–24; J. and E. Wolpert, op. cit.

[3] G. Brown *et al.*, op. cit., p. 10.

negotiate reality on behalf of the rest of society. Theirs is pre-eminently a moral enterprise, involved with the creation and application of social meanings to particular segments of everyday life. Just like physicians, they may be said to be engaged 'in the creation of illness as a social state which a human being may assume'.[1] Indeed, in view of the indefinite criteria employed to identify and define 'mental illness', its status as a socially con-structed reality is, if anything, plainer than in the case of somatic illness, and the latitude granted the expert correspondingly wide. I would argue that for all the psychiatric profession's claims (and their complex verbal gymnastics notwithstanding), the boundary between the normal and the pathological remains vague and indeterminate, and mental illness, partly as a consequence, an amorphous, all-embracing concept. Under such conditions, there exists no finite universe of 'crazy people', and the process of identifying who is and who is not to be defined as insane cannot, in the nature of things, be an activity governed by some objective, uniform, and unchanging standard.

I have suggested here how important this theoretical indeter-minateness of the concept of insanity was in the nineteenth century, with the boundaries of mental disturbance stretched to encompass all manner of decrepit, socially inept and incompetent, and super-fluous people, as well as victims of a whole spectrum of physical pathologies later assigned to a different ontological status (that of 'real' physical illness). It has proved equally significant in this century. As the psychiatric profession has advanced its social status and as it has succeeded in persuading a wider public to take seriously its claims to possess an expertise resting upon a scientific basis, so the psychiatric view of deviance has had a steadily growing influence on public policy. At least since the end of the Second World War, we have been moving away from a punitive and to-wards what Kittrie has termed a therapeutic state; that is, one which enshrines the psychiatric world view. Just as in 'the eighteenth and nineteenth centuries, a host of phenomena – never before con-ceptualized in medical terms – were renamed or reclassified as mental illness',[2] so in the present most other forms of deviance are

[1] E. Freidson, *Profession of Medicine*, New York, Dodd, Mead, 1970, p. 205.
[2] T. Szasz, op. cit., p. 137.

being assimilated to a quasi-medical model, being relabelled as illness, and so 'treated' rather than punished.[1] Moreover, the 'thrust of the expansion of the application of medical labels has been toward addressing (and controlling) the *serious* forms of deviance, leaving to the other institutions [law and religion] a residue of essentially trivial and narrowly defined technical offences'.[2]

With sardonic wit and much insight, Peter Sedgewick has recently proclaimed that '*the future belongs to illness . . .*', as the range of conditions subject to medical control and intervention is expanded, generating pressures to redefine various behaviours 'into medical (and thus controllable) pathologies'.[3] As I have demonstrated here at some length, such expansion is not necessarily tied to success; nor is the arena of medical action limited to those pathologies where its intervention is demonstrably efficacious. Indeed, in view of the demonstrable utility to those who benefit most from the existing social order of an explanatory schema which locates the source of the pathology in intra-individual forces, and which would allow the redefinition of all protest and deviation from the dominant social order in such individualistic and pathological terms, the restraints on the expansion of the notion of illness deriving from physicians' inability to 'cure' the forms of deviance so relabelled are significant only in so far as too blatant and repeated a failure might cast doubt on the underlying explanatory model. Frequently enough, pseudo-expertise will do. More generally, to the extent that medicine can develop successful techniques of intervention to modify 'socially undesirable behaviour', and/or to the extent to which the criteria of success are ambiguous or readily lend themselves to manipulation, one can only anticipate a further expansion of current tendencies towards a therapeutic state.

[1] See N. Kittrie, *The Right to be Different*, Baltimore, Johns Hopkins University Press, 1971; I. K. Zola, 'Medicine as an Institution of Social Control', *The Sociological Review*, 20, 1972, pp. 487–504.

[2] E. Freidson, *Profession of Medicine*, p. 249, emphasis in the original.

[3] P. Sedgewick, 'Mental Illness *Is* Illness', *Salmagundi*, 20, 1972, p. 220.

Index